S

# BACKGROUNDS OF ENGLISH
# LITERATURE, 1700–1760

# BACKGROUNDS OF
# ENGLISH
# LITERATURE

## *1700-1760*

### CECIL A. MOORE, *1879-*

PROFESSOR EMERITUS OF ENGLISH
UNIVERSITY OF MINNESOTA

THE UNIVERSITY OF MINNESOTA PRESS
*Minneapolis*

*Copyright 1953 by the*

# UNIVERSITY OF MINNESOTA

PRINTED AT THE LUND PRESS, INC., MINNEAPOLIS

*Library of Congress Catalog Card Number: 53-5943*

*To*

N. K. M.

# Preface

O F THE five studies included in this volume, four are reprints of
articles published longer ago than I like to be reminded. "Shaftesbury and the Ethical Poets in England" is taken from the *Publications of the Modern Language Association of America*, Vol.
XXXI, 1916; "The Return to Nature in English Poetry" from
*Studies in Philology*, the University of North Carolina, Vol. XIV,
1917; "John Dunton: Pietist and Impostor" from the same journal, Vol. XXII, 1925; and "Whig Panegyric Verse" from the *Publications*, Vol. XLI, 1926.

It was conventional in the eighteenth century for a writer to
announce modestly that he was republishing his works because
he had been "importuned" to do so. This is more than I can claim
for the present undertaking, but some of my associates have been
kind enough to recommend that the material be made more acces-
sible to students of the period than it has been. The articles are
arranged in the order of their original publication and are reproduced with only minor changes, except for the revisions in the
article on John Dunton. For these I am indebted to suggestions
I received, immediately after the article was published, from Mr.
Theodore M. Hatfield, who was then making a special study of
the bibliographical puzzle created by Dunton's dishonest practices
and was kind enough to give me the benefit of his research. When
I wrote these articles, I was aware that there was some repetition,

but this was hardly avoidable since the first two, and to some extent the third, deal with ideas closely related in origin and since each of the articles was intended to be self-contained.

In "The English Malady" I have used part of the material collected over a number of years with the original intention of tracing the history of melancholy in the medical literature of England from the sixteenth century through the eighteenth. Here I have confined myself to the eighteenth century and have treated the subject in broad outline only, avoiding as far as possible the minute technical details of medical theory. In one respect this essay differs noticeably from the others. Since the typographical eccentricities of early medical books would serve only to confuse the reader, I have taken the liberty of modernizing the quoted texts in the use of capitals and italics and occasionally in punctuation where clearness demanded a change.

Though not integrated, these pieces are accidentally united by a common purpose, one I have attempted to express in the title chosen for the collection. They all relate in some way to what came to be known in the seventeenth century as "the climate of opinion." Shelley had in mind the same thing when he said that all writers of any given period are subjected to "a common influence which arises out of an infinite combination of circumstances belonging to the time in which they live." This observation is nowhere more strikingly confirmed than in English literature of the eighteenth century. When dramatists, novelists, and poets as well as essayists are convinced that it is the function of literature to provide practical instruction, they will draw heavily upon the common stock of contemporary ideas and ideals, and this community of interest will be reflected in their writing. In the following studies I have examined some of the most popular sources of literary ideas — philosophy, science, politics, and religion — for the purpose of showing the part these borrowings played in the content of popular literature, especially poetry.

With the intrinsic merit of the poetry I am concerned only incidentally. The artistic results were both good and bad. If poetry was enriched by some of these influences, there can be no doubt that it suffered severely from others. The imperfections arose partly from inexperience in a new field, but more from a mistaken notion of what can and what cannot be converted into poetry. Some of the ideas that were transplanted now look more attractive in their original setting than in the poetical version, and the faults are most conspicuous of course in the work of the underlings. A strict application of Shenstone's dictum that it is "idle to be assiduous in the perusal of inferior poetry" would, I am afraid, exclude from consideration some of the extracts quoted from Shenstone himself, to say nothing of many specimens from poetasters. Yet for historical purposes the worst productions are often the most valuable because only in them are the inherent dangers of the didactic habit fully exposed. Besides, unsuccessful experiments served a useful purpose at the time by convincing others as well as Dr. Johnson that poetry cannot be made out of hops, parsley, and cabbage.

My obligations to friends for advice and help in connection with this book are too many for me to acknowledge all of them individually. I am very grateful to my former assistant, William B. Bjornstad, now Professor of English at Drake University, for valuable aid of various kinds. I am particularly indebted also to the following members of the Department of English at the University of Minnesota for their active interest: Samuel H. Monk, Huntington Brown, and John W. Clark. To Franz J. Montgomery I am under additional obligation for his generous help in the task of proofreading. It is a pleasure to add that the members of the staff of the University Press have earned my lasting gratitude by their hearty cooperation and the painstaking accuracy of their work.

C. A. M.

*April 5, 1953*
*St. Paul, Minnesota*

# Contents

# BACKGROUNDS OF ENGLISH
# LITERATURE, 1700–1760

# Shaftesbury and the Ethical
# Poets in England

Oɴᴇ of the notable changes in English literature during the eighteenth century is a growth in altruism. It is a change which involves not only a breaking down of the old aristocratic indifference to the lower classes of society during the Restoration, but the establishment of a new ethical theory; literature displayed a broader human interest and assigned a new reason for its sympathy. It is usually assumed that the difference is due principally to the influx of French philosophy. This assumption at least minimizes the importance of a development which had taken place in the literature of England itself before the general interest in Rousseau. The change, especially in poetry, is to be traced largely, I think, to the *Characteristics* (1711) of Lord Shaftesbury, whose importance as a literary influence in England has never been duly recognized.* It has long since been established that his system of philosophy constitutes a turning point in the

* The ethical works of Anthony Ashley Cooper, third Earl of Shaftesbury (1671–1713), which were known to the eighteenth century were first published in the following order: (1) *An Inquiry Concerning Virtue*, printed without authority by John Toland, 1699; (2) *A Letter Concerning Enthusiasm*, 1708; (3) *The Moralists: A Philosophical Rhapsody*, 1709; (4) *Sensus Communis, an Essay upon the Freedom of Wit and Humour*, 1709; (5) *Soliloquy, or Advice to an Author*, 1710; (6) *Characteristics of Men, Manners, Opinions, Times*, 1711. This contains the previous essays and also *Miscellaneous Reflections*.

history of pure speculation, especially in ethics; it has more recently been shown also that he is responsible for many of the
moral ideas that inform the popular literature of Germany from
Haller to Herder.[1] But his influence upon the popular writers of
his own country has received scant notice.

The purpose of the present investigation is to show that the
adoption of his ideas by popular writers in England was actually
widespread, and that, since theology and ethics were subjects of
vital interest, the *Characteristics* had a large part in determining
the content of English literature. In general, popular works were
affected very much as the more formal treatises of philosophy
were; various writers reproduced most of Shaftesbury's tenets,
but collectively they were indebted to him chiefly for a new
standard of morals. Their response, like that of the philosophers,
was due mainly to his "virtuoso" theory of benevolence. Through
the constant repetition of this doctrine by his imitators, the
"founder of the benevolent school of philosophy" became largely
responsible for the vigorous literary interest in philanthropy
that characterizes all English literature of the mid-century.
Previously neither society nor literature had been indifferent to
social evils, as the early work of Defoe and the essays of Addison
and Steele testify; but the essayists were proceeding upon a
rationale which was already weakening under the attacks of deism,
and which could never have engaged the lively interests of literature. Shaftesbury's scheme of the social affections infused a new
vigor into the cause and established philanthropy upon a basis
that allowed a larger play of sentiment. The quickening of literary interest that resulted is especially evident in poetry; versified "benevolence" was a literary innovation that sprang directly
from the new and fashionable ethics of the *Characteristics*.
Largely for this reason, I have confined myself here to a special
study of verse only.

An exhaustive treatment of the subject would demand as a
preliminary to the study of the poetry itself a detailed examination of Shaftesbury's system and its relation to current theory and
practice. Such an examination would show clearly why his popu-

larity was delayed until several years after his death and then became general. But it must suffice here to deal with his philosophy and these historical conditions in mere outline.

### I

Aside from the attractiveness of his style, Shaftesbury appealed to his age chiefly because he effectually antagonized two schools of thought out of harmony with growing tendencies of the time — the strict orthodoxy of the Church and the egoistic philosophy of Hobbes. These themselves were in open strife on various fundamental questions, and Shaftesbury was quite as much opposed to one as to the other. In his own system there is little that is strictly original; most of it is merely the assimilation and perfected statement of ideas which the Cambridge Platonists, Cumberland, and other Latitudinarians had imported from Greek philosophy.* The views he advanced in opposition to both Hobbes and the Church met with a favorable response because they satisfied an inclination of the age that needed only authoritative guidance.

His system of benevolence, formulated in opposition to Hobbes, rests upon a theology which was then dangerous heresy. The starting point is the deistic conception which in its full development assumes that the Deity is sufficiently revealed through natural phenomena, and that human reason unaided is capable of forming an adequate notion of God. Revelation, therefore, and all miraculous intervention it sets aside as not only superfluous but derogatory to the character of the Deity.[2] The "free thinkers" found their chief inspiration in the regularity and harmony of the physical universe; to them nature was man's only "open Bible," and the contemplation and worship of it supplied the place of more formal religious devotion. Shaftesbury, for example, calls

---

* Shaftesbury edited Whichcote's sermons in 1698. For references to Cudworth, see *Characteristics*, ed. J. M. Robertson (2 vols.; New York, 1900) (to which all references below), II, 50, 196; and Letter to Jean Le Clerc, March 6, 1705-6, in *Life, Unpublished Letters, and Philosophical Regimen*, ed. Benjamin Rand (London, 1900) (referred to hereafter as *Regimen*), p. 352. For More's influence, see *Characteristics*, II, 197–199, and Editor's note, I, 5. Robertson's novel view (I, xxxix ff., and notes) that Shaftesbury was indebted mainly to Spinoza is unconvincing.

it the "wise Substitute of Providence." This is a conception more poetic than the one which it opposed, and it had the additional advantage of satisfying the growing interest in natural science. While the orthodox found difficulty in adjusting the biblical account to recent discoveries in chemistry, physics, and astronomy, especially those of Newton, the deists hailed in all these marvels the appropriate marks of the Creator with whom they had replaced the provincial God of the Hebrews.

Associated with this conception of God as a being of unlimited power and majesty worthy of the physical universe he had created was the complementary moral view that he was the embodiment of supreme goodness. In the process of rehabilitation the ancient Deity was rapidly stripped of such stern attributes as vengeance, if not justice, and regarded merely as the Spirit of Benevolence. Out of this conception grows naturally the Platonic idea that the Creator acted for the happiness of man and placed him in the best possible of all worlds. The apparent ill of the individual part is necessary to the system of the universe as a whole; our view is limited, and "a mind which sees not infinitely can see nothing fully, and must therefore frequently see that as imperfect which in itself is really perfect." [3] A mere link in the vast chain of being, man is guilty of sheer folly when he laments his physical weakness or otherwise complains of the economy of nature. [4] This conclusion, which we instantly associate with Pope's *Essay on Man*, represents the popular theology that underlies most of the poetry to be examined; it gave rise to a pseudo-science and an optimism inseparably connected with the ethical ideas of the entire school. Such theology was, of course, not confined to Shaftesbury or even to the deists; but the *Characteristics* apparently did more to popularize it than all the other philosophical works combined.

Shaftesbury's ethical theory is the direct result of this theology, which, by undermining faith in the Scriptures, destroyed the force of biblical precept as a guide in conduct. In his protest against various harsh views of the Christian dogma and the egoism of Hobbes, he anticipated much of Rousseau's respect for natural man. On the theoretic side his system derives largely from Plato and Plato's imitators; * but for the practical part it is indebted even more to Epictetus and Marcus Aurelius.[5] The essence of it, so far as it affected poetry, is comprehended under the following views:

(1) Man is naturally a virtuous being, and is endowed with a "moral sense" which distinguishes good from evil as spontaneously as the ear distinguishes between harmony and discord.[†] Although the "moral sense," in common with all other endowments, requires cultivation, man becomes virtuous merely by following the preferences of this instinct. To be good he needs only to be natural.[6]

(2) Just as the "moral sense" is independent "even of any settled notion of God" or any other idea acquired by experience, Virtue itself is an independent good, immutable and eternal. It is to be sought, therefore, for its own intrinsic beauty — what Plato calls τὸ καλόν and Horace the *dulce et decorum* of virtue — regardless of all considerations of future reward and punishment.[‡] This doctrine gave immediate offense to the Church, which, according to Shaftesbury, was employing a method of "the rod and sweetmeat" that destroyed the natural relish for goodness itself and reduced virtue to a mercenary consideration.[7] Instead of the sordid utilitarianism of the orthodox, Shaftesbury proposed as the only reward of virtuous conduct the immediate satisfaction it produces, which is the only genuine happiness to be attained by man.[8]

(3) The natural beauty of virtue was further recommended to the smart set of "free thinkers" by his "virtuoso" identification of the Good and the Beautiful. To him virtue meant merely a perfect development of aesthetic sensibility. It is, therefore, the

* It is inaccurate to speak of his entire system as Platonism, though this was the practice in the eighteenth century. In my own use of the term I have tried to confine it to ideas of Shaftesbury's which are to be found in Plato.

† Shaftesbury is supposed to have invented the phrase "moral sense"; but see More's *Divine Dialogues*, Dial. II, Sec. xviii.

‡ He would retain the ancient doctrine of the Church only to terrify the ignorant and depraved (*Characteristics*, II, 265).

mark *par excellence* of a gentleman. There is, he said, a harmony of "inward numbers" as of outward, an observance of symmetry and proportion in morality as in architecture. The moral world as a whole is but another manifestation of the beauty which pervades and harmonizes the "bright, outward and visible world." In it also appears imperfection of detail; but in spite of apparent confusion, if apprehended "the order of the moral world would equal that of the natural." [9] Goodness, then, is harmony with nature; "knavery is mere dissonance and disproportion." [10] Man should cultivate his taste in morality as in any other fine art. [11]

(4) In opposition to Hobbes's view that man is by nature wholly selfish, and that compassion is a sign of weakness, Shaftesbury asserted that compassion, or benevolence, is not only instinctive in man, but is the highest virtue to which he attains. Man is provided, said Shaftesbury, with two sets of affections — the selfish and the social passions — both instinctive and both necessary for the preservation of the race.* To resolve all human motive into selfishness and deny the naturalness of the unselfish propensities, as Hobbes, Rochester, and the other egoists had done, was to contradict the palpable facts of nature. Moreover, there is no conflict between the two sets of instincts; for the good of the individual can be secured only by promoting the welfare of society. [12] The very fact that man is born helpless is an indication that he was intended never to exist out of the social state; Hobbes's theory of a "state of nature" and a "social compact" is a mere figment, for unsocial man is inconceivable. [13] In defining the conduct which leads to the perfection and happiness incident to virtue, Shaftesbury has, therefore, remarkably little to say concerning those acts which spring from the selfish motive and apply to man as he is considered apart from his fellows; the whole force of his teaching is to exalt the naturalness and beauty of universal benevolence, [14] which he calls the perfection of the "natural temper." Since compassion is the supreme form of moral beauty, the neglect of it is the greatest of all offenses against

* He includes also a third, the "unnatural affections" (*Characteristics,* I, 286), but makes no use of them.

nature's ordained harmony. While the Church was urging that charity returns to the donor a hundredfold, Shaftesbury appealed to the well-bred by representing the compassionate man as the perfection of human nature, and the selfish man as an unnatural monster. He accused the Church of destroying virtue in the interest of religion; forty years later Warburton in turn condemned the *Characteristics* as a "Scheme of Virtue without Religion." [15]

The fact that this genial theory did not secure literary adoption in Anne's reign is readily explained. Although deism had infected a large proportion of the upper classes, the Queen's zealous protection of the Established Church and the machinery of the law against heresy (1697) deterred most of the recalcitrant spirits from championing a belief that banished Collins in 1713, and threatened the position of Shaftesbury himself.* Outwardly the Church was at the height of power. [16] It was also the golden age of ecclesiastical charity, most of it being conducted through the agency of the Religious Societies and preached on the basis which provoked Shaftesbury's contemptuous reference to the "rod and sweetmeat." It is a significant fact that the word *benevolence* had not come into general use, and in spite of the actual relief afforded and the excellent character of men like Robert Nelson who were engaged in the undertaking, there is undoubtedly some truth in Shaftesbury's contention that such charity was a mere bargaining with God. The persuasive used is typified by one of Nelson's own appeals: "God returns to us a hundred-fold, even by open and glaring methods, that which charity hath secretly slided into the hands of the poor. An unexpected inheritance, the determination of a law-suit in our favour, the success of a great adventure, an advantageous match, are sometimes the recompenses of charity in this world." [17]

To poetry this regime offered at most the possibility of describing with conventional imagery the dread occasion of the final judgment, when rewards and punishments would be dealt

---

* See *Regimen*, pp. 369, 371, 384. Shaftesbury's birth was one protection, yet he probably would have suffered but for the interposition of his friend Lord Somers (*Regimen*, pp. 400–402, 420–421).

out. It was evident, too, that such a rationale could not defend
its philanthropy against the obnoxious doctrine of the egoists;
the Church was, in fact, utilizing the very doctrine it professed
to abhor. A vague uneasiness on this account is discernible in
some of the essays of Addison and Steele which recommend
the cause of the poor; they gradually abandoned the traditional
formula, but were too much concerned for their own standing
to employ any of Shaftesbury's argument. The only evidence
of his theory in any of their publications is to be found in two
numbers of the *Spectator* (588, 601) contributed by the dissenter
Henry Grove, and published after the Queen's death (1714).

The new conditions ushered in by the accession of George I,
however, produced a variety of effects that eventually cleared
the way for the reception of Shaftesbury. The authority of the
Church suddenly declined. The foreign sovereign's indifference
to matters of religion, Walpole's conversion of the Church into
an instrument of state policy, the Whig suspicion of all ecclesiastical measures fostered by the Tories of the previous reign, and the
internal dissensions which had long been brewing in the Church
resulted in a collapse of the old hierarchy and its dependent
charities,* a loss of prestige which the Established Church has
never succeeded in fully restoring. The chief of these causes was
the open fight between the deists and the orthodox. When the
conflict began to subside, without definite victory for either party,
the most tangible results of the fray were a liberty of thought
which had been questioned under Anne and a freedom of social

---

* The most popular philanthropy during Anne's reign was the Charity
School (see *An Account of Charity Schools lately erected in England,
Wales, and Ireland*, Ann. Pub. London, 1707; *Tatler*, Nos. 138, 261, 372;
*British Apollo*, II, 1, 15; *Spectator*, Nos. 294, 380, 430; *Guardian*, No. 105;
Robert Nelson, *An Address to Persons of Quality*, p. 183 and Appendix).
These schools were distrusted by the victorious Whig party under George I
as hotbeds of Jacobitism and discountenanced (see *Charity still a Christian
Virtue*, a pamphlet of 1719 formerly attributed to Defoe; footnote to a
*Poem humbly inscribed to . . . the Oxfordshire Society*, anonymous, 1723).
For other failures of the Church program, see Overton and Relton, *History
of the English Church*, etc., p. 20. On the general decay of the Church,
see J. H. Overton, *The Evangelical Revival*, etc., Introduction; Sir R. J.
Phillimore, *Memoirs of Lord Lyttelton*, I, 354–363; and Addison's *The
Drummer* (1716).

reform from the exclusive control of theological dogmatism. Temporarily the disintegration resulted in widespread immorality and a general indifference to questions of philanthropy; but it afforded the necessary transition from the prudential motives of the dogmatists to the safe adoption of Shaftesbury's more liberal views.

The one additional impulse needed for his triumph was furnished by his bitterest opponent, Bernard Mandeville, whose *Fable of the Bees* (1723) contains an attack on the *Characteristics.** While opposing Shaftesbury's theory of benevolence, Mandeville gave the cynical doctrine of Epicurus, Hobbes, and La Rochefoucauld such literal application in his attack on charities and so openly justified the grossness of the time that he offended the self-respect of the better classes.† In this way he drove to the defense of "benevolence" men of the most divergent views, who found in the *Characteristics* a common rallying ground. The most important of Shaftesbury's champions among the philosophers was the deist Francis Hutcheson; his influence in the spread of the benevolent theory was second only to that of Shaftesbury himself. It is still more significant, perhaps, that even the orthodox thinkers began slowly to perceive that much of Shaftesbury's ethical system, when "abstracted from the framework of its theology," could be used against Mandeville by the Church as well as by the "free thinkers." And it will be found

---

* The earlier edition (1714) is merely *The Grumbling Hive* (1705), a doggerel poem, supplemented by copious notes, and is primarily economic in purpose; the edition of 1723 added *An Essay on Charity Schools and a Search into the Nature of Society*. After a severe reprimand by the Grand Jury of Middlesex, the author published a vindication in the *London Journal* for Aug. 10, 1723, and in 1728 added to the *Fable* a second part. For comments, see *Tea Table*, No. 25 (1724) and *Comedian*, No. 9 (1733). The book went into a sixth English edition in 1729, and a ninth in 1755.

† The *Fable* provoked the following replies: John Dennis, *Vice and Luxury Public Mischiefs*, etc. (1724); William Law, *Remarks on the Fable of the Bees* (1724); Richard Fiddes, *A General Treatise of Morality*, etc. (1724); Francis Hutcheson, *Essays* (1725) and *Observations on the Fable of the Bees* (1725-1727); Archibald Campbell, *Aretelogia* (1728); George Berkeley, *Alciphron*, Dial. II (1732); John Brown, *Essays on the Characteristics*, etc., Secs. iv, v (1751), and *An Estimate*, etc. (1757), ed. 1758, I, 190, II, 86. It was attacked also by Rousseau in the *Discours sur l'inégalité* (1752).

that most of the philosophers who afterward opposed him did so on some ground other than that of his ethics.*

An idea of his vogue thereafter is to be had from general testimony of various kinds. The *Characteristics* went into a fourth English edition in 1727, a fifth in 1732, and by 1790 reached the eleventh.[18] It was translated into French and German,[19] and was referred to constantly by English and European writers. The fascination of what Lamb calls the "genteel style" of the author led Goldsmith to observe, in 1759, that Shaftesbury had had "more imitators in Britain than any other writer" he knew; "all faithfully preserving his blemishes, but unhappily not one of his beauties." [20] Montesquieu went so far as to call him one of the four great poets of the world.[21] Even Warburton, who was moved to righteous indignation by the theology of the *Characteristics*, could not entirely withhold his praise: "In his writings he hath shown how largely he had imbibed the deep sense, and how naturally he could copy the gracious manner of Plato." [22] Bishop Hurd was of the opinion that one of the only three dialogues in English that deserved commendation was *The Moralists* of Lord Shaftesbury.[23] John Byrom's *Enthusiasm* (1752) gives a more specific reason for his popularity:

> The Mercer, Tailor, Bookseller, grows rich,
> Because fine clothes, fine Writings can bewitch.
> A Cicero, a Shaftesbury, a Bayle —
> How quickly would they diminish in their Sale!
> Four-fifths of all their Beauties who would heed,
> Had they not keen *Enthusiasts* to read?

The Preface to the edition of 1733 asserts triumphantly, "All the best judges are agreed that we never had any work in the English language so beautiful, so delightful, and so instructive as these *Characteristics*."

Through Warburton we have Pope's testimony that "to his knowledge the *Characteristics* had done more harm to revealed religion in England than all the works of infidelity put to-

* Berkeley is a conspicuous exception (see *Alciphron*, Dial. III).

gether." [24] Herder, one of Shaftesbury's devoted followers, thinking of the aesthetic system of ethics proposed by him, declared in 1794 that this "virtuoso of humanity" had contributed much to the philosophy of Leibnitz, Diderot, Lessing, and Mendelssohn, and indeed had "exercised a marked influence upon the best heads of the century, upon men who with resolute honesty concerned themselves with the True, the Beautiful, and the Good." [25] Shaftesbury's countryman John Armstrong, who was not so friendly to his philosophy, gave similar, but less elegant, testimony by admitting in *Taste* (1753) that "Ashley turned more solid heads than one." It is safe to assert that, with the possible exception of John Locke, Shaftesbury was more generally known in the mid-century than any other English philosopher.

II

These various conditions indicate why Shaftesbury's vogue in popular literature was delayed until the closing years of George I's reign and then suddenly became general.

In the earlier period I have already noted a faint reflection of his influence on Henry Grove's essays in the *Spectator*; but it is a very general resemblance and cautiously avoids any possibility of offense to the Church. Apparently the first actual literary follower of Shaftesbury was the obscure poet Henry Needler (1690–1718). In a thin volume of verse and prose, original date of publication unknown, there is a letter of December 3, 1711, in which he thanks a correspondent for a copy of the *Characteristics* (published in that year). As a token of his appreciation, he attempted a prose imitation of Shaftesbury's apostrophe to nature in *The Moralists*, and used the same material for *A Poem in blank verse, proving the Being of a God from the Works of Creation. And some brief Remarks on the Folly of Discontent.* These puerile performances assemble all the propositions of Natural Religion: the Deity reveals himself through his works; the revelation of his character is made clear to his creatures, who are endowed with an all-sufficient reason; and the only legitimate attitude of man is the assurance that this scheme of nature is unexceptionable. Other resemblances to Shaftesbury are evident in Needler's prose essay *On the Beauty of the Universe* and his poems *On the True Cause of Natural Effects* and *A Vernal Hymn in Praise of the Creator.*

I suspect Needler's fate served for a time to deter further experiments of the kind; there seems to be no trace of his first edition, he committed suicide, and the editor of the second edition was much concerned to vindicate the "extreme piety" of the poet. Although his entire work is feeble and makes relatively little of Shaftesbury except as to theology, it is important as an index. In spite of the danger which almost certainly attended the adoption of deism, he could not resist the appeal of Shaftesbury's poetical treatment of nature. At the time of the second edition (1728), such ideas were no longer contraband, and poetry was already flooded with a more or less scientific study of universal harmony. Needler's explicit reference of these views to Shaftesbury is in itself a good reason for supposing that, although some of the later poets do not acknowledge the indebtedness, the entire school derived much of its inspiration from the same source. It is probable, too, that the following publisher's Advertisement included in the 1728 edition of Needler stimulated productivity: "The Essay on the Beauty of the Universe, though very just and rational, is but a sketch (as Mr. Needler himself owns) . . . I wish it may incite some able hand to treat more amply so useful and entertaining a Subject."

Shaftesbury's popularity, however, was to depend primarily on his ethical teaching, for which this theology served merely as a poetical background. Popular writers, like the philosophers, turned to him in the late twenties as a refuge from the nightmare occasioned by Mandeville's doctrine, which in view of contemporary selfishness was disconcertingly plausible, and therefore all the more distressing to national pride. A good general impression of the popular attitude is afforded by extracts from two poems that came somewhat late in the movement. In *Honour, a Poem* (1743), which denounces various pests of society, John Brown bestows chief place upon Hobbes and Mandeville:

Errour in vain attempts the foul disguise
Still tasted in the bitter wave of vice;
Drawn from the springs of Falsehood all confess
Each baneful drop that poisons happiness;
Gordon's thin shallows, Tindale's muddy page,
And Morgan's gall, and Woolston's furious rage;
Th' envenom'd stream that flows from Toland's quill,
And the rank dregs of Hobbes and Mandeville.
Detested names! yet sentenc'd ne'er to die;
Snatch'd from oblivion's grave by infamy.*

The author adds, in a footnote to the passage, "The reader who is acquainted with the writings of these gentlemen will probably observe a kind of climax in this place; ascending from those who attempt to destroy the several fences of virtue, to the wild boars of the wood that root it up." Shaftesbury, on the other hand, was hailed as the champion of moral rule. In a poem of 1735, referring to Newton's discoveries, is the following tribute by William Melmoth:[26]

Order *without* us, what imports it seen,
If all is restless anarchy *within?*
Fired with this thought great Ashley, gen'rous sage,
Plan'd [*sic*] in sweet leisure his instructive page.
Not orbs he weighs, but marks with happier skill
The scope of *action* and the poise of *will;*
In fair proportion here described we trace
Each *mental* beauty, and each moral grace,
Each useful passion taught its tone designed
In the nice concord of a well tun'd mind.
Does mean self-love contract each social aim?
Here publick transports shall thy soul inflame,
Virtue and Deity supremely fair,
Too oft delineated with looks severe,
Resume their native smiles and graces here.

The moral question at issue between these two systems of philosophy — the egoistic and the benevolent — became soon after

---

* Similar attacks on the egoists are contained in James Bramston's *The Man of Taste* (1733); David Mallet's *Tyburn: To the Marine Society* (1762); Samuel Wesley, Jr.'s *On Mr. Hobbes*; William Dobson's *Translation of Anti-Lucretius, Of God and Nature* (1757).

the publication of the *Fable* the most absorbing topic of public discussion. Apparently no poet had the courage to support Mandeville's entire theory.* Naturally Shaftesbury's most ardent defenders were deists who accepted the doctrine of the *Characteristics* entire. It was therefore due principally to the deists that "benevolence" became the most fashionable topic of poetry; but their view gradually spread. The result was not merely a revival of social and literary interest in philanthropy and a revulsion from the moral coarseness of the time, but the replacing of the old prudential argument by a more disinterested motive that lent itself to the sentimental belief in natural goodness. The change meant a break with theological dogma and a definite step toward the naturalism of Rousseau.

In poetry the beginning of this ethical movement is to be assigned definitely to James Thomson. By adopting the theory of the social affections, he became the first important humanitarian poet in English. When the original edition of *Winter* appeared (1726), Thomson was not sufficiently in touch with English social problems to deal with them; his first utterance on the subject is in *Summer* (1727), and is stated in very general terms. After upbraiding the cruelty of those who neglect charitable offices, he adds:

> But to the generous still-improving mind,
> That gives the hopeless heart to sing for joy,
> Diffusing kind beneficence around,
> Boastless, as now descends the silent dew —
> To him the long review of ordered life
> Is inward rapture only to be felt.
>
> (Lines 1641–1646)

Simple, and even commonplace, as this passage is, it sounds a new note in English poetry. From this time forward Thomson himself was continually pleading, not merely for the spirit of benevolence, but for every special humane movement of his day. Most of such comment in *The Seasons*[27] is in passages supplementary

* Lord Paget's *An Essay on Human Life* (1734), which according to Horace Walpole was written in imitation of Pope, is probably to be excepted; there is one passage which adopts Mandeville's view in explicit terms. Later, however, the author apparently contradicts himself.

to the original content of the poems,[28] the chief additions being made to *Winter*: the first edition, the second, and the final contain, respectively, 405, 781, and 1,069 lines, and the increase is due principally to the insertion of humanitarian passages. Among the special philanthropies he encouraged in *The Seasons* and elsewhere are Oglethorpe's prison reforms,[29] the founding of Georgia for debtors,[30] and the erection of the Foundling Hospital.[31] In no poet before Thomson, and in few poets since, does social reform hold so large a place in comparison with other literary interests; moreover, in no popular writing had the cause of social reform been argued on the basis adopted by him.

Thomson was regarded by Voltaire as "a true philosophical poet," [32] and that he drew his inspiration largely from the *Characteristics* was recognized by Herder,[33] whose own reproduction of Shaftesbury's ideas in both prose [34] and verse [35] establishes his competence as a critic in the matter. One of Thomson's recent biographers, however, is disturbed by what he considers a modern tendency to associate the poet with the philosophers. "To represent him as primarily a 'philosophical poet' is," says G. C. Macaulay, "a strange aberration of criticism which has been reserved for our own times." [36] The truth is, it would be a strange oversight in criticism not to do so. If in a period when most of the literature was didactic there is any poet more frankly committed to philosophy than Mark Akenside, it is James Thomson. In a juvenile lay he laments his philosophic inability:

> Ah! my loved God! in vain a tender youth
> Unskilled in arts of deep philosophy,
> Attempts to search the bulky mass of matter,
> To trace the rules of motion; and pursue
> The phantom Time, too subtle for his grasp.*

In a later poem he indicates that he has supplied the deficiency:

> With thee, serene Philosophy, with thee,
> And thy bright garland, let me crown my song!
> Effusive source of evidence and truth!

* *Fragment of a Poem on the Works and Wonders of Almighty Power*, published in the *Plain Dealer*, No. 46.

And after explaining the nature of his philosophical conclusions, he adds:

> Tutored by thee, hence poetry exalts
> Her voice to ages; and informs the page
> With music, image, sentiment, and thought,
> Never to die; the treasure of mankind,
> Their highest honour, and their truest joy.*

There are few pages in his poems which will not furnish further evidence, including the mention and reproduction of various philosophers, ancient and modern. What Macaulay probably meant is that Thomson does not expound any particular system of philosophy in dry detail, that he is not a mere versifying philosopher. This statement, however, is true only in the sense that his philosophy is not collected in one continuous passage, but is relieved and illustrated by many devices of poetic art; the entire corpus of his verse is pervaded by philosophic assumptions frequently stated and maintained with as great consistence as one finds in most speculation of the period.†

That Thomson accepted the theology of deism is established by the testimony of his poetry and his contemporaries. Macaulay cited the latter class of evidence, but took little account of the former. Negatively, Thomson's deism is indicated by the fact that, after he came to England, he expressed no belief in Christ or in revelation — an omission of some consequence when we recall that the religious controversy was then intense, that he was constantly dealing with questions immediately related to theological belief, and that in his early life he had written poems on the orthodox pattern. Positively, it is indicated by his insistence on the sufficiency of reason.‡ His friend Lord Lyttelton lamented his heresy and hoped that he would retract it publicly; but Lyttel-

* See the entire passage, *Summer*, 1730–1805.

† Pope's contradictions are notorious. Thomson vacillates between pantheism and a belief in the personality of God (Léon Morel, *James Thomson, sa vie et ses oeuvres* [Paris, 1895], pp. 397–399); the same inconsistence runs throughout Shaftesbury's philosophy. Their pantheism is a matter largely of poetic phrasing; but the orthodox found in these deistic expressions grounds for identifying deists and atheists.

‡ There is more than a hint of his theology in *Liberty* IV.561–573.

ton's only satisfaction was that Thomson on his deathbed made a vague profession of Christianity to one or two personal friends.[37] To shield the poet's reputation after his death, Lyttelton omitted from the collected edition of Thomson's work the *Hymn* which concludes *The Seasons*; but Murdoch reinstated it, claiming that "the theology of it, allowance being made for poetical expression, is orthodox." On this particular point Lyttelton's judgment was obviously sound; but this one omission would have had slight effect, for the deistic presupposition is at the root of all Thomson's verse.

It is highly probable, too, that the poet took his theology, as Needler did, directly from Shaftesbury. The fundamental principle he might have had from various sources, for it was by this time a commonplace. The literature and coffeehouse discussions which carried on the "learned scuffle" during the reign of George I, however, were strictly polemical and usually very coarse. Shaftesbury had, on the other hand, quietly assumed the doctrine, and as a theologian had devoted his main energy to giving it poetic application in his impassioned treatment of the Deity and Nature. An equally aesthetic and insidious presentation is not to be found in any of the argumentative deists who followed him. Thomson's theology is of the same unobtrusive, artistic kind.

The similarity between the nature worship in *The Seasons* and in the *Characteristics*, especially between the *Hymn* and the apostrophe in *The Moralists*, is too obvious to require more than a statement; but it will become still more impressive if these two pieces are studied in connection with Herder's *Naturhymnus von Shaftesburi* (1800). The indebtedness is particularly evident in Thomson's virtual identification of God and Nature in such passages as the following, which occur frequently:

Hail, Source of Beings, Universal Soul
Of heaven and earth! Essential Presence, hail!
(*Spring*, 556ff)

O Nature! all-sufficient! over all!
(*Autumn*, 1351)

> These, as they change, Almighty Father, these
> Are but the varied God. The rolling year
> Is full of Thee.
>
> *(Hymn)*

The dependence upon the *Characteristics* manifests itself still more clearly in passages like the following from *Summer*, which repeats Shaftesbury's protest against the short-sighted vanity of man in questioning the perfect ends of nature:

> Let no presuming impious railer tax
> Creative Wisdom, as if aught was formed
> In vain, or not for admirable ends.
>
> *(Lines 318–320)*

The most connected discourse in the manner of the *Characteristics* is the treatment of the thesis already noted in the study of Shaftesbury — that the physical and moral world are but two expressions of the same cosmic order. Thomson would study with his friends the world of physical nature —

> Its life, its laws, its progress, and its end,

and adds in continuation:

> Then would we try to scan the moral world,
> Which, though to us it seems embroiled, moves on
> In high order; fitted and impelled
> By wisdom's firmest hand, and issuing all
> In general good.
>
> *(Winter, 572–616)*

This agreement in theology, however, has for the present purpose only the secondary importance of confirming Thomson's debt to the *Characteristics* for his system of morality. On this purely ethical ground the relation between the two can hardly be questioned, although it has been disregarded by such a thorough student as Morel.* The main business of Thomson as well as Shaftesbury was to make his entire speculation subservient to virtuous practice: in each case theology was important only as a starting point for ethics. In his statement of man's moral obli-

---

* There is a slight reference to Shaftesbury and Thomson's tribute to him, p. 399, and note. Grudzinski (pp. 7–8, *op. cit.* in note 1) follows Herder.

gations the poet's indebtedness to the philosopher would be sufficiently clear from internal evidence; it is, moreover, explicitly
acknowledged by Thomson. In a long catalogue of illustrious
philosophers, statesmen, and poets of England, Shaftesbury is the
only one commended for his moral teaching:

> The generous Ashley, thine, the friend of man;
> Who scanned his nature with a brother's eye,
> His weakness prompt to shade, to raise his aim,
> To touch the finer movements of the mind,
> And with the moral beauty charm the heart.
>
> (*Summer*, 1550–1555)

The end of all Shaftesbury's theology and ethics is the "moral
beauty" which entitles man "to be justly styled the friend of
mankind"; the moral purpose which invigorates and unifies all
of Thomson's poetry is the same universal benevolence.

In strict accord with Shaftesbury's theory of natural virtue,
Thomson urges as the sole persuasive of all humanitarian conduct
the "moral beauty" of goodness. He makes even slighter concession to the orthodox notion of future reward and punishment
than Shaftesbury does; the conclusion of *Winter*, altered as it
now stands, allows a life of bliss to compensate the evils endured
by the virtuous in this world, but Thomson makes no attempt
to enforce morality by reference to a future life. The orthodox
poets of a slightly earlier period, and a few in his time, recommend social duties by depicting the awful scenes of the Judgment
Day, when the charitable will be given eternal happiness with
God, and the uncharitable will be consigned to everlasting fire;
Thomson regularly proposes as the ultimate reward of generous
aid the "inward rapture only to be felt." His belief in the sufficiency of virtue is contained in this prayer:

> Father of light and life! thou Good Supreme!
> O teach me what is good! teach me thyself!
> Save me from folly, vanity, and vice,
> From every low pursuit; and feed my soul
> With knowledge, conscious peace, and virtue pure,
> Sacred, substantial, never-fading bliss!
>
> (*Winter*, 217–222)

It may be objected that the present argument exaggerates the evidence of internal resemblance and of Thomson's own statement of discipleship by attributing to Shaftesbury's suggestion many ideas that are commonplaces in philosophy and poetry. The very fact that they are commonplaces is due largely to these two writers. Before Thomson's time there is no popular writer who exhibits his system in its entirety or even the full statement of his moral doctrine. It is equally true that he himself could have borrowed his main assumptions *in toto* only from Shaftesbury. His theology he might have had from anywhere, but in a very desiccated form. Some details of his ethics he might have had from early philosophers. But the pagan moralists whom he mentions are the very writers whose doctrines inform the *Characteristics*; and among Shaftesbury's successors the only moral philosopher who could have contributed directly to Thomson's special view of benevolence was Francis Hutcheson, who began his defense of the *Characteristics* the year Thomson came to London, and whose influence, if proved, would be merely additional.

The argument of relation between Shaftesbury and Thomson is further confirmed by their agreement on matters extraneous to the subject of this study — including their critical utterances on literature, politics, and the connection between the arts and social progress. In *Advice to an Author*, an essay recommended to struggling writers by its eloquent plea for literary patronage, Shaftesbury urges particularly the employment of blank verse and the conversion of all poetry into a medium for moral instruction. Thomson's conformity with these views and the defense of his practice, set forth in the prose dedications and the poetry itself, may be accidental; at any rate, the coincidence adds another link to the chain of association. Possibly a greater significance attaches to the fact that Thomson's defense of the Whigs, his unhappy efforts to trace the genesis and progress of society, his treatment of the connection between culture and freedom, and various other enthusiastic ideas of *Liberty* are faithful in spirit to the earlier statements of the more practical Whig philosopher.[38]

If we take into account at one view this general agreement on the incidental matters discussed by the two writers, the widespread interest in the Shaftesbury-Mandeville dispute, Thomson's evident imitation of Shaftesbury's theological and ethical doctrine, and his own acknowledgment of his indebtedness, there is no reason for rejecting Herder's opinion or for denying to Shaftesbury's influence the moral system which underlies all of Thomson's benevolent poetry. To do so would be to assume that the poet Thomson evolved a theory of ethics which the philosophers themselves, Hutcheson and others, were copying from Shaftesbury.

This is a matter of the first importance in defining the effect of the *Characteristics* upon popular literature. This relation once admitted, it follows that "the founder of the benevolent school of philosophy" exerted through *The Seasons* an indirect influence upon many other poets, great and small, who were immediately fired by the reception of Thomson, but did not always refer their ideas to Shaftesbury as the original source. It was due largely to Thomson's example that "benevolence" and "good-nature" stamped themselves on all English literature. In a biography prefixed to the 1740 edition of his poems, Thomas Murdoch explains the poet's popularity on two grounds: "In a short time the applause became unanimous; everyone wondering how so many pictures, and pictures so familiar, should have moved them but faintly to what they felt in his descriptions. His digressions, too, the overflowings of a tender benevolent heart, charmed the reader no less; leaving him in doubt, whether he should more admire the Poet or love the Man." Lord Lyttelton referred to Thomson as one who taught "fair Virtue's purest laws," [39] and paid a compliment to his "fine and delicate sentiments of a most tender and benevolent heart." [40] Shiels's *Musidorus* (1748) [41] commended Thomson's humanity. David Mallet addressed the author of *The Seasons* as a benefactor who "dared to embrace the general welfare of thy kind." [42]

Similar praise is to be found in Shenstone's *Verses Written towards the close of 1748, Elegy* XIV, XXIII, and *Pastoral Ode* to *Richard Lyttelton*; Richard Savage's *Of Public Spirit*; Mrs. Elizabeth Rowe's *To Mr. Thomson*; Joseph Giles's *The Leasowes*; Joseph Mitchell's *To Mr. Thomson*; and the anonymous *On Beneficence*.[43] The encouragement of the poetasters to imitate Thomson's benevolent writing and also to capitalize his example is seen in the following passage from James Ralph's Preface to a volume of poetry (1729) including *Night*, which was written in imitation of Thomson's *Winter*:

"Poetry is at once intended for our delight, and instruction; but a vicious fancy of amusing the world with trifles in lieu of such subjects as are in themselves truly noble and sublime, has of late been too much indulg'd; for which reason, I hope, 'twill be equally needless, to make any excuse for my choice of so grave a subject, or use any persuasives to influence its success; especially if the dress it appears in should prove any way becoming to its dignity; and 'tis consider'd with what applause Mr. Thomson's admirable poems were generally received by the favorers of learning and good sense; an undeniable argument, that if the 'Muse' is really the inspirer, the world, even to a serious author, will not be wholly ungrateful." *

Of Mark Akenside's direct indebtedness to the *Characteristics* there is abundant evidence. He himself speaks of Shaftesbury as "the noble restorer of ancient philosophy." † According to Gray, *The Pleasures of the Imagination* (1744) is "too much infected with the Hutchison jargon." [44] Warburton calls Akenside "a follower of Ld. S[haftesbury]." [45] John Gilbert Cooper regarded Shaftesbury's doctrine as best reproduced by Hutcheson and Akenside.[46] *The Pleasures of the Imagination* versifies not only the incidental theology of the *Characteristics*, but the attacks on superstition and the defense of ridicule as a corrective in all reli-

---

* Compare Thomson's Preface to the second, third, and fourth editions of *Winter*, Aldine ed., I, cxi–cxvi.

† Author's note on *The Pleasures of the Imagination* I.374 ("Truth and Good are one"): he praises Hutcheson for the same doctrine. In a note on III.18, he connects Shaftesbury with Marcus Aurelius and Epictetus and declares that in Shaftesbury "the stoical doctrine is embellished with all the elegance and grace of Plato." See also the note on II.325. For the suggestions of another kind derived from Addison, see the Preface.

gious discussion.* It is least poetic in those parts which discuss
the harmony of the physical universe discovered by Newton;
Akenside attempts to illustrate the general truth by minute details,
and turns out a product frequently neither scientific nor poetic.
Thomson had exhibited the same fault, but less extensively.

Although Akenside devotes much more of his time to these dry
details than to the moral ideas and practical lessons arising from
his system of nature, there are some passages which reproduce
very accurately Shaftesbury's theory of innate benevolence. In
the following passage Akenside takes issue with the cynicism of
Hobbes and Mandeville:

> Dost thou aspire to judge between the Lord
> Of Nature and His works? To lift thy voice
> Against the sovereign order He decreed,
> All good and lovely? To blaspheme the bonds
> Of tenderness innate and social love,
> Holiest of things! by which the general orb
> Of being, as by adamantine links,
> Was drawn to perfect union and sustain'd
> From everlasting? Hast thou felt the pangs
> Of softening sorrow, of indignant zeal
> So grievous to the soul, as thence to wish
> The ties of Nature broken from thy frame;
> That so thy selfish, unrelenting heart
> Might cease to mourn its lot, no longer then
> The wretched heir of evils not its own?
> O fair benevolence of generous minds!
> O man by Nature form'd for all mankind!
>
> (II.246–262)

In another passage he is equally pointed in his attack on the
assertion of the egoists that all pity is to be resolved into selfishness. Mandeville had illustrated the point by saying that if a man
rescues a baby from falling into the fire, he acts, not out of compassion for the baby, but out of the selfish desire to save himself
from an unpleasant sensation. To this Akenside retorts:

* This view of Shaftesbury's was especially irritating to the orthodox,
and was constantly attacked by them. For a similar protest in verse, see
W. Whitehead, *On Ridicule* (1743).

> Ask the crowd
> Which flies impatient from the village walk
> To climb the neighboring cliffs, when far below
> The cruel winds have hurl'd upon the coast
> Some helpless bark; while sacred Pity melts
> The general eye, or Terror's icy hand
> Smites, every mother closer to her breast
> Catches her child, and, pointing where the waves
> Foam through the shatter'd vessel, shrieks aloud
> As one poor wretch that spreads his piteous arms,
> For succour, swallow'd by the roaring surge,
> As now another, dash'd against the rock,
> Drops lifeless down: O! deemest thou indeed
> No kind endearment here by Nature given
> To mutual terror and compassion's tears?
> No sweetly melting softness which attracts,
> O'er all that edge of pain, the social powers
> To this their proper action and their end?
>                     (Rev. ed., 1765, II.624–642)

The closest rendering of Shaftesbury's theory is found in *Concord* (1751), a poem written by his nephew James Harris.* The general resemblance is indicated by the opening lines:

> The deeds of discord, or in prose or rhyme,
> Let others tell. 'Tis mine (the better theme)
> Concord to sing; and thus begins the song:
> Congenial things to things congenial tend:
> So rivulets their little waters join
> To form one river's greater stream: so haste
> The rivers, from their different climes, to meet,
> And kindly mix, in the vast ocean's bed;
> To fires etherial, each terrestrial blaze,
> Such elemental Concord. Yet not here
> Confin'd the sacred sympathy, but wide
> Thro' plant and animal diffusely spread.
> How many myriads of the grassy blade

---

* Not included in the edition of Harris's works by his son, but assigned to him in F. Fawkes and W. Woty, *The Poetical Calendar* (London, 1763), XII, 53–59. Johnson considered Harris "a prig, and a bad prig" (Boswell, ed. Morley; III, 206). In 1744 he published *Three Treatises, the first concerning Art, the second concerning Music, Painting, and Poetry, the third concerning Happiness*; the first of these is dedicated to Shaftesbury.

Assemble, to create one verdant plain?
How many cedars' towering heights conspire,
Thy tops, O cloud-capt Lebanon! to deck?
Life-animal still more conspicuous gives
Her fair example. Here the social tie
We trace, ascending from th' ignoble swarms
Of insects, up to flocks and grazing herds;
Thence to the polities of bees and ants,
And honest beavers, bound by friendly league
Of mutual help and interest. Cruel man!
For love of gain, to persecute, to kill,
This gentle, social, and ingenious race,
That never did you wrong. But stop, my Muse,
Stop this sad song, nor deviate to recount
Man's more inhuman deeds; for man too feels
Benign affection, nor dares disobey,
Tho' oft reluctant, Nature's mighty voice,
That summons all to harmony and love.
Else would to Nature's Author foul impute
Of negligence accrue, while baser things
He knits in holy friendship, thus to leave
His chief and last work void of sweet attract,
And tendence to its fellow.

The identity of the Good and the Beautiful, one of the chief doctrines of the *Characteristics*, is stated thus:

And as the tuneful string spontaneous sounds
In answer to his kindred note; so he
The secret harmony within him feels,
When aught of beauty offers. This the joy,
While verdant plains and grazing herds we view,
Or ocean's mighty vastness; or the stars,
In midnight silence as along they roll.
Hence too the rapture, while the harmonious bard
Attunes his vocal song; and hence the joy,
While what the sculptor graves, the painter paints,
And all the pleasing mimickries of art
Strike our accordant minds. Yet chief, by far,
Chief is man's joy, when, mixt with human kind,
He feels affection melt the social heart;
Feels friendship, love, and all the charities
Of father, son, and brother. Here the pure

> Sincere congenial, free from all alloy,
> With bliss he recognizes. For to man
> What dearer is than man? Say you, who prove
> The kindly call, the social sympathy,
> What but this call, this social sympathy,
> Tempers to standard due the vain exult
> Of prosperous fortune? What but this refines
> Soft pity's pain, and sweetens every care,
> Each friendly care we feel for human kind?

The similar purport of *The Power of Harmony, In Two Books* (1745), by John Gilbert Cooper, one of the chief "benevolists," is indicated sufficiently by the concluding statement of the Design prefixed to the poem: "From what has been premised, it would be needless to explain the comprehensive meaning of the word harmony. For an explanation or a proof of the relation of the imitative arts to moral philosophy, the reader is referred to the dialogues of Plato, and the other philosophers of the academic school; to lord Shaftesbury and Hutchison, their great disciples among the moderns." The authority of Shaftesbury is avowed also by the minor poet Andrews in *To the Late Lord Shaftesbury's Ghost*, printed as a conclusion to *Eidyllia* (1757), and in the anonymous poems *An Ode on Benevolence* (1753) and *An Essay on Happiness, In Four Books* (1762).

### III

The poetry so far cited, ranging in time from 1726 to 1762, represents a definite "school." Of the distinctive characteristics which these writers imitated from Shaftesbury the most common are a quasi-scientific theology and a moral system ending in the doctrine of universal benevolence. That many other writers, who do not state their authority, fell under the same influence would naturally follow from the evidence of Shaftesbury's popularity furnished by these poets and by the testimony of other writers cited in connection with various matters throughout this study. In view of such a vogue, it is clearly legitimate to refer to the same source contemporary poems exhibiting with minute precision the same characteristics. Whether they spring directly from

Shaftesbury or his imitators is of small concern. Undoubtedly most of them were stimulated by Thomson's *The Seasons*. The very titles of some indicate the nature of their contents: Henry Baker's *The Universe* (1727), Henry Brooke's *Universal Beauty* (1728, 1735),* Soame Jenyns's *An Essay on Virtue* (1734), and the anonymous *Order* (1737), *Essay on Happiness* (1737), *On Beneficence* (1740), *Nature, A Poem* (1747), and *Poetic Essays on Nature, Men and Morals* (1750). There is further evidence of imitation in David Mallet's *The Excursion* (1728) and William Hamilton's *Contemplation, or The Triumph of Love* (1747). The allegiance to Hutcheson is acknowledged by Mrs. Constantia Grierson in a poem *To the Honourable Mrs. Percival* and by the anonymous author of *On Reading Hutchison*.[47]

Of this group, only two pieces call for discussion. Henry Baker's *The Universe*, one of the first minor poems to indicate the movement, has intimations of both Shaftesbury and Needler. Moreover, crude as the following passage is, it looks forward to *An Essay on Man*:

> Alas! what's *Man* thus insolent and vain?
> One single link of Nature's mighty chain.
> Each hated toad, each crawling worm we see,
> Is needful to the Whole no less than he.

The passage immediately succeeding gives further evidence of relation to Shaftesbury and raises a point so far purposely ignored in the discussion of his philosophy and that of his imitators.

> Calmly consider wherefore gracious Heav'n
> To all these Creatures has existence giv'n.
> Eternal Goodness certainly design'd,
> That ev'ry one, according to its kind,
> Should happiness enjoy: — for God, all-just,
> Could ne'er intend His creatures to be curs'd.

---

* According to the *Cambridge Hist. of Eng. Lit.* (IX, 207), Brooke's poem is "by no means atheistic or even deistic"; but it has the characteristics of this school of deistic literature from Needler's essay *On the Beauty of the Universe* to Pope's *Essay on Man*, to which Brooke refers, V.60. Compare his pseudo-science with that of Shaftesbury, Thomson, and Akenside. Note also V.1–32. Did the Advertisement attached to Needler's poem influence Brooke?

> When life, He gave, He meant that life should be
> A state productive of felicity.
> And, though to kill there may be some pretence,
> When raging hunger bids, or self-defence;
> No cause beside can justify the deed.
> 'Tis murder if not urg'd by real need.
> If the same Pow'r did ev'ry being give,
> If all for happiness did life receive,
> Then ev'ry thing has equal right to live.
> And how dares man, who's but himself a breath,
> Destroy through wantonness, and sport with Death!

That this particular form of humanity is an integral part of Shaftesbury's scheme is self-evident, for the social affections must of necessity include the lower animals as a part of universal nature. He specifically makes this application in opposition to Descartes,[48] and Needler develops the doctrine at some length.[49] Like all of Shaftesbury's program, this idea came largely from the seventeenth-century study of Greek philosophy. It is found repeatedly in the Cambridge Platonists,* who were indebted for it chiefly to the Pythagoreans.† On the other hand, the elaboration and widespread diffusion of it in eighteenth-century literature were due to so many contributory influences ‡ besides Natural Religion that an adequate examination of it would require more space than can be given here. The movement was undoubtedly stimulated by deistic notions, and is represented most strikingly in deistic poets like Thomson.[50] It is cited here, however, merely to confirm the argument that Baker is quite in harmony

* For example, Cudworth, *The True Intellectual System of the Universe* (3 vols., 1845), II, 61, 357, III, 307–308, 449–453, 469; Henry More, *A Collection of Several Philosophical Writings*, Bk. II, Ch. 12; *Divine Dialogues*, Dial. II, Sec. xi, Dial. III, Secs. iii, xxx. J. Maxwell, the translator of Cumberland's *De Legibus Naturae* (tr. 1727), regrets, in General Remarks on Ch. 5, that the author did not include animals.

† A popular source for the Pythagorean doctrine was Dryden's translation of Ovid's *Metamorphoses*, Bk. XV. Compare Thomson, *Spring*, 336–378.

‡ One of the most important was *The Turkish Spy*, by Giovanni Paolo Marana, which went through twenty-six English editions between 1687 and 1770, and was widely imitated (see Martha Pike Conant, *The Oriental Tale in England*, Appendix B. I). Another was Montaigne's Essays, translated by Cotton (1685–1686) (see Bk. I, Ch. 22; Bk. II, Chs. 11 and 12, especially pp. 135–175, Bohn's Library).

with Shaftesbury and that he may be regarded, therefore, as an early member of the school.

Soame Jenyns's *Essay on Virtue*, written when deism was at its height, demands particular mention because it is the most vicious of all this group of poems in its attack on Christian ethics. His principal grievance is the old charge of the deists, that so-called religion makes a man unnatural and therefore immoral. To be good, according to Jenyns as well as Shaftesbury, man needs only to follow the dictates of nature: *

> How easy is our yoke! how light our load!
> Did we not strive to mend the laws of God!
> For his own sake no duty he can ask,
> The common welfare is our only task:
> For this sole end his precepts, kind and just,
> Forbid intemp'rance, murder, theft, and lust,
> With ev'ry act injurious to our own
> Or others' good, for such are crimes alone:
> For this are peace, love, charity, enjoin'd,
> With all that can secure and bless mankind.
> Thus is the public safety virtue's cause,
> And happiness the end of all her laws;
> For such by nature is the human frame,
> Our duty and our interest the same.
> "But hold," cries out some puritan divine,
> Whose well-stuffed cheeks with ease and plenty shine,
> "Is this to fast, to mortify, refrain,
> And work salvation out with fear and pain?"
> We own the rigid lessons of their schools
> Are widely diff'rent from these easy rules;
> Virtue, with them, is only to abstain
> From all that nature asks, and covet pain;
> Pleasure and vice are ever near a-kin,
> And, if we thirst, cold water is a sin;
> Heaven's path is rough and intricate, they say,
> Yet all are damn'd that trip, or miss their way;

* "What Soame Jenyns says upon the subject is not to be minded; he is a wit. No, Sir; to act from pure benevolence is not possible for finite beings. Human benevolence is mingled with vanity, interest, or some other motive." — Dr. Johnson (Boswell, III, 40). Jenyns's view underwent a change (see *A Free Inquiry into the Nature and Origin of Evil*, Letter v).

God is a being cruel and severe,
And man a wretch, by his command plac'd here,
In sunshine for a while to take a turn,
Only to dry and make him fit to burn.

Pope's *Essay on Man* (1732–1734) falls in the same category; it is a deistic poem evidently indebted to Shaftesbury, but there is no reference to him.* It raises a number of special considerations due to the additional influence of Bolingbroke and others; but fortunately, in order to come at Shaftesbury's effect on Pope's theory of benevolence, we may take for granted various facts which have become fully established. In the first place, it is certain that Bolingbroke, whom Pope cited as the sole authority for his ideas, drew much of his own system from Shaftesbury; but on account of a passage in the *Characteristics* † which reflects on him for deserting the Whigs, he deliberately omitted from his tedious review of philosophy all direct reference to Shaftesbury's system. J. M. Robertson asserts that the *Essay* is "in large part pure Shaftesbury filtered through Bolingbroke." [51] In the second place, it is known that Pope borrowed directly from various sources, and that one of the most important is *The Moralists*. This view, advanced by Voltaire, Warton, Warburton, and others in the eighteenth century, is not questioned.[52] That Pope elsewhere mentioned Shaftesbury only to ridicule him needs no further explanation than the attitude of his patron. In addition, there are two other important authorities cited for the *Essay*: King's *De Origine Mali* (1702) and Leibnitz's *Théodicée* (1710). The contribution of the latter is, I think, purely conjectural; but the insertion of neither King nor Leibnitz affects the main question under present consideration. The passages rightly or wrongly attributed to them relate only to details of theology, particularly

---

* Elsewhere Pope ridiculed *The Moralists*. "After borrowing so largely from this treatise, our author should not, methinks, have ridiculed it as he does, in the Fourth Book of the Dunciad, ver. 417" — J. Warton (*Essay on Pope* [1806] II, 94n). Without citing his evidence, Professor T. Fowler says that Pope did mention both the *Inquiry* and *The Moralists* as sources for the *Essay* (*Shaftesbury and Hutcheson*, p. 152n). Grudzinski makes the same unsupported assertion (p. 100, *op. cit.* in note 1).

† II, 262. Bolingbroke is not mentioned by name; but see Editor's note.

to the question of God's providence; from the nature of their work they could have yielded no more.

Pope's theory of benevolence is clearly due to Bolingbroke or Shaftesbury or both. Curiously enough, the commentators have confined themselves to the triangular agreement of the three; no attempt has been made to study Pope's views in the light of certain differences which distinguish Bolingbroke's theory of benevolence from Shaftesbury's. And the study of these at once explains some inconsistencies of the *Essay* and demonstrates the hold which the *Characteristics* had established on the popular mind.

Bolingbroke's suggestions were conveyed to Pope partly in conversations, "often interrupted, often renewed," and partly in writing. Pope is said by Lord Bathurst to have had before him at the time of writing a special outline drawn up by Bolingbroke;[53] but the only record which we have of the instructions given is in the *Letters* and the *Fragments* which were "thrown upon paper in Mr. Pope's lifetime, and at his desire," and published for the first time in the posthumous edition of Bolingbroke's works (1754). There are in the *Fragments*, as the author admits, some alterations, and parts were written after what we have of the incomplete *Essay* had already been published; these were evidently for the further guidance of Pope, who planned originally to extend the poem. There is no reason for supposing that this printed material, which fills two huge volumes of the latest edition of Bolingbroke,[54] does not represent an accurate statement of his instructions; and it is on the basis of these that we must calculate the differences between the views of Bolingbroke and Shaftesbury.

There are differences in both theology and ethics, and in the main, though not consistently, Pope follows Bolingbroke. Theologically Shaftesbury would not have encouraged Pope's adoption of the very ancient view:

> Know then thyself. Presume not God to scan,
> The proper study of mankind is man.

He insisted constantly on the study of man;[55] but he had little or none of Bolingbroke's vicious contempt for the supposition that human reason is capable of arriving at a knowledge of the divine nature, a view which Bolingbroke attacked with wearisome frequency in his opposition to Clarke.[56] It will be observed that here, and wherever else the two differ, Shaftesbury is far more flattering to man's nature. Under this difference are comprehended all of Bolingbroke's covert attacks on the ethics of the *Characteristics*.

Bolingbroke followed the Cambridge Platonists and Shaftesbury only to the extent of considering benevolence the supreme Law of Nature and the one possibility of human happiness; beyond this point he pursued a system at times almost in harmony with Hobbes and Mandeville. Allowing the desirability of benevolence, he makes it very difficult of attainment. With him it is not a matter of instinct. He had no greater tolerance for Shaftesbury's moral sense and intuitive benevolence than Mandeville had. These were mere "Platonic whimsies." "They affirm," he said, "that they have . . . a moral sense, that is, an instinct by which they distinguish what is morally good from what is morally evil, and perceive an agreeable or disagreeable intellectual sensation accordingly, without the trouble of observation and reflection. They bid fair to be enthusiasts in ethics, and to make natural religion as ridiculous, as some of their brothers have made revealed religion, by insisting on the doctrine of an inward light."[57] Instead of the two sets of affections provided by Shaftesbury's formula, self-love and social, man has, according to Bolingbroke, only an instinctive self-love. This, he admitted, has a rudimentary social tendency in that it prompts man to associate with his fellows; but this instinct is no more than that of the lower animals and is limited to physical enjoyment. It not only fails to conduct man beyond this embryonic social state, but is an active enemy to true social development. The virtue of benevolence, and indeed all virtue, is to be acquired only by means of the reason. There is an incessant conflict between the various passions arising from natural self-love, which seeks mere pleasure, and the dictates of reason, which seeks genuine happiness.[58] In this conflict the selfish passions have the advantage in that they act quickly under the influence of immediate pleasure, whereas the reason acts slowly under the influence of a greater but more remote good.[59] The sentimentalist Shaftesbury declares that goodness is the natural state of man; the rationalist Bolingbroke, that goodness results from a conquest of natural instinct by reason: they are the proto-types, respectively, of Rousseau and Voltaire.

In this difference is found the key to the most distinctive doc-trine of Pope's ethical system. Warton's note to the contrary, Bolingbroke's theory is seen clearly in Pope's

> Two principles in human nature reign;
> Self-love, to urge, and reason, to restrain;
> Nor this a good, nor that a bad we call,
> Each works its end, to move or govern all:
> And to their proper operation still,
> Ascribe all good; to their improper, ill.
>
> . . . . . . . . . . . . . .
>
> Self-love still stronger, as its objects nigh;
> Reason's at distance, and in prospect lie:
> That sees immediate good by present sense;
> Reason, the future and the consequence.*

Nor is Pope guilty of inconsistence when he grafts upon this doctrine Mandeville's contention that the virtues themselves arise from vices properly controlled by reason.† Bolingbroke does not develop the thesis, but it is implied and thoroughly in keeping with his assumptions.

In the *Essay* and the *Epistles* Pope's occasional emphasis on the "ruling passion" as the source of the chief virtue or of the chief vice, according as it is or is not controlled by reason, is a faithful development of this rationalistic view of ethics as opposed to the sentimentalism of Shaftesbury and Hutcheson. Like the old Cal-vinistic doctrine of man's depravity, it justifies Bolingbroke and Pope in their practical suspicion of human nature — a suspicion

---

* Second Epistle, 53–74. Both Bolingbroke and Pope were probably in-fluenced by Bacon (see Bowles's note).

† See, however, a remark of Pope's quoted by Spence, *Anecdotes*, p. 9.

far more natural to them than Shaftesbury's genial flattery, and corroborated no doubt by their intimate knowledge of themselves. Thus it came that though both Bolingbroke and Shaftesbury attached supreme moral importance to nature's law of benevolence as the only means of happiness, the theory of intuitive social affection led Shaftesbury to regard the ideal of universal philanthropy as a practical dream, while the insistence upon the conflict between instinct and reason led Bolingbroke to the gloomy conclusion that, since social virtue is pitted against great odds, at best our lot here will always be "a mixed happiness." In poetry Thomson reflects the first view, and Pope, despite much criticism to the contrary, reflects the second. So far his teaching, which undoubtedly accords with his predilections, is consistent also with the philosophical tenets of his model.

He was unable, however, to maintain throughout the *Essay* the fine distinction involved, and his failure to do so explains one inconsistence of the poem which has never been assigned to its exact cause. Pope's awkwardness is due largely to himself, for he was incapable of sustained logic; but partly also to Bolingbroke, whose phrasing at times obscures his original quarrel with the Platonists. For example, such sentences as the following read like Shaftesbury's formula: "Sociability is the great instinct, and benevolence the great law, of human nature, which no other law can repeal, or alter." [60] The fact is Bolingbroke found it a very delicate matter to represent natural instinct as being at once an embryonic social motive and also an impediment to genuine social development. Even if such a discrimination is valid, it is difficult to handle. To refute Hobbes, he needed the first assumption; to refute the Platonists, he needed the second. In his attempt to appropriate for his own purpose most of Shaftesbury's refutation of Hobbes, he came perilously near admitting the very doctrine of Shaftesbury's that he was constantly denying. In the same manner his poetical disciple sets out boldly with self-love opposed to reason; but later, in his anxiety to emphasize the beauty of benevolence, he finds his hypothetical man duly equipped with self-love and social, both of which seem to be instinctive.

For example, the third Epistle closes:

> So two consistent motions act the soul;
> And one regards itself, and one the whole.
> Thus God and Nature linked the general frame,
> And bade Self-love and Social be the same.*

The most illuminating comment on this passage is one made by Bolingbroke himself, who was quick to detect signs of Pope's defection from the cause of reason to that of moral instinct.

"That true self-love and social are the same, as you have expressed a maxim, I have always thought most undeniably evident; or that the author of nature has so constituted the human system, that they coincide in it, may be easily demonstrated to any one who is able to compare a very few clear and determinate ideas. But it will not follow, that he to whom this demonstration is made, nor even he who makes it, shall regulate his conduct according to it, nor reduce to practice what is true in speculation. We are so made, that a less immediate good will determine the generality of mankind, in opposition to one that is much greater, even according to our own measure of things, but more remote, and an agreeable momentary sensation will be preferred to any lasting and real advantage which *reason alone can hold out to us, and reflection alone can make us perceive.* . . . The influence of reason is slow and calm, that of the passions sudden and violent. Reason therefore might suggest the art that served to turn the passions on her side." †

Pope's *Essay on Man* thus becomes a conspicuous proof of the literary ascendancy attained by the *Characteristics*. It is indebted to Shaftesbury in three ways: in the first place, many of the ideas contributed by Bolingbroke came originally from his opponent; in the second place, the phrasing of Pope indicates that he sometimes borrowed from Shaftesbury directly what he might have found also in Bolingbroke; and in the third place, Pope, who was under the special tutelage of his friend, could not wholly refrain from that particular aspect of Shaftesbury's theory which Bolingbroke endeavored to controvert. The extent to which he

* Warton's note is clearly and radically wrong.
† Vol. III (Philadelphia, 1841), Essay iii, p. 224. The italics are not in the original.

did actually succeed in applying Bolingbroke's theory of benevolence as opposed to Shaftesbury's is what differentiates the *Essay* from the other poems so far examined in this study. The other poets were not subjected to Bolingbroke's own statement until after the publication of his works by Mallet in 1754, and they seem in the meantime not to have been affected by Pope's vague and inconsistent reproduction.* Though his example must have encouraged the later productions of the "benevolists," it is significant that the small poets cite as their authority Shaftesbury, Hutcheson, and Thomson rather than Pope. Those who wrote after the publication of Bolingbroke showed no greater inclination to adopt him, and Isaac Hawkins Browne made a special point of attacking him.[61]

## IV

The poetry of benevolence so far considered, though not written necessarily by avowed deists, is based on the assumption of Natural Religion and antagonizes the old orthodox position. Since these deistical poems, however, represent by no means the whole output of poetry written under George II to recommend benevolence, it remains now to be considered whether Shaftesbury probably influenced those poems which are less definitely associated with his peculiar theology.

His opposition to revealed religion continued to be a thorn in the flesh of the orthodox.† Naturally enough, some of them also attacked his system of independent ethics. Dr. Johnson's *Rasselas* introduces a philosopher whose moral code is summed up in "this simple and intelligible maxim — that deviation from nature is deviation from happiness"; but after considerable explanation, the prince decided "that this was one of those sages whom he should understand less as he heard him longer." [62] Fielding ridiculed the doctrine of "the fitness of things" by assigning it to Square, and to the assertion that virtue produces happiness and vice, misery,

* Lord Paget's *An Essay on Human Life* (1734) is an exception.
† See *The Cure of Deism*, etc. (1736, 1737, 1739); *Deism Revealed*, etc. (1751); J. Ogilvie, D.D., *An Inquiry into the Causes of Infidelity . . . of the Times*, etc. (1783).

he offered "but one objection, namely, that it is not true." [63]
Smollett put "the greatest part of that frothy writer's rhapsody"
in the mouth of the philosophical doctor in *Peregrine Pickle*, and
accounted for the ruin of Miss Williams in *Roderick Random* by
making her a disciple of Shaftesbury, Tindal, and Hobbes.[64] Mrs.
Mary Barber, a writer of temporary importance, vented her
prejudice against deistical morality in the following passage from
a poem inappropriately addressed *To Mr. Pope: Intreating him
to write Verses to the Memory of Thomas, late Earl of Thanet*
(published 1734):

> Ye vain pretenders to superior sense,
> Ye empty boasters of beneficence,
> Who, in the *scorners seat*, exulting, sit,
> And vaunt your impious raillery for wit,
> The Gospel-Rule defective you pretend,
> When you the social duties recommend:
> In Thanet see them heighten'd and refin'd;
> In Thanet see the friend of human kind;
> Heighten'd by Faith, see ev'ry virtue's force:
> By Faith, the surest sanction, noblest source.
>
> . . . . . . . . . . . . . . .
>
> Free-thinkers, Moralists, on you I call,
> Can Thanet's worth be equall'd by you all?

Similar protests abound in the minor poetry of the period,* and
a few small poets still persisted in recommending social duties by
means of the old-fashioned forecast of the Day of Judgment.†

The most formidable opposition offered by poetry to deism in
general is that of Edward Young, whose *Night Thoughts* (1742–
1745), written primarily to rebuke Pope's omission of immortality from the scheme of his *Essay*, was regarded as the official
apology for Christianity. Admitting the force of reason in re-

---

* See, for example, *To The Rev. Mr. Layng. Occasion'd by his Sermon
on Mutual Benevolence* (anonymous, 1746), in Fawkes and Woty, *Poet.
Cal.*, V, 118; Thomas Hobson, *Christianity the Light of the Moral World*
(1745).
† In 1757 two poems entitled *The Day of Judgment* were presented for
the Seatonian Prize at Cambridge, by G. Bally and R. Glynn. The first was
published independently, London, 1757; the second appears in *Poet. Cal.*,
XII, 20–30.

ligion, the uselessness of miracles, and the eternal laws imprinted
on nature, he contended that Christianity is as reasonable and
natural as deism, but that the addition of faith is essential, and
that mercy is not, as the deists implied, the sole attribute of God.
In his ethical utterances he sternly denounced the theory of natural goodness; in fact, the orthodox could not maintain their
opposition to Mandeville on this one point without doing violence
to their accepted theology and probably their real conviction.
Young's chief quarrel, however, was with the assumption of the
Shaftesburian moralists that virtue is its own reward and not in
need of future recompense.

> "Has virtue, then, no joys?" — Yes, joys dear bought.
> Talk ne'er so long, in this imperfect state,
> Virtue and vice are at eternal war,
> Virtue's a combat; and who fights for nought?
> Or for precarious, or for small reward?
> Who virtue's self-reward so loud resound,
> Would take degrees angelic here below,
> And virtue, while they compliment, betray,
> By feeble motives and unfaithful guards.
>
> .   .   .   .   .   .   .   .   .   .   .   .   .
>
> Rewards and punishments make God ador'd;
> And hopes and fears give conscience all her power.
>                                         (Night VII)

Opposing his orthodoxy to the special argument of intuitive social
affection, Young declared,

> Some we can't love, but for the Almighty's sake.

But such opposition was less thorough than these opponents
themselves believed. That new ethical principles were invading
the stronghold of the "Gospel-Rule" is evident from the examples
of Butler and the other Christian moralists; without setting aside
the authority of precept, they were giving ethics an independent
foundation in nature. In taking this step, they were indebted
chiefly to Shaftesbury, whose theology they abhorred. In the
Preface to the 1729 edition of *Fifteen Sermons* (1726), Butler,
for example, acknowledged that, despite his exception to some de-

tails of Shaftesbury's system, it is in the main authoritative.*
Likewise "Estimate" Brown's review of the *Characteristics*,
though at many points antagonistic, stoutly champions Shaftesbury's general conclusion against the doctrine of Mandeville.†
Their example, which probably had no effect on literature, is
symptomatic of Shaftesbury's gradual conversion of orthodoxy
to independent ethics in general and to his special emphasis upon
benevolence as a natural impulse. Just as the orthodox had all
along endeavored to prove that the deists had no monopoly on
reason, they were now equally determined to contest the superior
claim of the deists to natural benevolence, and it was with particular reluctance that they mentioned Shaftesbury among the opponents of revealed religion.‡

The resulting compromise so far obliterated the line between
the ethical assumptions of the more liberal Christians and of the
moderate deists that the poetry of benevolence came to be less
distinctive of the author's religious affiliations. Many of the
less specialized poems occupy this middle ground. To whichever
party the writers adhered, whether they were deists or Christians
or "Christian deists," they presented the beauty of benevolence,
or "good-nature," in a manner different from the earlier orthodox
formula, but confined themselves to a statement so general and
so free from minute controversial details that, if we except a few
old-fashioned sticklers for the unaided "Gospel-Rule," their poems
were now inoffensive to all parties. The volume of such poetry is

* Note the importance attached to Butler's statement by William Hazlitt,
"Self-Love and Benevolence," *New Monthly Mag.*, Oct. and Dec. 1828.

† *Essays on the Characteristics*, by John Brown, M.A. (1751). Those parts
of his criticism which were unfavorable provoked three replies: Charles
Bulkley, *A Vindication of Lord Shaftesbury on the Subject of Ridicule*
(1751) and *A Vindication of Lord Shaftesbury on the Subjects of Morality
and Religion* (1752); and *Animadversions on Mr. Brown's Three Essays on
the Characteristics*, authorship unknown.

‡ "It gives me a real concern, that among the writers who have appeared
against revealed religion, I am obliged to take notice of the noble author
of the *Characteristics*. Some indeed are not willing to allow that he is to be
reckoned in this number . . . and yet it cannot be denied, that there are
many things in his books, which seem to be evidently calculated to cast
contempt upon Christianity and the holy Scriptures." J. Leland, *A View of
the Principal Deistical Writers* (London, 1754), I, Letter v.

immense and was written by men of the most varied beliefs. Some of the writers were in complete sympathy with Shaftesbury, some were skeptical of various details, and some were on occasion openly hostile to him. Acknowledged or not, however, their indebtedness to "the founder of the benevolent school of philosophy," at first hand or second, is obvious.

In the first place, the fashion which they followed in poetry was popularized by Shaftesbury's deistical adherents; in the second place, their ability to adopt the fashion without giving open offense to the orthodox was due to his partial conquest of the traditional belief. The class is sufficiently illustrated by Henry Fielding's *Of Good Nature* (1743); * Lyttelton's *A Monody* (1747); † John Armstrong's *Of Benevolence* (1751); Christopher Smart's *On Good Nature* (1760); William Dodd's *Sacred to Humanity*, *The Man of Southgate*, and *An Hymn to Good Nature* (1760); William Stevenson's *On Riches* and *The Progress of Evening, or The Power of Virtue* (1765); Sir Charles Hanbury Williams's *On Benevolence*; and Thomas Blacklock's *An Hymn to Benevolence* (1746). In some of these poems, as well as in those which are openly deistical, there are evidences of the *Characteristics* not only in idea, but also in phrasing. Even Young was not wholly immune. His designation of God as "the great Philanthropist" is, according to his editor, the Reverend J. Mitford, an example of very bad taste; [65] certainly it is a concession to deistic theology out of harmony with some of his strictures. With similar inconsistence, Young, in the following passage, recommends the natural impulse to benevolence exactly as the disciples of Shaftesbury were doing:

> Nothing in nature, much less conscious being,
> Was e'er created solely for itself:
> Thus man his sovereign duty learns in this
> Material picture of benevolence.

* One of a collection of poems published by Millar. Later the author spoke of them apologetically as "productions rather of the heart than of the head," and they have since been omitted from some of the best editions of Fielding's works.

† Ridiculed by Smollett in his *Burlesque Ode*.

And know, of all our supercilious race,
Thou most inflammable! thou wasp of men!
Man's angry heart, inspected, would be found
As rightly set, as are the starry spheres;
'Tis nature's structure, broke by stubborn will,
Breathes all that uncelestial discord there.
Wilt thou not feel the bias nature gave?

(*Night* IX)

Isaac Hawkins Browne's *De Animi Immortalitate* (1754), written, like Young's *Night Thoughts*, to demonstrate Pope's error in omitting considerations of future reward and punishment, exhibits Young's tendency much more clearly. This was one of the most popular didactic poems of the time; there were three translations of it in the year of its publication and a fourth in 1765.* The fact that Soame Jenyns immediately translated it should have been enough to cast suspicion on its pure orthodoxy. The following passage coincides exactly with the fashionable doctrine of Natural Religion in its sanction of benevolence as a dictate of nature:

The laws of life why need I call to mind,
Obeyed by birds, and beasts of every kind;
By all the sandy desert's savage brood,
And all the numerous offspring of the flood;
Of these none uncontroul'd and lawless rove,
But to some destin'd end spontaneous move.
Led by that instinct, heaven itself inspires,
Or so much reason, as their state requires;
See all with skill acquire their daily food,
All use those arms, which Nature has bestow'd;
Produce their tender progeny, and feed
With care parental, whilst that care they need!
In these lov'd offices completely blest,
No hopes beyond them, nor vain fears molest.
Man o'er a wider field extends his views;
God through the wonders of his works pursues;
Exploring thence His attributes and laws,
Adores, loves, imitates th' Eternal Cause;

* The first three, by Soame Jenyns, Richard Grey, and William Hay; the fourth, by J. Cromwell.

For sure in nothing we approach so nigh
The great example of divinity,
As in benevolence: the patriot's soul
Knows not self-centered for itself to roll,
But warms, enlightens, animates the whole:
Its mighty orb embraces first his friends,
His country next, then man; nor here it ends,
But to the meanest animal descends.
Wise Nature has this social law confirm'd,
By forming man so helpless and unarmed;
His want of others' aid, and power of speech
T' implore that aid, this lesson daily teach.
Mankind with other animals compare,
Single how weak and impotent they are!
But, view them in their complicated state,
Their powers how wondrous, and their strength how great,
When social virtue individuals joins,
And in one solid mass, like gravity combines!
This then's the first great law by Nature giv'n,
Stamp'd on our souls, and ratify'd by Heav'n;
All from utility this law approve,
As every private bliss must spring from social love.

Moreover, the following extract from Grey's translation indicates that the author practically contradicts his main thesis of the necessity of future reward:

Base and mean
Is that man's virtue, who does therefore well
That after Death he may be paid for't. He
Is truly good, whom, future hopes apart,
Virtue's sweet charms, and Honesty's plain path,
Lead of themselves to what is fair and fit,
Superior to regard of every kind.

v

An exhaustive study of benevolent theory in poetry would necessitate the further inclusion of poems on charity and social reform like those referred to in the discussion of Thomson; in these the same arguments for benevolence are to be found, but the main object of the writers is to encourage and direct the practice itself. For the present purpose it is sufficient merely to intimate the extent of such literature and its possible effect on the moral conduct of the period.

Malone expressed great contempt for the "benevolists" as men who talked much about virtue and did little to promote it.* As a general charge, this would be manifestly unjust. There was a very intimate contact between the ideals of literature and of society. The same writers who persistently lauded the benevolent disposition converted it into a practical force for the encouragement, if not the initiation, of all the numerous philanthropies of the day. These appeals are made, not only in literature professing such charitable purpose, but in the most unexpected connections, where frequently the moral lesson is at the sacrifice of artistic effect. They are to be found in the work of all versifiers, from Pope † and Thomson to the mere scribblers, some of the poets proposing charity on the old theological ground of future reward, but most of them on the more fashionable principle that active compassion is the perfection of the "natural temper." Some of this sentiment was, of course, affected for literary popularity; such imitation, however, is a tribute to the practical appeal and genuine motive of the movement as a whole, and the avidity with which the public read this versified philosophy indicates that the age found in such literature a faithful presentation of its chief social slogan.

There is, moreover, a direct connection between this constant poetizing of benevolence and charity and the extensive practical charity which signalized the reign of George II. In the *Champion* for February 16, 1740, Fielding says: "This virtue hath shone

* His opinion is quoted by Sir James Prior, *Life of Edmund Malone* (London, 1860), p. 427: "Mr. Gilbert Cooper was the last of the *benevolists,* or sentimentalists, who were much in vogue between 1750 and 1760, and dealt *in general* admiration of virtue. They were all tenderness in *words*; their finer feelings evaporated in the moment of expression, for they had no connection with their practice." A. W. Ward takes exception to this stricture (*The Poems of John Byrom*, Chetham Soc., I [2], 449).

† Pope's case is instructive; he was apparently following the example of Thomson. In his early poetry there is no plea for charity; but after he began to "moralise" his song, such passages became frequent (see *Moral Essays*, Epistles III, IV, and *Epilogue to the Satires*). Fielding praises these passages, especially the first, in *Joseph Andrews*, Bk. III, Ch. 6.

brighter in our time, than at any period which I remember in our annals." Johnson testifies similarly in the *Idler* for May 6, 1758: "But no sooner is a new species of misery brought to view, and a design of relieving it proposed than every hand is open to contribute something, every tongue is busied in solicitation and every art of pleasure is employed for a time in the interest of Virtue." Even John Brown's *Estimate*, which is pessimistic, concedes in 1757 that the charitable foundations recently established "are such indisputable proofs of a national humanity, as it were the highest injustice not to acknowledge and applaud." It is evident that charity was becoming, as a few writers of that period note, a mere fashion.* It was degenerating into sentimentalism unguided by discriminating judgment. To argue Shaftesbury's authority for either the good or the bad qualities of this sentimental program would be to repeat the evidence already adduced; if he stimulated many of the "benevolists" directly and most of them indirectly through Hutcheson and through poetical followers, he had a proportionate share in determining the general preoccupation of these same writers and their public with the practical application of his theory.[66]

That the humanitarian program of Shaftesbury's school had its old-fashioned limitations is true. Most of the solid benefits acquired during the ascendancy of his philosophy were confined to the accomplishment of private endeavor. The poets who followed him have been accused of hypocrisy for holding up a lofty ideal of individual benevolence and at the same time extolling a government which legalized abuses against the plainest dictates of humanity. This is notably the case of Thomson's *Liberty*, and the example was set by Shaftesbury himself. If this is a fault, however, it is a fault due, not to sentimental philosophy, but to Whiggism, which affected most of the poetry of the time.

* See T. W., Gent., *The Country Priest* (1746); Joseph Warton, *Fashion, A Satire*; William Kenrick, *On Moral Sentiment* (1768); Robert Lloyd, *Charity, A Fragment*; Christopher Smart, *Care and Generosity*; and the *Connoisseur*, No. 98 (1755). Note also a pamphlet published anonymously, *Considerations on the Fatal Effects of the Present Excess of Public Charities*, etc. (London, 1763).

There was, in fact, some moral excuse for this loyalty: throughout much of this period the Act of Settlement was still contending with the Jacobite adherence to divine right, and certainly the future of social reform was safer in the hands of the Whigs than it would have been in those of the Stuarts. The Whig poets were justified also in praising British liberty at the expense of any previous regime in England and contemporary conditions in Europe. They were not wholly mistaken or insincere in defending Whig commercialism as a national philanthropy to relieve the distress of the lower classes. In supporting the Whig government they were fighting to hold the measure of individual right England had already acquired; * it is natural that the reforms proposed at this stage should have confined themselves principally to enlarging the sympathies of individual readers, and that literature, therefore, should have had more to say in favor of benevolence and charity than against legalized abuses.

On these, however, the writers were not silent. Shaftesbury himself supported a successful bill for giving the accused right of counsel.[67] Thomson and his contemporaries protested against the inhumanity of prison laws, slavery, the criminal code, and various other evils. Although they did not effect any material alterations in the law, they performed a practical service by educating the public conscience for the social reforms which logically followed — reforms with which we usually associate Howard, Wilberforce, Romilly, and others who perfected movements initiated long before. The agitation during the reign of George II was not wholly new in literature, nor was it confined to the followers of Shaftesbury. But the revival of interest in such matters after the moral laxity under George I was contemporaneous with the triumph of his sentimental benevolence. The interest displayed by poets, which was entirely new, was due chiefly to the example

* Of Shaftesbury, Dr. Rand says: "The political measures which he most strongly supported at home were those which had for their aim the protection of the rights and liberty of the individual" (*Regimen*, pp. vii–viii). That he was not a dogmatist in politics is evident from the Letter to Tiresias, Nov. 29, 1706 (*Regimen*, pp. 367–368); his defense of the British monarchy was based, not on theoretic grounds, but on the belief that no other form of government could subsist in England.

of Thomson. If we except the strictures of Defoe, the measures proposed were more openly critical of the law than any that had appeared before; and the still more radical agitation which followed, in and out of literature, derived its authority from the general belief in benevolence as the supreme virtue.

Against this conclusion, the popular view of deism immediately urges the "shallow optimism" of Shaftesbury as an obstacle to reform. The objection is not without support from high authority; but that it is often exaggerated is so evident as hardly to deserve proof. By "Whatever is, is right" none of the deists meant more than to assert the goodness and providence of the Deity against the claims of grumbling atheists who, like Epicurus, saw in the evils and moral confusion of the world a negation of God. The assumption that this is "the best possible of all systems" is in its intent and application primarily theological and not political or social. Deists were not so besotted as to believe the details of human conduct and society literally in need of no alteration. They were, in fact, boastingly identified with the cause of social improvement; this claim was one of their chief weapons against the orthodox. Beyond this purely theological argument of God's providence, their views concerning the perfectibility of society represent all the various shades of confidence from optimism to pessimism. Relatively speaking, and in this sense, Shaftesbury was an optimist, and so were Thomson and various other poets of this school. We know that they underestimated the tenacity of evil and exaggerated man's instinctive response to the cause of suffering, but it was this optimism which gave the humanitarian movement in literature its real vigor.

Those who cite deism as inefficient for the purposes of reform judge by an absolute rather than a historical standard. What is to be said of the traditional attitude of the Church with which deism came into open conflict? Far from trying to equalize the lot of human beings or to remove the abuses incident to the social system, the Church defended all inequalities as part of a divine dispensation which wisely subjects every soul to that particular influence best adapted to its spiritual development: the rich man's wealth affords him an opportunity to cultivate the virtue of charity, and the poor man's poverty nurtures in him the fine flower of Christian resignation.* Such a view anticipated no real change of conditions; it contemplated merely the temporary assuagement of extreme suffering and complacently looked forward to a continuation of social evils predetermined by a wise Creator for the spiritual good of both victim and patron. The rectifying solvent was conveniently deferred to a future life. Christianity as it was then interpreted exerted a paralyzing influence on genuine reform, and real progress became possible only after deism had forced upon the dogmatists some of its more liberal ideas of human relations in this life.

The total evidence of Shaftesbury's influence would be greatly increased also by extending the study of literature beyond 1760; the selection of this year as a concluding date is largely arbitrary. In the later period his influence is slightly confused by the additional effect of Rousseau's example; but the general indications are that the popular appeal of the *Characteristics* continued unabated to the last decade of the century. It was supplemented, but not displaced, by more radical ideas of Rousseau's. A candid estimate of their relative influence would probably assign greater practical results to the Englishman: not only had he initiated the sentimental program which concluded with the violent performance of Rousseau, but he represented that degree of sentimentalism which satisfies the conservative bent of the ordinary Briton. The revolutionary doctrine superimposed by Rousseau affected, after all, no more than a small coterie, and for a brief period only. The case of Henry Brooke's *The Fool of Quality* is not an unfair example of English timidity in the presence of Rousseau's proposals. The ideal Henry Moreland begins life with a strong inclination to discard clothes and revolt against organized society, but terminates his career by attaching himself to the cause of the English throne and turning Methodist. The very fact, however, that the early school of humanitarians did not go to the extent

---

* See Robert Nelson, *Address*, etc., pp. 78, 79; J. Balguy, *Divine Rectitude* (London, 1730), pp. 58–59; William Dodd, *Gratitude. An Ode* (1760).

of denouncing Society root and branch, as Rousseau did a little later, partly accounts for the neglect of Shaftesbury by critics. There is in Rousseau's doctrine a touch of audacity which distracts attention from the amateur lectures of the earlier benevolists. He was indirectly responsible also for the sudden termination of Shaftesbury's long ascendancy: when the English perceived the revolutionary possibilities of sentimental benevolence, which had escaped Shaftesbury to be fully expounded by Rousseau and applied by the Revolutionists, their distrust extended to the comparatively innocuous doctrine of the *Characteristics*. Between 1711 and 1790 it commanded eleven English editions; after 1790 no new edition appeared for a century.[68]

## VI

Even if Shaftesbury had in 1760 suddenly yielded his position to the superior influence of French sentimentalism, he would still deserve more attention than is accorded him by the historians of English literature. His importance arises not so much from novel proposals advanced as from the sureness with which he interpreted the vague predisposition of the age toward new modes of thought and feeling.

The evidence adduced in this study — including the undeniable fact of his general popularity, the explicit citation of his ethics by various writers, the minute agreement of others, and the reluctant adoption of the essentials by still others — leads directly to a conclusion that affects only so-called historical criticism of literature. It seems to evince unmistakably that in an early stage of English philanthropy when the orthodox conception of moral obligation was considered inadequate, Shaftesbury afforded a doctrine with which poetry, as well as philosophy, argued the cause of social reform against the egoism of Epicurus, Hobbes, La Rochefoucauld, and Mandeville; that by gradually ingratiating himself with all parties of benevolists, he became the main authority for English ideas of philanthropy during a period that witnessed a broadening of human sympathies, a preoccupation of society and literature with the cause of social amelioration, and the first general use of poetry as an organ of humanitarian theory. His connection with this change and its ultimate permanent effects on literature and society give additional weight to Dr. Rand's remark that the third Earl was "a most worthy predecessor to the noble and philanthropic seventh Earl of Shaftesbury." [69] If we confine ourselves wholly to his effect on literature, it may be well to recall that, whatever criticism may say about the strictly "literary" influences and changes, the fact of human moment in literature of the eighteenth century is that it became genuinely sympathetic.

This moral effect was not accomplished without some detriment to the literature which it humanized. Goldsmith's shrewd judgment concerning the injury to English prose through the continual but unsuccessful imitation of Shaftesbury's style notes one of the least faults which followed in the wake of the *Characteristics*. The constant lauding of compassion and the apotheosis of benevolence resulted in a monotony of theme and phrase to be properly deprecated only by those who have read the minor verse of the mid-century. Although literary criticism has little or nothing to say on the subject, this influx of benevolence and charity was one of the principal causes for that excess of sentiment described by Sir Leslie Stephen as "a kind of mildew which spreads over the surface of literature at this period to denote a sickly constitution."

What we condemn as sentimentalism in literature is the logical product of a society committed to the notion that God's one attribute is benevolence and man's chief perfection an imitation of it. The distinction between the humanitarian and the posturing sentimentalist is always difficult to define, for the enthusiastic preachments of the "benevolists" shade imperceptibly into the cant of mawkish sentiment. In the literature before Shaftesbury's vogue as well as in philosophy, there were already faint signs, especially in comedy, that public taste was moving toward a more sentimental interpretation of life. But unrestrained sentimentalism did not become a national characteristic until Shaftesbury's philosophy, which was itself merely one manifestation of the new ideal, had provided an authoritative defense of it. The habitual study and reproduction of this theory was at least a powerful agent in the formation of the popular temper which encouraged the flaccid emotionalism we find in most poetry of the period and in such prose fiction as *Pamela*[70] and *The Man of Feeling*. It is probable, indeed, that most humanitarian literature is too special and temporary in its appeal to be of permanent significance, and the faults to which it is liable naturally manifested themselves strikingly in the first reaction against the harshness of egoistic philosophy and traditional theology.

Whatever the literary gain or loss, the humanitarian thesis, inclining always to an unreflective sensibility and requiring the constant check of the judgment, has since occupied a large place among the interests of English poetry. If ethical instruction is conceded to be a legitimate function of poetical art, Shaftesbury and his school deserve unqualified praise for cementing a connection between poetry and social questions that has performed a recognized service in the reformation of English morals. In whatever light the addition of this function may be viewed by the appreciative critic of literature, the historical fact remains that Shaftesbury's ethical theory was primarily responsible for a moral tone which is one of the chief distinctions between the literature before and after the adoption of him by English poets, and which with various modifications has persisted to our own time.

# The Return to Nature in English Poetry of the Eighteenth Century

RECENT investigation has corrected the old idea that no appreciation of nature is to be found in the early part of the eighteenth century. Studies made by Miss Reynolds and Dr. Havens have shown that critics once exaggerated the differences between the age of Pope and that of his successors.[1] In the early part of the eighteenth century "God's outdoor world" was not, as commentators once held, uniformly despised or neglected. What we once considered two distinct "schools" really shade into each other imperceptibly, and many individual writers defy strict classification. It is now evident that the "return to nature" — a reaction from classicism — began earlier than we formerly supposed, and developed more gradually. Like other changes in literature, it was an evolution rather than a revolution.

From another point of view, however, our investigation of the subject has been less satisfactory. The attempt of criticism to account for this growth of interest in nature, including uncultivated nature, has not yet gone beyond the traditional explanation that it came from the renewed study and imitation of earlier literary practice. The inadequacy of this supposition is generally recognized. The revival of such poets as Shakespeare, Milton, and Spenser, and the additional influence also of the few medieval writers who were actually known to English poets, leave still to

53

be accounted for in the eighteenth century, and later, some of the most distinctive qualities in our poetry of nature.

In the first place, this explanation fails to account for the modern poetical interest in mountains. As all critics agree, the development of the feeling for nature in recent literature is to be gauged largely by the attitude toward the austere phases of it — winter, storms, deserts, seas, and especially mountains. Although the change of sentiment that brought these "deformities" into general favor was neither so late in point of time nor so sudden as early critics held, there evidently was such a change somewhere between the Restoration and the close of the eighteenth century.

The striking fact is that this new literary fashion had never before been prevalent in any literature. Appreciation of the grand and rugged was virtually unknown to Greek and Roman writers.[2] Humboldt and Biese have discovered a few instances in out-of-the-way medieval prose;[3] but the tendency was short-lived, because it was opposed by the Church, and no one will contend that these few obscure cases were known by English poets of the eighteenth century. In Scottish literature, one might naturally expect, on account of local scenery, to find such appreciation developed early; but Veitch states it as a "curious and puzzling" fact that "imaginative sympathy for the grand and powerful in nature — as mountain height and cataract, the foaming flood, the force of ocean, and the dark wind-swept wood as it sways in the storm — " was very rare in Scottish letters before the closing years of the eighteenth century.[4] This modern note is absent also from our early English literature. Ruskin has pointed out the deficiency in Shakespeare.[5] In the same connection, Shairp says it is certain "that the power of mountains is not expressed in that poetry which expresses almost every other conceivable thing, and that the mountain rapture had to lie dumb for two more centuries before it found utterance in English song."[6] One or two exceptions in Milton's verse are apparent rather than real.[7]

According to Perry, the first traces of the new spirit in English literature are to be found "towards the middle" of the eighteenth century. "Before that time," he adds, "we find mountains spoken of in terms of the severest reprobation." [8] Phelps discovered the first notable interest of the kind in Gray's comments on the Alps in his journal and letters of 1739.[9] The forward date set by most, if not all, of these statements is inaccurate; but the consensus of all investigation is that this liberal attitude began to be prominent in the first half of the eighteenth century,[10] and that it was virtually an innovation.*

In the second place, the ordinary explanation fails equally to account for the modern habit of regarding nature as a great moral and spiritual force acting upon the life of man — another trait of our poetry that came into prominence between the Restoration and the time of Wordsworth. Like the affection for mountains, this sentiment is of distinctly modern growth. Again, the Middle Ages have yielded a few exceptions to the general statement; [11] but through the disapproval of the Church, the theory died in embryo, and the few who proclaimed it could have had no influence on those poets who fostered a similar doctrine in English literature.† There are intimations of it also in the writings of Henry Vaughan, who was impressed by the spiritual force of material things; but Vaughan's interpretation, hardly more than a hint of the full theory, is exceptional in English, just as a passage or two in the sonnets of William Drummond of Hawthornden and

---

* Some additional evidence of Restoration dislike of the rugged in nature is to be found in the Duchess of Newcastle's *The Life of the First Duke of Newcastle* (1668), Everyman's, p. ix, and Grammont's *Memoirs*, Bohn's Library, pp. 193–199. The following passage from Mrs. Haywood's *Life's Progress through the Passions: or the Adventures of Natura* (1748) is an excellent illustration of the change in popular taste: "Whether you climb the craggy mountains or traverse the flowery vale; whether thick woods set limits to the sight, or the wild common yields unbounded prospect; — whether the ocean rolls in solemn state before you, or gentle streams run purling by your side, nature in all her different shapes delights. . . . The stupendous mountains of the Alps, after the plains and soft embowered recesses of Avignon, gave perhaps a no less delightful sensation to the mind of Natura." (Cited by G. F. Whicher, *The Life and Romances of Mrs. Eliza Haywood* [Columbia Univ. Press, 1915], p. 157n.) See also *Gentleman's Mag.*, XX (1750), 506, and XXI (1751), 211–213, and earlier examples cited below.

† As Biese points out, these Catholic mystics were very different from such later mystics as Jacob Behmen. Moreover, the influence of Behmen, although he was translated by William Law, was confined to a very small set of Englishmen, who were apart from the current of popular literature.

a generally neglected passage in Charles Cotton's *The Retirement* are exceptions to seventeenth-century inappreciation of mountains. Examples cited later will demonstrate that by the middle of the eighteenth century, on the contrary, this ethical and spiritual valuation of the physical world had become the rule in English poetry rather than the exception.

If, then, these two characteristics did not come from the imitation of earlier popular literature, did they originate with the modern poets themselves, or were they due to some influence which has been neglected in our study of literary origins? My contention is that both of them sprang originally from the common source of learned philosophy. Appreciation of the uncouth forms of nature and the worship of all nature are inseparable phases of a general movement. It is not a mere coincidence that the two developed contemporaneously. There had existed a traditional prejudice against the uninhabitable and inaccessible regions of the world, and the idea of beauty was seldom associated with them until this prejudice had been removed by a new conception of nature in general. To account for this change of feeling, we need to go beyond the borders of all popular literature. The source of it is to be found in certain philosophic conclusions first established by learned speculation in the latter part of the seventeenth and the early part of the eighteenth century, and then popularized by poetical imitators.

By neglecting this source of influence, critics have given only a partial explanation of a literary evolution that can be explained in full. The "return to nature" in popular works, far from being the simple process of mere reversion implied by the phrase, represents a great variety of appreciation, some degrees of which were entirely new. The modern poetic conception is the composite result of many forces. In the literature of the early eighteenth century it would be possible to distinguish among these with considerable precision. Some of them existed still in a detached and initial state. This was a formative period, when the various elements were beginning to coalesce into that rich interpretation of the natural world most familiar to us through the poetry of

Wordsworth. To study these separate elements in detail, there would be required such elaborate classifications of the feeling for nature as those proposed by Shairp[12] and Veitch.[13] But for the present purpose of distinguishing between those character-istics that arose from earlier popular writers and those that were added through imitation of the learned philosophers, it is suffi-cient to group all the various modes of treatment under two inclusive heads — the descriptive and the synthetic.

The first class is characterized by the "simple and childish de-light" which men in all ages have felt, in varying degrees, under the tonic influence of blue skies, budding flowers, green grass, and the other benign manifestations of the outdoor world — what Léon Morel characterizes in Chaucer as "une naïve et superficielle sensualité."[14] Literary treatment of this kind attempts only to reproduce in detail the sensuous or emotional effect occasioned by the individual thing contemplated; there is no reference to the system of nature as a vast, organic whole, and the degree of feel-ing expressed is comparatively slight. In this class fall practically all the illustrations of the "romantic revival" collected from the early eighteenth century. Miss Reynolds recognizes that in the early cases she has cited — roughly speaking, before 1725 — there is no attempt to interpret nature in terms of man's moral and spiritual life. The passages show only that the writers had grown weary of the descriptive formulas imitated from Vergil, Horace, and the other Latin poets, and were becoming restive under the restraint of the neoclassic rule. With the slight exception of Parnell's *Hymn to Contentment* (1722), of which I shall speak later, the entire list of illustrations emphasized by Miss Reynolds indicates that in the early stages of the "return" the only marked disposition was to be more truthful in reporting what men saw and heard. The additions made by Dr. Havens are of the same kind; the attitude of the writers is "unreflective," and nature is praised only for its picturesqueness.

These passages are far more numerous than was formerly sup-posed, and they are of great importance historically. But they represent only one element of the modern conception, and that not the most significant. Denoting as they do merely a revolt from the negativeness of the neoclassic prescription, they are what we might expect in any period of literature when the natural impulse is not repressed by an artificial code. In them we have actually a *return* to previous literary practice. The treatment accorded is fragmentary and superficial; of the universal system and spirit nothing is said. Consequently here, as in our still earlier literature, there is little incentive to extend the appreciation to nature as a whole. Even Allan Ramsay, responsive as he was to the charms of the outdoor world, was unaffected by the beauty of its "deformities." "Though brought up in a rugged part of Scotland," says Miss Reynolds, "he seems to have had none of the modern feeling for mountains." [15]

Under the second head — the synthetic treatment — I include collectively all the varied conceptions of nature which regard, not merely the sensuous beauty of the individual object or scene, but the ultimate significance of such parts considered as details or links of a universal system which is to be appraised rightly only in its completeness. The simplest and least poetic form of this theoretic valuation is the argumentative statement that every detail, however unlovely or even repulsive in itself, is to be defended as serving some indispensable function in the vast economy of the entire scheme. The highest and most poetic form is the assumption that all nature is an intimate revelation of God to man — a power for good, therefore, in its constant appeal to man's moral and spiritual faculties. Those who adopt this view recognize a divine spirit permeating and identifying all creation. Shairp's characterization is excellent: "The best and highest way in which Nature ministers to the soul and spirit of man is when it becomes to him a symbol translucent with the light of the moral and spiritual world." [16] This reverence may express itself in the doctrine of the Deity immanent in nature, or it may very easily, especially in poetry, take the form of a vague pantheism virtually identifying Creator and created. Evidently the utilitarian theory can have only an indirect value in the history of poetry; it is important only as preparing the way for something better. But the other conclusion is of the greatest importance, for it is one of the chief distinctions of recent poetry.

For this whole range of synthetic interpretation — the utilitarian and the more poetic form — popular literature is demonstrably indebted to the Augustan philosophers. In brief, it was through poetical imitators of these that English poetry acquired the various forms of defense and praise of the irregular and grand aspects of nature and likewise the apotheosis of nature in general.

Before undertaking to adduce evidence on the point, however, it is necessary to note an inevitable prejudice against this view. The body of learned philosophy to which I refer is designated as rationalism. The intimate appreciation of nature, especially the stern phases, is ordinarily catalogued as one of the distinctive marks of romanticism. According to the usual classification, *rationalism* and *romanticism* are irreconcilably opposed. Quite naturally, therefore, most accounts of popular literature which do not wholly ignore the existence of such philosophy actually represent all phases of the romantic movement as a revolt from its influence.\* The ordinary view, stated or implied, is that the development of the feeling for nature was due, positively, to the reassertion of an earlier literary ideal, and, negatively, to a complete divorce of literature from the arid formulas of the rationalists. Speaking of the romantic movement as a whole, Professor Beers explains it as a reaction "against the rationalistic, prosaic, skeptical, commonsense spirit of the age, represented in England by deistical writers like Shaftesbury, Mandeville, Bolingbroke, and Tindal, in the department of religious and moral philosophy,"[17] etc. A later critic in the field, Dr. W. H. Durham, holds that "rationalism is another name for crude dogmatism."[18] He evidently applies the word *rationalism* to philosophy as well as to literary criticism, for he very prettily explains the deterioration of Charles Gildon in the following manner: "Once a Catholic, he became a Deist; once a critic, he became a criticaster . . . Certainly in both

---

\* See, however, W. J. Courthope, *A History of English Poetry* (1905), Vol. V, Ch. 10.

cases he substituted a barren and superficial rationalism for conceptions at once more fruitful and more profound."

The element of truth contained in such derogatory estimates of the rationalists has misled us into the natural error of over-generalizing, either by formal statement or by implication. Setting out with the complete antithesis authorized by the dictionary, we have assumed that it is valid also with reference to two schools of thought in all their historical ramifications, and hence to the individual writers composing those schools. The pitfalls of such a method are obvious. Since *romanticism* is used loosely to include many vaguely related notions, it is unwise to assume that these various aspects are reducible to any one general cause, or that, conversely, whatever clashes with the romantic idea at one point opposes it at all others. The difficulty is enhanced also by the similar inclusiveness of the term *rationalism*. In some respects the line of cleavage is easily definable. In the treatment of nature it is not. Any broad statement that even implies a hard-and-fast demarcation of the kind falls into the old error of insisting too much upon final definition and the use of exclusive terms.

This pigeonhole method assumes a sharper historical conflict between the "pure reason" of the rationalists and the "imagination" of the romanticists than actually existed. The general supposition that the doctrine of reasonableness utterly precluded imaginative activity on the part of the individual thinker is, at least in all that relates to physical nature, unjust. The faulty conclusion arises partly from our virtual identification of the neoclassic view and the rationalistic. It must be remembered that rationalism was merely one of several ingredients composing the neoclassic prescription. The express inhibitions concerning nature came from the literary lawgivers rather than the philosophical. The philosophy of the rationalists, considered historically, was, I hold, not only unopposed to an intimate appreciation of the outdoor world, but was actually the chief agent in eventually forcing the minute study and love of nature as a whole upon popular attention.

A comparative study of learned and popular literature of the Augustan age will demonstrate: (1) that even the earliest and simplest phase of rationalistic theory — that which was inoffensive to the Church — contributed something to our poetic creed by offering an apology for those parts of creation which before had been condemned as "deformities"; (2) that the unorthodox length to which this speculative doctrine was carried by the "free think-ers," or deists, was the main incentive to our positive love of the grand and rugged, and also to our apotheosis of nature as a whole. If romanticism may be taken in the popular interpreta-tion of including our modern sympathy for all nature and a belief in its moral and spiritual associations with human life — such a creed as we find, for example, in Wordsworth, Byron, and Shel-ley — then deism may be said to be the starting point for our modern romantic treatment of nature.

### I

Insistence on the beauty of universal nature was a necessity of rationalistic theory. The triumph of this philosophy in the seventeenth century was due to the fact that the Church, in order to maintain her prestige in a scientific age, was compelled to de-fend herself against a growing suspicion that Christian dogma was incompatible with recent discoveries in natural science. In their endeavor to reconcile the two claims, the Christian apologists at the outset allowed almost equal weight to natural revelation and supernatural, holding that there is no real conflict between the two. In their deference to the evidence afforded by scientific knowledge all rationalists agreed up to the point of regarding the outward world as a faithful record of the Creator's power and beneficence, a visible embodiment of Divine perfection. This argument from nature was soon developed so convincingly, how-ever, that it threatened to render all other evidence of God superfluous, and thereby produced dissension in the Church as to how far it might be pursued. The extreme, or deistic, view was that human reason requires no other revelation than the outward and visible world. Even those rationalists who still accepted the Bible held its utterances to be merely a confirmation of universal truths already set forth to the reason of man in the Book of Nature. The line between these two positions – the heretical and the orthodox – was not always clearly marked. But whether a given philosopher became a "free thinker" and denied the doctrine of supernatural revelation or whether he managed by compromise to maintain his standing in the Church, the difference was one, not of kind, but of degree. The beauty of the natural universe, as expounded by the new science, occupied the central position in all rationalistic speculation.

Evidently a universal system full of flaws could not meet the demands of such reasoning. From the first there was a tendency to hold nature perfect in every detail, and the necessity of doing so became gradually more evident. Such optimism, however, was confronted at once by traditional opposition. No difficulty was found in applying the theory to the serene and physically agreeable aspects of nature; the real problem was how to include the sterner phases, especially an angry sea or the jagged pinnacles of the mountain. The Calvinist looked upon these as imperfections due to original sin, and the earlier atheist as a proof that our world was not created by God. Whether or not either of these views was held by any considerable portion of English society, they were proclaimed with sufficient persistence to stimulate controversy and bring into sharp relief the issues of a long and spirited debate. They thus served to denote the chief point of attack upon which the "physico-theology" of the rationalists was to be directed throughout the first half of the eighteenth century.

The case of extreme reprobation is set forth most nakedly by Thomas Burnet in *Telluris Theoria Sacra* (1681–1689), which very curiously grafts the biblical doctrine of original sin upon what purports to be a scientific hypothesis. Burnet's theory of the antediluvian world was that it had consisted of a perfectly flat surface. In the goodly pristine state, the work of the Creator was not disfigured by ugly protuberances of rocks and mountains.*

---

\* "In this smooth earth were the first Scenes of the World, and the first Generations of Mankind; it had the Beauty of Youth and blooming Nature, fresh and fruitful, and not a Wrinkle, Scar or Fracture in all its Body; no Rocks nor Mountains, no hollow caves, nor gaping Channels, but even and uniform all over" (*The Sacred Theory of the Earth*, 4th ed., 2 vols.

Such unsightly objects were the lasting monuments of the wrath which later moved God to alter the habitation of man. Puerile as this explanation is, Burnet's book was held in great esteem. Addison contributed a Latin ode to the edition of 1689. In *Spectator* No. 38 Steele recommended the "learned Dr. Burnet" and in No. 146 quoted a long extract approvingly. Joseph Warton spoke of Burnet as combining Milton's imagination with solid powers of understanding.[19] An English translation of his book, made by the author himself and dedicated to Queen Mary, was published the year the complete Latin version appeared (1689). By 1726 the English version had reached its sixth edition, and in the meantime Burnet's theory had been the occasion of much controversy.*

The other argument—that of the atheists—was popularized chiefly by Lucretius's *De Rerum Natura.* Lucretius's poem is little more than a versified résumé of Epicurus and other pagan atheists

[1719–1722] Vol. I, Bk. I, Ch. 6, pp. 90–91). It should be added, however, that Burnet was impressed by the majesty of the seas and mountains in spite of his theory. "The greatest objects of Nature are, methinks, the most pleasing to behold; and next to the great concave of the Heavens, and these boundless Regions where the Stars inhabit, there is nothing that I look upon with more pleasure than the wide sea and the Mountains of the Earth. There is something august and stately in the Air of these things, that inspires the Mind with great Thoughts and Passions; we do naturally, upon such occasions, think of God and his Greatness" (Vol. I, Bk. I, Ch. 11, p. 191). For his full treatment of mountains, see Vol. I, Bk. I, Chs. 4, 5, 6, and especially 11.

* The extent of discussion is indicated by the following works: Herbert Crofts, Bishop of Hereford, *Some Animadversions upon* . . . *"The Theory of the Earth"* (1685); Erasmus Warren, *Geologia, or a Discourse concerning the Earth before the Deluge and Defence of the Discourse* . . . *wherein the Form and Properties ascribed to it, in a Book entitled, The Theory of the Earth, etc., are excepted against* (1690); Thomas Burnet, *An Answer to the late Exceptions made by Mr. Erasmus Warren against "The Theory of the Earth"* (1690); John Beaumont, *Considerations on a Book entitled The Theory of the Earth* (1693), and *Postscript* to same (1694); John Keill, *An Examination of Dr. Burnet's Theory of the Earth* (1695); Robert St. Clair, *The Abyssinian Philosophy considered and refuted; or Telluris Theoria neither sacred nor agreeable to reason* (1697); S. P., Gent., *Six Philosophical Essays upon several subjects, viz. Dr. Burnet's Theory of Earth, etc.* (1699); Anonymous, *Reflections upon the Theory of the Earth; occasioned by a late Examination of it* (1699); Burnet's replies to Warren and Keill, appended to ed. 6 of the *Theory* (1726). For still other opponents, see John Ray, *The Wisdom of God manifested in the Works of Creation* (1691) and *Three Physico-Theological Discourses concerning,* 1.

who saw in the physical as well as the moral imperfections of the world a negation of God and therefore resolved all nature into "a fortuitous concourse of atoms." Their objection to the world consisted largely in the repulsiveness of the same features condemned by Burnet, especially mountains. Both of these unfavorable views of nature — the extreme orthodox and the atheistic — were opposed all the more vigorously because these were integral parts of two general systems that were opposed by rationalism on various other grounds.

The defense against such charges derived its main impetus from the Cambridge Platonists, in whose works English rationalism began to take definite form. The most influential of these was Ralph Cudworth's *The True Intellectual System* (1678); his philosophy had a marked effect on all subsequent speculation in the Augustan period. In Cudworth's assumptions is found at least the germ of all that was afterwards said by the champions of natural creation — both the orthodox rationalists and the deists. The orthodox could not safely go beyond the argument of mere utility; quite naturally, therefore, this doctrine was the first to be perfected and to secure general adoption. However imperfect individual details of the natural world may appear, they were defended as serving some imperative purpose in the intricate economy of the universal plan. Cudworth appropriated this general statement from Greek philosophy, chiefly from the Platonists, and he used it only in opposition to atheism.[20] Later, however, it served equally well to refute all other doctrines that questioned the perfection of nature.

Those who challenged the theory of Burnet immediately applied this general thesis to the specific case of mountains. For example, John Keill, in 1695, charged Burnet with "presuming boldness" for asserting that "mountains are placed in no order one with another, that can either respect use or beauty." Keill

---

*The primitive Chaos, and Creation of the world. 2. The general Deluge, its causes and effects. 3. The Dissolution of the World and future Conflagration; wherein are largely discoursed the production and rise of Mountains* (1692); John Woodward, *An Essay towards a Natural History of the Earth* (1695); William Whiston, *A New Theory of the Earth* and *A Vindication* of same (1696).

saw fit seriously to contest only the first point. "Notwithstanding this strange assertion," he says, "I am sure, if we were without these shapeless and ill figur'd old Rocks and Mountains, as he calls them, we should soon find the want of them. It being impossible to subsist or live without them. For setting aside the use they may have in the production of various Plants and Metals, which are useful to mankind, and make a part of the compleat whole, and the Food which they yield to several Animals, which are design'd by Nature to live upon them; *The high hills being a refuge for the wild Goats, and the Rocks for the Conies* . . . Without them it is certain we should have no rivers," etc.[21]

A similar, but much more influential, statement of this apology was made by William King in *De Origine Mali* (1702), a book known in the original or in its English translation (1729) by most readers of the eighteenth century. In opposition to the ultra-Calvinistic theologians, King held the waste places of the globe, such as mountains and deserts, to be a part of the original scheme of things; in opposition to the atheists, he considered even these disagreeable aspects proofs of the Creating Mind. "God," he says, "has given those parts to the Brutes which were unfit for Men; and that there might be nothing useless, which yet could not be alter'd without detriment to the whole, he has adapted Animals to every Part and Region of it; and since the Habitations could not conveniently be converted into any other form, he provided such Animals as wanted, and were agreeable to these Habitations. Hence Mountains, Woods and Rocks give Harbour to wild Beasts, the Sea to Fishes, the Earth to Insects."

Archbishop King, however, obviously did not make out a strong case against the atheists, for they would have brushed aside both the habitation and its inhabitants as useless and ugly. By admitting that "the Habitations could not conveniently be converted into any other form," he actually made the Creator a workman subject to human limitations. God seemed to disguise one fault by committing another. King's translator, Edmund Law, from whose Chapter 4 I have quoted,[22] attempted to supplement King's reasoning so as to bring it into complete harmony with

Cudworth's general thesis. "Our Author's argument here might be convey'd," he thought, "much farther, and the Infinite Wisdom of the Creator demonstrated, not only from his having made nothing in vain, or useless in *itself*, but also from the distinct and *various* relations which every thing bears to *others*, and its contribution to the good of the whole." Then follows in Law's note a passage that may be taken as a final statement of the utilitarian argument in defense of mountains. "Thus the Mountains mention'd in the Objection of *Lucretius*, and which many Moderns also have misrepresented as deformities of Nature, have not only their own peculiar Inhabitants, but also afford to other Animals the most commodious Harbour and Maintenance, the best Remedies and Retreats. To them we owe the most pleasant Prospects, the most delicious Wines, the most curious Vegetables, the richest and most useful Metals, Minerals, and other Fossils; and, what is more than all, a wholesome Air, and the convenience of navigable Rivers and Fountains."

This doctrine of usefulness soon found its way into the works of orthodox English poets, and it is practically the full measure of appreciation shown by the few who were tolerant of mountains during the reign of Anne. For example, John Philips, who found his native hills "not unamiable," was proceeding upon the expressed hypothesis that "naught is useless made"; hence, just as King had defended mountains as places of habitation and refuge for animals, the poet Philips justifies the existence of the "cloud-piercing hill Plinlimmon" because it yields "shrubby browze" to the goats (*Cyder* I.98ff). Yalden's apology is similar.* He is consoled for the ugliness of the hills by the consideration that they are filled with precious metal. A still clearer example is the pious Sir Richard Blackmore's *Creation*, in seven books (1712). The avowed purpose of his "endless line" is to refute the atheistic argument of Lucretius and "the Lucretian tribe," especially their objection to the unsightliness and inconvenience due to mountains. In the Preface Blackmore disclaims any attempt at originality. Previously his argument has been stated, he says, in a

---

* *To Sir Humphrey Mackworth.*

manner "obscure, dry and disagreeable"; he himself will give it the advantages peculiar to poetry, and adapt it more "to the general apprehension and capacity of mankind"—an undertaking in which he is encouraged by the belief that "the Epicurean philosophy had not lived so long, nor been so much esteemed, had it not been kept alive and propagated by the famous poem of Lucretius." The gist of Blackmore's opposition to Lucretius is contained in the following passage:

> You say, "The hills, which high in air arise,
> Harbour in clouds, and mingle with the skies,
> The Earth's dishonour and encumbering load,
> Of many spacious regions man defraud,
> For beasts and birds of prey a desolate abode."
> But can the objector no convenience find
> In mountains, hills, and rocks, which gird and bind
> The mighty frame, that else would be disjoin'd?
> Do not those heaps the raging tide restrain,
> And for the dome afford the marble vein?
> Does not the river from the mountain flow,
> And bring down riches to the vale below?
> See how the torrent rolls the golden sand
> From the high ridges to the flatter land.
> The lofty lines abound with endless store
> Of mineral treasure, and metallic ore;
> With precious veins of silver, copper, tin,
> Without how barren, yet how rich within!
> They bear the pine, the oak and cedar yield,
> To form the palace, and the navy build.*

This pragmatic argument, which contains slight nourishment for poetry, represents the first, or orthodox, stage of rationalism. The poetry written in imitation of it, though only apologetic and of no intrinsic worth, is of some value. Even this attitude was more promising than the earlier hostility to mountains. It served also as a stepping-stone to the poetic appreciation developed by the extreme rationalists, or deists, who are to be considered next.

* III.407–426. This is merely a brief summary of the elaborate treatment already made in Bk. I. The same view is expressed in Haller's *Die Alpen* (1729).

## II

The poetic qualities of deism were developed mainly by the Earl of Shaftesbury, the first English philosopher to realize at all fully the aesthetic possibilities of nature and natural law. His essays began appearing in 1699 and were collected as *Character-istics of Men, Manners, Opinions, Times*, in 1711. The fullest treatment of nature is contained in *The Moralists: A Philosophical Rhapsody* (1709). Since his conception has had a profound effect upon subsequent literature, both learned and popular, it requires here a somewhat detailed examination.

Shaftesbury's rationalism took the heretical stand that the Deity has written himself out so plainly in the Book of Nature that further revelation would have been superfluous. On the dry dialectics of his thesis he spends comparatively little time. Likewise, although King's utilitarian argument underlies all of Shaftesbury's reasoning, he makes little of it in his discussion. His main purpose is to illustrate in detail the matchless beauty and harmony inherent in all creation. This aesthetic purpose is manifest also in Cudworth, who in turn was indebted to the Platonic τὸ βέλτιστον: all that is implied by Cudworth's "plastic nature" as an emanation of the Deity is fully developed by his pupil in *The Moralists*.[23]

In a spirit that defied the prevailing horror of "enthusiasm" and a style of composition utterly disregarding the model of restraint set up by the prose-writers of his day, Shaftesbury's frequent rhapsodies exhibit every detail of nature as not only useful to some great end, but as supremely beautiful. He is a poet among philosophers. Montesquieu regarded him as one of the four great poets of the world.[24] In the "universal order and coherence of things," he found all he needed to know of God. "All Nature's wonders serve to excite and perfect this idea of their author. 'Tis here he suffers us to see, and even converse with him in a manner suitable to our frailty. How glorious it is to contemplate him in this noblest of his works apparent to us, the system of the bigger world."[25] The "anti-enthusiastic poet" Lucretius * stirred his profound contempt; for "'tis impossible," he said, "that such a divine order should be contemplated without ecstacy and rapture, since in the common subjects of science and the liberal arts, whatever is according to just harmony and proportion is so transporting to those who have any knowledge or practice in the kind." [26]

Such passages are scattered throughout his works. The most connected treatment of the subject is to be found in the well-known apostrophe to Nature in *The Moralists*, the "enthusiasm" of which is indicated by this paragraph:

"O glorious Nature! supremely fair and good! All-loving and all-lovely, all-divine! Whose looks are so becoming and of such infinite grace; whose study brings such wisdom, and whose contemplation such delight; whose every single work affords an ampler scene, and is a nobler spectacle than all which ever art presented! O mighty Nature! wise Substitute of Providence! impowered creatress! Or thou impowering Deity, supreme creator! Thee I invoke and thee alone adore. To thee this solitude, this place, these rural meditations are sacred; whilst thus inspired with harmony of thought . . . I sing of Nature's order in created beings, and celebrate the beauties which resolve in thee, the source and principle of all beauty and perfection." [27]

The full significance of such general statements can be understood only by reference to his system as a whole.[28] The "divine order" of which he speaks, anticipating not only the idea but the very phrasing of Wordsworth, is really the basic assumption upon which Shaftesbury erected his entire philosophy. The theological import I have already indicated; harmonious nature is the one record wherein man's reason may discern the character and purposes of God. This adoration of nature is still further increased by the aesthetic and ethical doctrine likewise rooted in his naturalistic theory. Setting aside all moral precepts and the doctrine of future reward and punishment, he held that the Good and the Beautiful are identical, that moral virtue is merely the perfect

* *Characteristics* (ed. J. M. Robertson), II, 175. As a matter of fact, Lucretius was "enthusiastic" in spite of his theory (see J. C. Shairp, *On Poetic Interpretation of Nature* [1877], p. 145).

expression of aesthetic sensibility, and that such perfection is a "harmony of inward numbers" resonating to the perfect harmony of the physical world. The resolution of his system into these component parts makes it clear that the "union and coherence of things" is the sole basis of a philosophic scheme embracing theology, aesthetics, and ethics. This idea of the "sacred order" of nature removed, there would be nothing left of his entire speculation. In his view the worship of nature replaces the necessity of formal creed and is invested with a significance involving the supreme moral and spiritual needs of man. To follow Nature was literally to follow God.

Such a conception obviously does not preclude imagination. Some of the critics whom I have quoted imply that those who followed the doctrine of reasonableness to a denial of the miraculous surrendered with Christian "faith" their sense of mystery and yearning after the infinite. Instead, the "free thinkers" transferred their imaginative reverence from biblical legends of the supernatural to the equally great, but as they thought more credible, mysteries of the natural universe. Evidence of God was to be found, they claimed, not in the occasional suspension of natural law, but in its continuous and harmonious operation. Whatever the other results may have been, this change in theology meant at least a theoretic gain for the significance of nature. And in spite of their suspicion of the word *mystery* as applied to theology, deists did not cut themselves off from an imaginative interest in the mysterious processes of nature. It is a habit of critics to speak of the rationalistic conception as if it were diametrically opposed to the romantic. They would have it appear that one school of writers rationalized all physical phenomena and another spiritualized them, the first set treating nature objectively and the second subjectively. Such terms and distinctions are valuable for the purposes of criticism, but they cannot be taken as a basis for rigid historical classification.

Shaftesbury is a clear illustration of the fact that the so-called rationalistic and the imaginative conception exist side by side. Rather they are two successive steps of one interpretative process, the rationalistic conclusion serving as a basis of fact for the more imaginative and intensive statement. Although Shaftesbury arrived at his belief through a process of pure reason, to him nature was not merely the "objective and phenomenal" demonstration of the Creator, but was itself an emanation of the Deity; and although he actually accepted the doctrine of a personal God, his phrasing, in passages already cited and others to follow, constantly hovers on the verge of pure pantheism.* Nor would anything be gained by labeling the imaginative part of his theory sentimentalism. A comparison of King and Shaftesbury will lead to a more reliable statement: the very thoroughness with which the deist applied the doctrine of pure reason cut him off from the traditional creed and left him either to become a downright materialist or else to satisfy his spiritual nature in a highly poetic conception of the natural universe. Following the latter course, he proposed a theory of nature which, I shall try to show, anticipated in detail much of what we call romanticism, in both material and mood.

Theocles, who in *The Moralists* represents Shaftesbury himself, does not confine his enthusiasm to mere platitudes about the heavens and the other accepted beauties of nature. At times the praise may run into trite observations justifying Sir Leslie Stephen's phrases "empty declamation" and "old fashioned classical magniloquence." [29] Shaftesbury would have been most extraordinary if he had wholly avoided rhetoric of this kind at a time when Newton's discoveries were still recent and the deists were using such scientific truths as a telling argument against the dogmatists. But there is much more in his apotheosis of nature. He exulted in phases of the natural world that had never become hackneyed subjects of art, or even subjects at all. Theocles avowed there is not a part of the entire "map of nature" unworthy of man's reverence. To establish his thesis, he descended from his contemplation of the heavens and conducted his pupil "through different climates, from pole to pole, and from the frigid to the torrid zone." [30]

* This aspect of deism was developed by John Toland in *Pantheisticon* (1705) — a work very offensive to the orthodox.

The least enthusiastic part of this survey is the apology for the frozen North. Even here, however, Shaftesbury was an innovator. The description itself anticipates the work of the "Winter Poets," who arose about sixteen years later, and any defense of the rigors of winter was at the time of Shaftesbury's writing (1709) a catholic note hardly to be found in all the range of English literature.[31] The polar regions are, he admitted, "the darkest and most imperfect parts of our map"; but even here are found "the kind compensating gifts of heaven" and such strangeness of life as to force man "humbly to adore the great composer."

In his comment upon the deserts of the earth there is a close approximation to the romantic affection for inanimate nature and also the lower animals. Of these places, he says: "All ghastly and hideous as they appear, they want not their peculiar beauties. The wildness pleases. We seem to live alone with Nature. We view her in her inmost recesses, and contemplate her with more delight in these original wilds than in the artificial labyrinths and feigned wildernesses of the palace."[32] It follows of necessity that this imaginative sympathy embraces all animal life as one part of the finely graduated system of nature. In this respect Shaftesbury was falling in with a tendency of the age to repudiate the Cartesian doctrine that animals are mere machines. In other essays he takes issue with Descartes,[33] condemns baitings and other forms of cruelty to animals,[34] and praises the humanitarian views in the essays of Montaigne.[35] In his application of this benevolent doctrine to the creatures of the desert he strikes a note of sympathy suggestive of Coleridge's moral in *The Ancient Mariner*. "The objects of the place," he declares, "the scaly serpents, the savage beasts, and poisonous insects, how terrible soever, or how contrary to human nature, are beauteous in themselves, and fit to raise our thoughts in admiration of that divine wisdom, so far superior to our short views."[36]

Still more significant is his attitude toward mountains. To many writers in his day and long afterwards they were "great ruins, the result of sin"; and at best they were subjects for apology. Theocles seeks the mountain top in the dawning, for he thinks the *genius loci* will "make us feel Divinity present in these solemn places of retreat." [37] Mountains are mentioned for repeated praise and are given the last word in the author's fervid apostrophe to all Nature. The very dangers of dizzy heights, sharp crags, and impending ledges are alluring. Even thoughtless men, "seized with the newness of such objects," are awakened from their moral lethargy. Such places may be horrible, but the horror is blended with a strange, religious pleasure. The vague melancholy of the later romanticist is clearly detected in the passage that follows:

"But, here, midway the mountain, a spacious border of thick wood harbours our wearied travellers, who are now come among the ever green and lofty pines, the firs, and noble cedars, whose towering heads seem endless in the sky, the rest of the trees appearing only as shrubs beside them. And here a different horror seizes our sheltered travellers, when they see the day diminished by the deep shades of the vast wood, which, closing thick above, spreads darkness and eternal night below. The faint and gloomy light looks horrid * as the shade itself; and the profound stillness of these places imposes silence upon men, struck with the hoarse echoings of every sound within the spacious caverns of the wood. Here space astonishes; silence itself seems pregnant, whilst an unknown force works on the mind, and dubious objects move the wakeful sense. *Mysterious voices are either heard or fancied, and various forms of deity seem to present themselves and appear more manifest in these sacred silvan scenes, such as of old gave rise to temples, and favoured the religion of the ancient world. Even we ourselves, who in plain characters may read divinity from so many bright parts of the earth, choose rather these obscurer places to spell out that mysterious being, which to our weak eyes appears at best under a veil of cloud.*" [38]

Though published in 1709, do these passages not contain at least a hint of what Pater calls "an intimate consciousness of the expression of natural things, which weighs, listens, penetrates, where the earlier mind passed roughly by"? Here there is, to be

---

* It has frequently been pointed out that the word *horrid* in eighteenth-century literature is not derogatory.

sure, no finely wrought description. But this is not to be expected: Shaftesbury was writing as a philosopher, and was therefore confined to general statement. It is the spirit of his interpretation that counts. It would be difficult — I think impossible — to find in any other literature of his day utterances so nearly akin to the mood of Wordsworth. Instead of the humanistic love of solitude as merely a retreat favorable to examination and discipline of self, one finds much more frequently in Shaftesbury an express statement of nature's spiritual power over man. Instead of being objects of hatred, mountains are the special dwelling place of the Great Spirit.

How far Shaftesbury's love of mountains had outdistanced the literary habits of his time can be clearly demonstrated. A more liberal conception was beginning, as I have shown, to creep into popular literature, but only in an apologetic form. Addison's appreciation was limited to a polite tolerance. "Mount Pausilypo makes," he says, "a beautiful prospect to those who pass by it . . ." "In sailing around Caprea we were entertained with many rude prospects of rocks and precipices," and the journey over the Apennines was "very agreeably relieved by the variety of scenes we passed through." [39] Since Wordsworth proclaimed Lady Winchilsea's merit in 1815, she has been regarded as the one poet of Queen Anne's reign who reflected the spirit of nature. Her published work was contemporaneous with that of Shaftesbury. Imaginative as some of her description is, and far removed from the literary cant of the day, her appreciation is exceedingly limited in range. Her latest editor admits that her imagination could not wholly escape the conventional impression of the sea, the storm, and the mountain. [40] To her, mountains meant something more than "huge, monstrous *excrescences* of nature"; but her tribute to them never went beyond the stilted apostrophe, "Ye native altars of the Earth." Pope's *Essay on Criticism*, published two years after *The Moralists*, makes only a doubtful concession:

> In prospects thus, some objects please our eyes,
> Which out of nature's common order rise,
> The shapeless rock, or hanging precipice.

The following passage from John Philips's *Cyder* (1708), Miss Reynolds considers "perhaps the earliest expression in the eighteenth century of that pleasure in high hills and wide prospects that were so marked a characteristic of later poetry": [41]

> Nor are the hills unamiable, whose tops
> To heaven aspire, affording prospects sweet
> To human ken.

The passage is unusual in popular literature; but, compared with the rhapsodies in *The Moralists*, the tribute is faint. The striking fact is that neither this nor any of the other passages cited from this period contains the spirit of actual worship. This is absent also from Lady Mary's praise of the Alps in 1716. She found the banks of the Danube merely picturesque — "charmingly diversified with woods, rocks, mountains covered with vines," etc.[42] Among the stock examples usually quoted we do not come across a spirit of "devout ecstacy" similar to Shaftesbury's until we reach Gray's notes on the Alps. His letter to Richard West, November 16, 1739, contains this comment: "Not a precipice, not a torrent, not a cliff, but is pregnant with religion and poetry. There are certain scenes that would awe an atheist into belief, without the help of other argument. One need not have a very fantastic imagination, to see spirits there at noonday." [43] This is clearly, I think, the strongest statement of Gray's impression. And yet this same theistic argument and poetical belief in mountain spirits had been anticipated thirty years earlier by one of the "rationalistic, prosaic, skeptical philosophers."

Shaftesbury himself realized that he was a pioneer. There is a prophetic note in the tribute which he has Philocles, the pupil, pay to his master, Theocles, the unfashionable worshiper of wild nature in the reign of Queen Anne:

"Your genius, the genius of the place, and the Great Genius have at last prevailed. I shall no longer resist the passion growing in me for things of a natural kind, where neither art nor the conceit or caprice of man has spoiled their genuine order by breaking in upon that primitive state. Even the rude rocks, the mossy caverns, the irregular unwrought grottos and broken falls of water, with all the horrid graces of the wilderness itself, as representing Nature more, will be the more engaging, and appear with a magnificence beyond the formal mockery of princely gardens." [44]

Philocles adds very pertinently, "But tell me, I entreat you, how comes it that, excepting a few philosophers of your sort, the only people who are enamoured in this way, and seek the woods, the rivers, or seashores, are your poor vulgar lovers?" The reply of Theocles conveys in a few words an arraignment of approved taste that meets the situation squarely. "All those who are deep in this romantic way," he laments, "are looked upon, you know, as a people either plainly out of their wits, or overrun with melancholy or enthusiasm."

Shaftesbury was not unaware that he was promulgating an aesthetic view at variance with the literary creed of his time; he realized that as a genuine lover of the solitudes and mysteries of uncultivated nature he was guilty of a heresy in literature comparable to his heretical attitude toward theology, ethics, and "enthusiasm." To neglect him in a treatment of popular literature is wrongly to assume that his ideas were not adopted by popular writers, and to pit him against the romanticists is to pervert the actual facts.

Shaftesbury himself, however, was but a part of a general movement. His phrase "excepting a few philosophers of your sort" conveys a shrewd judgment of the whole matter considered historically. The reference is to the deists, and the implication is sound. When once speculation had disentangled itself from the old theological creed that was suspicious of anything in its natural state, and had also disclaimed the doctrine of mere chance as a solution of life, it was committed to a theory of the universe leading straight to a love of all things natural for their intrinsic beauty. Another name for deism, one used much more frequently at that time, was the Religion of Nature. It was not a misnomer. Primarily as the result of deistical theory, all forms of nature — physical and moral — were given a more honorable place in European thought. Both King and Shaftesbury were greatly indebted to Cudworth's "plastic nature." Allowance made for personal accomplishments, such as style, Shaftesbury may be said to have surpassed King because his disavowal of the orthodox view was thorough, whereas King attempted to effect a compromise between natural and special revelation. They are typical of all contemporary philosophy. Rationalism as a whole was drifting away from the stern Calvinistic conception of God, man, and the world; but it was left to the heretical deists to develop the doctrine of "natural revelation" into a form suitable for the purpose of poetry.

In Shaftesbury's essays this naturalistic philosophy reached the high-water mark in English speculation of the eighteenth century, and from him most of the popular writers drew. None of the other deistic philosophers possessed the literary skill to rival him; their treatment of nature is at best an echo of his. Besides, most of them were fully occupied with the bitter controversy over fundamental points of theology which Shaftesbury had assumed as a starting point. Some, like his avowed champion Francis Hutcheson, were concerned primarily with the ethical doctrine of the *Characteristics*. The only other philosopher who calls for mention here is the orthodox Berkeley. He was violently opposed to Shaftesbury on various grounds, but his conception of nature, as intimated in *Alciphron*, Dialogue IV (1732), and *Siris* (1744), is drawn largely from Cudworth and the pagan philosophers whom both Cudworth and Shaftesbury imitated. Berkeley's example apparently had little or no effect on popular literature; it is important here only as an indication of the compromise gradually accepted by the orthodox when the controversy between the Church and the deists began to subside.[45] A comparison of King and Berkeley would demonstrate to what extent the Christians, who for a time had been seriously discomfited by the extreme argument of natural revelation, were finally able to appropriate its most poetic results. Berkeley himself, however, did not develop this part of his philosophy — "the language or discourse of nature" — until most of his ideas had begun to appear in popular literature through poetical imitation of deism.

Just as Blackmore and his like borrowed from the orthodox phase of rationalism, other English poets daringly appropriated the radical conclusions of the "free thinkers." In this way was derived the ethical and spiritual valuation of nature with which we are familiar in modern poetry, and which is far more distinctive of romanticism than is mere delineative description. That the full poetic possibilities of such a creed should be realized at once in popular literature was not to be expected; the new philosophy made its way gradually as it had done in learned writings. The parallel is seen also in that it is not wholly divorced from the unpoetic argument of utility. The belief in nature's usefulness always underlies the more artistic conception, and, especially in the early stages of poetical treatment, is constantly cropping out. Strict classification of individual poems is, therefore, impracticable. The two ideas — utility and beauty — are frequently found side by side. Also in poetry as well as formal speculation, nature may be presented both as a purely external and objective demonstration and as a symbol or even a part of the Deity. The various elements are confusingly intermingled. The full artistic possibilities were to be realized only after a long process of development during which the more poetic ideas were gradually abstracted and emphasized. But even from the first there are discernible certain elements of interpretation that foreshadow the perfected creed of Wordsworth.

### III

The first signs of the deistic view in popular literature of the eighteenth century are to be found in the work of Henry Needler (1690–1718).* Needler's productions have no intrinsic merit. Much of his philosophy also is confined within the safe limits of orthodox belief. Several of his poems are concerned with a set of theological ideas advocated by all the rationalists. In *A Vernal Hymn in Praise of the Creator*, he versifies the old attack on the atomic theory of "Chance or Parent-Nature." *A Poem in blank verse, proving the Being of a God from the Works of Creation. And some brief Remarks on the Folly of Discontent* follows the

---

* Apparently the date of the first edition of his works is not known. The second came out in 1728. For previous comment on Needler's discipleship to Shaftesbury, see above, pp. 13–14.

lead of rationalism in general very closely, as will be seen from
this extract:

> For what but an Eternal Mind, endu'd
> With utmost Reach of Wisdom exquisite,
> In Goodness and in Power praeeminent,
> Cou'd raise this stately pile; and, all its Parts,
> So visibly, in Order due, dispose;
> Cou'd spread this spacious Canopy, adorn'd
> With thousand glowing stars, that seem to shine
> With emulating lustre, and display
> Their bright Nocturnal Scene; cou'd clothe this Earth
> With grass; with forest crown the mountain-tops;
> With rivers grand, and murm'ring rivulets,
> Refresh the thirsty fields; that so the Whole
> To man a habitation might afford
> Commodious and delightful? How ingrate,
> And blind the Atheist! who denies the Pow'r
> Indulgent, that has made him, and bestow'd
> So many blessings on him undeserv'd!

To most of the ideas in these pieces the pious Sir Richard could
have subscribed; but elsewhere Needler leans to a heresy which
Blackmore had mentioned only for reprobation. And the difference between these two poets on this point serves admirably to
define the new line of thought in popular literature due to the
additional influence of deism.

Blackmore had taken occasion to mark the boundary beyond
which the theological argument from nature must not go. Pantheistic worship is as dangerous, he thought, as atheism. That he
was here glancing at Shaftesbury is not improbable, especially
since the Preface to *Creation* contains a long passage clearly aimed
at *Wit and Humour*; but he referred the obnoxious doctrine of
the pantheists to Spinoza and derisively summed it up as follows:

> The lucid orbs, the earth, the air, the main,
> With every different being they contain,
> Are one prodigious aggregated God,
> Of whom each sand is part, each stone and clod;
> Supreme perfections in each insect shine,
> Each shrub is sacred, and each weed divine.
>
> (III.806–811)

By condemning this very theory, however, Blackmore precludes all that is genuinely poetic in this whole field of speculation. The unmodified utilitarian view is too drily pragmatic for the purposes of art. The only justification of it is that for some of the other writers it served as a stepping-stone to the more aesthetic view which Blackmore deplored as heresy. Apparently the first of these was Needler, who derived his ideas from the *Characteristics*.

In a "Letter to Dr. Duncombe," dated December 3, 1711 (the year of the collected *Characteristics*), Needler thanked his correspondent for the "Philosophical Meditations of my Lord Shaftesbury" and composed a prose rhapsody in imitation of Shaftesbury's apostrophe. Beginning "Hail Sacred Solitude and Silence," Needler's thin song glorifies all Nature as a "Fair Copy of the Divine Ideas, and Image of the Deity!" The conclusion of the piece strikes a note which within a few years was to become general: "How vast a System then is the Universe! Profuse Beneficence! Luxuriant Bounty! . . . Thou minglest Thyself (as it were) with the Matter of the World; thy ever-active and Omniscient Power inspires the Whole; infusing Life and Motion into all its Parts."

Although this passage contains a mere hint of Cudworth's "plastic nature" and the bold assumptions erected by Shaftesbury upon it, Needler's imitation, if published during the reign of Anne, would probably account for some of the few facts we have concerning his life. Cudworth's book was a storehouse for the "free thinkers," and therefore condemned by the orthodox, and Shaftesbury was more than once in danger of prosecution.[46] Needler's imitation of one or both seems to have brought him into similar disfavor. Apparently there are no copies of his first edition, he committed suicide, and Duncombe, the editor of his second edition (1728), was suspiciously anxious to vindicate the "extreme piety" of the poet.[47] His offense was aggravated by a prose essay *On the Beauty of the Universe*, where these opinions are set forth more elaborately. In the edition of 1728, published when the Church was no longer able to enforce her coercive policy, the publisher inserted an Advertisement that may have had the effect of stimulating some of the similar productions to be cited later: "The Essay on the Beauty of the Universe, though very just and rational, is but a sketch (as Mr. Needler himself owns) . . . I wish it may incite some able hand to treat more amply so useful and entertaining a Subject."

After reading Shaftesbury and Needler, one is disposed to question the historical importance assigned by Miss Reynolds to Parnell's *Hymn to Contentment* (1722), which falls here chronologically. The following passage, praising the "Great Source of Nature," is typical:

> The sun, that walks his airy way,
> To light the world, and give the Day;
> The moon, that shines with borrowed light;
> The stars, that gild the gloomy night;
> The seas, that roll unnumber'd waves;
> The wood, that spreads its shady leaves;
> The field, whose ears conceal the grain,
> The yellow treasure of the plain; —
> All of these, and all I see,
> Should be sung, and sung by me:
> They speak their Maker as they can,
> But want, and ask, the tongue of man.

The poem as a whole Miss Reynolds finds "indeed remarkable": "for spirituality and insight, for what has well been called 'a sense of the thing behind the thing,' it was many years before it was paralleled." [48] In the list given by her it is exceptional. But does it reflect any more "insight" than is to be found in the philosophy of Shaftesbury or in the works of Needler? The theory proposed is less bold and poetic than Needler's. These two writers died the same year (1718); Needler's first edition appeared before his death; and Parnell's poem was first published, by Pope, in 1722. This chronology does not argue that Parnell ever heard of Needler; but it shows that Parnell's view was not anomalous in popular literature, and suggests that he himself was probably influenced by the philosophy expressly acknowledged by the more obscure poet. Parnell's ignorance of such speculative doctrine can hardly be supposed. It is at least probable that he found the story of *The Hermit* in the works of the Cambridge Platonist Henry More; his vicarage of Finglass was bestowed upon him by Archbishop King; and his association with Pope and other "free thinkers" renders it likely that he was not unacquainted with some of the later and less orthodox rationalists.

It was not until after 1725, however, that these tendencies exhibited by Needler and Parnell became widely prevalent in English poetry. There then arose a philosophical school of writers most of whom were avowed deists actuated by a well-defined theory. Their conception of nature is presented most fully in Thomson's *The Seasons* (1726–1730), Henry Baker's *The Universe* (1727), Henry Needler's works (second edition 1728), Henry Brooke's *Universal Beauty* (1728, 1735), Pope's *Essay on Man* (1732–1734), Mark Akenside's *The Pleasures of the Imagination* (1744, revised edition 1757), John Gilbert Cooper's *The Power of Harmony* (1745), and James Harris's *Concord* (1751). Traces of it are to be found in much other poetry of the time, notably in the anonymous poems *On Design and Beauty* (1734), *Order* (1737), *Nature, A Poem* (1747), and *Poetic Essays on Nature, Men and Morals* (1750), these being inferior imitations of better-known work. Collectively this body of verse represents a wide range of merit and considerable variation in details, but it is all inspired by the worship of cosmic nature as a unified and unexceptionably beautiful whole, the revelation of God to man. My contention is: first, that it sprang directly from deistic speculation; second, that it forms a connecting link between the formal theorists and the later poets usually designated romanticists.

That this entire school was drawing inspiration directly from the earlier deists I have argued in the preceding study, where I have discussed the same set of writers and considered also why deistic belief was not popularized until late in the reign of George I. My purpose there was to show that the popular ethical theme of "benevolence" in the poetry of the second quarter of the century was due mainly to the widespread imitation of the *Characteristics*, at first by deists only and later by poets in general. The same evidence is applicable in the present case. That those who versified Shaftesbury's theory of natural goodness should have admitted his reverence for external nature was an absolute necessity. None of the ethical poets who imitated him could have disregarded this phase of his teaching, for it is the basic principle of his entire system. The relative emphasis on the physical and the moral aspects varied with individual writers. Needler, his first avowed follower, and Herder, apparently the last, were interested most in the praise of natural objects. Other poets followed the example of the philosopher Hutcheson in putting the main emphasis upon ethics. But in all instances both phases are represented to some extent.

Among those who acknowledged their indebtedness to Shaftesbury are Thomson, Akenside, and John Gilbert Cooper. Thomson refers only to the ethical doctrine of the *Characteristics*, but his imitation of Shaftesbury's scheme of nature is not to be questioned. The underlying assumptions of the two writers are identical, each endeavoring to interpret the "harmonious whole" recorded in the Book of Nature. The deistic tendency of the *Hymn* is so obvious that Lyttelton tried to screen Thomson's memory by omitting it from the collected edition of his works, and this part of Thomson's indebtedness is now pretty generally recognized. Herder thought the best notes of Thomson's muse had been caught from those of Theocles; a comparison of *The Moralists*, the *Hymn*, and Herder's own *Naturhymnus von Shaftesburi* (1800) will afford convincing proof that he was right. It is not improbable, indeed, that Thomson derived a hint for the entire framework of *The Seasons* from Theocles's general survey of the map of nature "through different climates, from pole to pole, and from the frigid to the torrid zone." * In that part of *Winter* describing the polar region (lines 886ff), though some of the details are based on Maupertuis,[49] there are resemblances also to Shaftesbury's description of the frozen North, especially in Thomson's concluding moral (lines 1008ff).

Akenside's imitation of Shaftesbury and Hutcheson is expressly acknowledged in the notes appended to *The Pleasures of the*

* See above, pp. 71, 72.

*Imagination* by the author himself and commented on by several of his contemporaries.[50] He differs from the other poets of the deistic school, except Cooper, in that he undertook to versify almost the entire corpus of Shaftesbury's speculation. He included, for example, the doctrine that the perfect harmony of nature is the only revelation of the Deity required by a reasonable creature, a spirited attack on orthodox superstition, a defense of ridicule as a legitimate weapon in religious debate, and the aesthetic identification of the Good and the Beautiful. Like Akenside, Cooper refers to Shaftesbury and Hutcheson as his models.

Harris, the author of *Concord*, was a nephew of Shaftesbury, to whom he had previously dedicated one of his works. Although Shaftesbury is not referred to in *Concord*, long sections of the poem are little more than transcripts from the *Characteristics*. The annotated editions of Pope's *Essay*, especially Elwin's and Mark Pattison's, prove unmistakably that he derived his interpretation of nature from Shaftesbury and also Cudworth and King, as well as from Bolingbroke's instructions. J. M. Robertson considers the *Essay* "in large part pure Shaftesbury filtered through Bolingbroke." Brooke's source cannot be asserted so positively, but his poem is to be classed with the *Essay*. The deism of the two poems is of the same tone; Pope passed judgment on *Universal Beauty* before it was published; and Book V, line 60 of Brooke's poem (1735) pays a tribute to Pope's. Baker's *The Universe* contains one passage evidently based on King's *De Origine Mali*,[51] and there are various resemblances to Shaftesbury.

IV

These separate facts taken collectively mean that this whole body of versified philosophy was derived to some extent from Cudworth and King, but chiefly from the extreme doctrine and more engaging statement of Shaftesbury. It remains to be considered, then, what new elements this imitation contributed to the treatment of nature, and to what extent the details of this new conception anticipated the work of the so-called romanticists.

In the first place, interest in nature was greatly stimulated by the doctrine of the identity of Truth and Beauty. Through it aesthetic appreciation in general was made the distinguishing trait of the eighteenth-century gentleman. Not to be sensible of beauty was to be wanting in the chief article of the new and fashionable religion; and since the beauty of nature was the supreme beauty, indifference to it was a mark of special depravity.

In the poetry of Thomson there is no express statement that the Good and the Beautiful are one, but apparently the belief is in the background of Thomson's verse. Akenside states the doctrine in set terms. On the basis of his

> For Truth and Good are one;
> And Beauty dwells in them, and they in her,

Gosse called him "a sort of frozen Keats," [52] and Miss Reynolds credited him with being "the first one to emphasize the platonic doctrine of the identity of truth and beauty." [53] Neither insisted, however, that this anticipation of Keats was a matter of mere imitation. Akenside himself refers his aesthetic ideal to Shaftesbury and Hutcheson.[54] It runs throughout the *Characteristics*. The following statement is typical: "And thus, after all, the most natural beauty in the world is honesty and moral truth. For all beauty is truth." [55] The English origin of the doctrine was regularly ascribed to Shaftesbury, especially by his orthodox opponents. Quoting for the purpose of attack, John Balguy wrote (1730): "*All Beauty is Truth* says the penetrating author of the *Characteristics*." [56] Emphasis is to be placed, not only on Shaftesbury's responsibility for the English acceptance of this doctrine, but also on the fact that Akenside's poetical statement is not the solitary anticipation of Keats that some would have us think. The year after his poem appeared, Cooper's *The Power of Harmony* (1745), another imitation of Shaftesbury and Hutcheson, developed the same idea in a much more elaborated form than Akenside's statement of it.* It is an organic part also of James Harris's

---

* II.330–343. In addition to Shaftesbury and Hutcheson, whom the author had already cited as his principal sources among the moderns, he here included in a special note Plato's *Dialogues*, Xenophon's *Memorabilia*, and the French *Traité du Beau*.

*Concord* (1751), and is implied, if not expressed, by most of the poets under consideration.

In the actual treatment of nature, the first service of the deistic poets was to popularize Shaftesbury's view that every aspect of nature is worthy of man's reverence. In some instances this plea rests largely on the orthodox argument of mere utility. Thomson challenges the atheists much as Blackmore had done earlier in his *Creation*:

> Let no presuming impious railer tax
> Creative Wisdom, as if aught was formed
> In vain, or not for admirable ends.
>                              (*Summer*, 318–320)

Baker gives this argument a more detailed application:

> Here pause, and wonder! — then reflect again.
> Almighty Wisdom nothing makes in vain:
> The smallest Fly, the meanest Weed we find,
> From its Creation had some use assign'd,
> Essential to its Being, still the same,
> Co-equal, co-existent with its Frame.

In the passage that follows, Thomson's interpretation becomes less prosaic. He would spend the "winter glooms," he says, with "friends of pliant soul,"

> With them would search, if nature's boundless frame
> Was call'd late-rising from the void of night,
> Or sprung eternal from the Eternal Mind;
> Its life, its law, its progress, and its end.
> Hence larger prospects of the beauteous whole
> Would, gradual, open on our opening minds;
> And each diffusive harmony unite
> In full perfection to the astonish'd eye.
>                              (*Winter*, 575–582)

To Brooke every process of nature is a powerful revelation of the Deity:

> Like Nature's law no eloquence persuades,
> The mute harangue our ev'ry sense invades;
> Th' apparent precepts of the Eternal Will,
> His ev'ry work, and ev'ry object fill;

Round with our eyes his revelation wheels,
Our ev'ry touch his demonstration feels.*

Book II of Cooper's *The Power of Harmony* covers every phase
of the argument which I have discussed in the treatment of the
philosophers, including an attack on both the traditional view of
the Calvinists and the atomic hypothesis. According to Cooper,
when man is rightly attuned, he

> Looks thro' all
> The plan of Nature with congenial love,
> Where the great social link of mutual aid
> Through ev'ry being twines; where all conspire
> To form one system of eternal good,

and thus man learns to love and commune with all nature – from
"the effulgent sun" to "the pale glow-worm in the midnight
shade" (II.321–329).

Frequently the poetical form of this reverence is, like Shaftesbury's, virtually pantheistic. In Thomson we find

> O Nature! all-sufficient! over all!
> (*Autumn*, 1351)

Of the seasons he says:

> These, as they change, Almighty Father, these
> Are but the varied God. The rolling year
> Is full of Thee.
> (*Hymn*)

The following apostrophe scarcely distinguishes between the
Creator and his work:

> Inspiring God! who, boundless spirit all,
> And unremitting energy, pervades,
> Adjusts, sustains, and agitates the whole.
> He, ceaseless, works alone, and yet alone
> Seems not to work; with such perfection framed
> Is this complex, stupendous scheme of things.
> But, though concealed, to every purer eye
> The informing Author in His works appears.
> (*Spring*, 853–860)

* V.23–28. For his argument against the atheists, see II.271–333 and the
Author's long note on 271.

Brooke's constant manner of address is

> Nature, bright effluence of the One Supreme!
> (*Universal Beauty* II.261)

Pope's pantheism in the following well-known passage was one of the chief causes of Crousaz's attack:

> All are but parts of one stupendous whole,
> Whose body Nature is, and God the soul;
> That, changed through all, and yet in all the same,
> Great in the earth, as in th' ethereal frame,
> Warms in the sun, refreshes in the breeze,
> Glows in the stars, and blossoms in the trees,
> Lives through all life, extends through all extent,
> Spreads undivided, operates unspent.*

To give a practical application of this belief that the Deity is diffused throughout creation, Cooper devotes an entire book (Bk. II) of his poem to "The Harmony of Nature" in its immediate effect upon the moral and spiritual life of man. Probably, however, the most striking single statement of the new poetic creed is in the concluding lines of· Akenside's *The Pleasures of the Imagination*:

> Thus the men
> Whom Nature's works can charm, with God himself
> Hold converse; grow familiar, day by day,
> With his conceptions, act upon his plan,
> And form to his, the relish of their souls.†

This paganistic assumption that Nature, when properly understood, is a complete revelation of the Creator is the basis upon which the modern romantic worship of nature arose. Even those

---

* *An Essay on Man* I.267–274. Defending the passage, Warburton denies that Pope is a Spinozist, but admits his pantheism. *An Essay on Reason* (1735), by Pope's friend Walter Harte, affords an interesting parallel, although his poem was supposed to be thoroughly orthodox:

> Science like this, important and Divine,
> The good man offers, *Reason*, at thy shrine;
> Sees *Thee, God, Nature* (well explain'd) the same;
> Not chang'd when thought on, varying but in name.

† Compare *The Prospect. A Poem* (1735), published in the *Gentleman's Mag.*, XIII (Nov. 1743), 608.

early poets who did no more than proclaim this belief in dry terms of exposition were helping to popularize a theory that underlies the best poetry of Wordsworth, his American imitator Bryant, Byron, and Shelley. Dr. Durham apparently regards defection from Christianity to deism in the Augustan period as an inevitable loss of poetic vigor. I take the opposite view. There is more than a verbal connection between the Religion of Nature and the Poetry of Nature. The slightest exaggeration converts this new philosophic interpretation into the vague pantheism that manifests itself constantly in such poets as Wordsworth. Though probably none of the philosophers or poets actually substituted pantheism for a belief in a personal God, the poetical tendency to do so appears in Shaftesbury and his imitators just as it does in their successors. So far as mere thought is concerned, Wordsworth's *The Tables Turned* (1798), *Lines Written in Early Spring* (1798), and *Influence of Natural Objects* (1809) had been anticipated more or less exactly by all these philosophical poets. The following passage from *Tintern Abbey* (1798), often cited as typical of a new attitude, merely repeats what Cudworth meant by the "plastic life of nature" and what Shaftesbury and his poetical followers labored to express in detail:

> And I have felt
> A presence that disturbs me with the joy
> Of elevated thoughts; a sense sublime
> Of something far more deeply interfused,
> Whose dwelling is the light of setting suns,
> And the blue sky, and in the mind of man:
> A motion and a spirit, that impels
> All thinking things, all objects of all thought,
> And rolls through all things.

When deistic poets had thus envisaged all nature, they necessarily followed Shaftesbury in his insistence that the "horrid" aspects of the world, as well as the softer features, are to be revered as parts of the divine harmony. They naturally preferred the uncultivated portions of the earth, where the evidence of the Creator is least obscured by the hand of art. Such appreciation

is very different from the cautious apology used by the orthodox
writers. If the deistic poets had done no more than bring such
"deformities" as deserts, storms, and mountains into special favor,
they would have made a vast contribution to succeeding poetry.
This new attitude is discernible even in Needler; among the
proofs of the divine regimen he includes the forest-crowned
mountains as spectacles of beauty. Brooke explains the "all-
teeming wed-lock" of nature as comprising

> The lowly sweetness of the flowry vale,
> The mount elate that rises in delight,
> The flying lawns that wanton from the sight,
> The florid theatres, romantic scenes,
> The steepy mountains, and luxurious plains,
> Delicious regions.
>
> > (*Universal Beauty* I.133–139)

*The Pleasures of the Imagination* includes within "the goodly
frame" of nature the "sable clouds," the "flying storm," and the
mountains.* Following Shaftesbury's identification of taste and
morality, Cooper says the "tasteful" mind enjoys

> Alike the complicated charms which glow
> Thro' the wide landscape, where enamell'd meads,
> Unfruitful rocks, brown woods, and glittering streams,
> The daisy-laughing lawns, the verdant plains,
> And hanging mountains, strike at once the sight
> With varied pleasure.
>
> > (*The Power of Harmony* II.312–321)

Elsewhere, after dwelling on the charms of the soft and agreeable
aspects, he adds:

> Now change the scene,
> Nor less admire those things which view'd apart
> Uncouth appear, or horrid; ridges black
> Of shagged rocks, which hang tremendous o'er
> Some barren heath; the congregated clouds
> Which spread their sable skirts, and wait the wind
> To burst th' embosom'd storm; a leafless wood,
> A mould'ring ruin, lightning-blasted fields,

---

* Bk. II, line 274 is not really an exception.

Nay, e'en the seat where Desolation reigns
In brownest horror, by familiar thought
Connected to this universal frame,
With equal beauty charms the tasteful soul,
As the gold landscape of the happy isles
Crown'd with Hesperian fruit; for Nature form'd
One plan entire, and made each sep'rate scene
Co-op'rate with the gen'ral force of all
In that harmonious contrast.

(II.124–140)

This trait is particularly striking in the poetry of Thomson. In common with Shaftesbury, he liked especially to study the "obscure places of nature" — the gloom, the solitude, the melancholy remoteness of desert and mountain. Mountains appear throughout *The Seasons*, and in spite of Miss Reynolds's remark that "towards mountains and the sea Thomson held almost the traditional attitude," [57] they are usually invested either with solitary grandeur or with a religious significance. I venture the assertion that by no English poet before Thomson are mountains referred to so often and so affectionately. In a spring landscape,

the Cambrian mountains, like far clouds
That skirt the blue horizon, dusky rise.

(*Spring*, 961–962)

In summer

The dripping rock, the mountain's misty top,
Swell on the sight, and brighten with the dawn.

(*Summer*, 54–55)

The most forlorn aspects of nature are ennobled by the return of the summer season:

The precipice abrupt
Projecting horror on the blackened flood,
Softens at thy return. The desert joys,
Wildly, through all his melancholy bounds.

(*Summer*, 163–166)

In the following passage Thomson's love of mountain solitude goes no deeper than a feeling of physical luxuriousness, such as Keats might express:

> Thrice-happy he, who on the sunless side
> Of a romantic mountain, forest-crowned,
> Beneath the whole collected shade reclines;
> And fresh bedewed with ever-spouting streams,
> Sits coolly calm; while all the world without,
> Unsatisfied and sick, tosses in noon.
>
> (*Summer*, 458–463)

But usually, like Theocles, he seeks such spots because they are sacred to the best thought and deepest inspiration of the philosopher. Emerson's charge that "Thomson's *Seasons* . . . are simply enumerations by a person who felt the common sights and sounds, without any attempt to draw a moral or affix a meaning" [58] is, as Morel observes, only Emerson's way of saying that Thomson was not a transcendentalist. [59] If any poet ever moralized his song and made all things subservient to "Divine Philosophy," it was Thomson. To quote Morel again, "Il a quelque chose de la méthode du savant qui reconnaît dans chaque phénomène un anneau d'une chaine." This spiritual valuation of nature frequently reveals itself in his treatment of mountains, and in such passages, whatever we allow to Thomson's originality or his indebtedness to early poets, there are undoubted traces of Shaftesbury's special suggestion. Alone with nature, Thomson surrenders himself to a solemn mood best described by Collins * when he hailed him as "a Druid." He is overpowered by

> A sacred terror, a serene delight.
>
> (*Summer*, 541†)

Shaftesbury thought the *genius loci* of the mountain would "make us feel divinity in these solemn places of retreat"; Thomson has the same kind of reverential feeling —

> Oh! talk of Him in solitary glooms,
> Where o'er the rock, the sacred waving pine
> Fills the brown shade with a religious awe.
>
> (*Hymn*)

---

* In *Ode on the Death of Mr. Thomson.*
† See also lines 522ff.

In mountain solitudes, Theocles hoped to "charm the genius of the place . . . to inspire us with a truer song of Nature"; the "various forms of deity" which he thought "more manifest in these sacred silvan scenes" address themselves to the poet in the following strain:

> Be not of us afraid,
> Poor kindred man! thy fellow-creatures, we
> From the same Parent-Power our beings drew;
> The same our Lord, and laws, and great pursuit.
> Once some of us, like thee, through stormy life
> Toiled, tempest-beaten, ere we could attain
> This holy calm, this harmony of mind,
> Where purity and peace immingle charms.
> Then fear not us; but with responsive song,
> Amid these dim recesses, undisturbed
> By noisy folly and discordant vice,
> Of Nature sing with us, and Nature's God.
> Here frequent, at the visionary hour,
> When musing midnight reigns, or silent noon,
> Angelic harps are in full concert heard,
> And voices chanting from the wood-crowned hill,
> The deepening dale, or inmost sylvan glade;
> A privilege bestowed by us, alone,
> On contemplation, or the hallowed ear
> Of poet, swelling to seraphic strain.
>                               (*Summer*, 544–563)

The appreciation of nature was extended also to the severities of climate and season. "In 1725, or shortly before, were written three poems on Winter," says Miss Reynolds, in reference to Armstrong's *Winter* (published 1770), Riccaltoun's *A Winter's Day* (published 1726), and Thomson's *Winter* (published 1726).[60] All of these denote a broadening of sympathetic interest, and all of them were by Scotsmen, whose sympathy was due partly to local environment; but it is significant that the praise is strongest in the avowed deists, and that such appreciation is wanting in Scottish literature before the rise of deism. After the success of Thomson's poem the sentiment became common. Akenside's *On the Winter Solstice* (1740) states the philosophic attitude of all the "Winter Poets":

> But let not man's unequal views
> Presume o'er Nature and her laws;
> 'Tis his, with grateful joy, to use
> The indulgence of the Sovereign Cause;
> Secure that health and beauty springs,
> Through this majestic frame of things,
> Beyond what he can reach to know;
> And that Heaven's all-subduing will,
> With good, the progeny of ill,
> Attempereth every state below.

Evidently, so far as praise of inanimate nature is concerned,
little was left to the inventiveness of later poets except in the
matter of phrasing and refinement upon details. The various characteristics I have so far noted are admirably summed up in a
passage of Cooper's, which has a further claim to attention because
it anticipates Wordsworth's theory of enjoyment through retro-
spection. The work of Memory, who acts as a handmaid to Art,
is thus described:

> Thro' Nature's various paths,
> Alike, where glows the blossom'd pride of May,
> Or where bleak Winter from the widow'd shrubs
> Strips the gay verdure, and invests the boughs
> With snowy horrour; where delicious streams
> Thro' flow'ry meadows seek their wanton course,
> Or where on Afric's unfrequented coasts
> The dreary desert burns; where e'er the ray
> Of beauty gilds the scene, or where the cloud
> Of horrour casts its shade; *she* unrestrain'd
> Explores, and in her faithful mirrour bears
> The sweet resemblance, to revive the soul,
> When absence from the sight forever tears
> The source of rapture.
>                    (*The Power of Harmony* I.214–227)

This all-embracing sympathy for nature was made, finally,
to include also the lower animals. It thus stimulated a humanitarian movement which probably owed its inception to oriental
literature. That Shaftesbury's deism contributed something is
fairly evident from the fact that the movement in poetry was due

largely to his imitators. Thomson's poetry, as I have shown in the preceding study, is saturated with the sentiment, and the same doctrine is developed in the earlier verse of Needler. Baker's insistence upon the significance of the meanest objects led him into a similar strain of moralizing; in his tenderness for the very worms of the earth there is the spirit of Blake's *The Book of Thel* and Coleridge's *The Ancient Mariner*. One passage of the kind has already been quoted from Cooper. Henry Brooke points the same moral, but in execrable phrase:

> The flocks that nibble on the flowery lawn,
> The frisking lambkin, and the wanton fawn;
> The sight how grateful to the social soul,
> That thus imbibes the blessings of the whole;
> Joys in their joy, while each inspires his breast
> With blessings multiply'd from all the bless'd!
> (*Universal Beauty* IV. 300–304)

### V

Whether we do or do not consider this increased sympathy for nature romantic depends entirely upon our definition of romanticism, and for my purpose the use of the term is of little consequence. Certainly it was a new conception, far more catholic than any that had ever prevailed in English poetry and similar to the views expressed by later poets usually classified as romanticists. The supposition that it resulted from the renewed study and imitation of the elder poets clearly misses the fact. Earlier literature had shown little inclination to condone the asperities of nature or to embrace natural creation as a whole. The poetry of the eighteenth century represents more than a recrudescence of early sentiment.

After the first quarter of the century, when the recent discoveries in science were becoming generally known and men were beginning to apprehend the marvelous intricacies of natural law, nature took on a larger significance. Whether literature gained or lost by the addition — and that it did for a time lose spontaneity, no one questions — there is this obvious distinction, that the new poetry was painstakingly illustrating a hypothesis. Its interest in nature, like all other rationalistic interests, presupposed the sanction of logic and scientific information. The appreciation of the earlier periods had been determined much less by scientific law and the philosophic arguments occasioned by it. The nightmare of the atomic theory had scarcely been known, and theology had had no occasion to recommend all nature as the reflex of the Deity; it had, in fact, opposed this view. Appreciation of natural objects had, therefore, been less sophisticated. The poet of the eighteenth century, on the contrary, was committed to a moralized interpretation of all natural phenomena as parts of a stupendous revelation of God, the beauty of which consists in its complex unity and its nice conformity to the laws of science. In early literature appreciation was partial; it now became universal. Poetry, in other words, was beginning to assimilate the results of the increased scientific learning which had given impetus to the entire train of rationalistic philosophy.

But, it may be objected, the very presence of this scientific element is what distinguishes such poetry from that of the romanticists, which is said to be dominated wholly by the imagination. This objection, however, is based upon mere definition rather than historical fact. Probably a romanticist ought, for our convenience, to avoid all intercourse with the discoveries of the scientist; but in actual practice those poets whom we call romantic do not. Our modern poetry of nature takes full cognizance of scientific discovery. Shairp has shown that there is no conflict between "poetic wonder" and "scientific," but that the real business of the poet is to find and express the poetic in all knowledge.[61] Such an adaptation or fusion is essential, he thinks, to the very existence of poetry; like a religious creed, poetry that no longer responds to the accompanying state of human knowledge becomes impotent. Wordsworth recognized this law. "If," he declares, "the time should ever come when what is now called Science becomes familiarized to men, then the remotest discoveries of the chemist, the botanist, the mineralogist, will be as proper objects of the poet's art as any upon which it can be employed. He will be ready to follow the steps of the man of science, he will be at his side, carrying sensation into the midst of the objects of Science itself. The poet will lend his divine spirit to aid the transfiguration, and will welcome the being thus produced as a dear and genuine inmate of the household of man." [62] In this process of transfiguration Wordsworth himself was a prominent teacher, and so were Tennyson and various other poets who wrote of nature in the nineteenth century. Science did not throttle their imagination but gave it a larger scope in the new material revealed by a profounder intelligence.

The philosophical poets of the eighteenth century,

Led by the hand of Science and of Truth,*

were the pioneers in this movement. In the early stages of the assimilation the resulting product was frequently neither good science nor beautiful poetry. Much of this verse is exceedingly dry and seems to have little enough of the romantic. Its very faults are due largely to the philosophers who were imitated. Cudworth is uninspiring. King is invariably dry as dust. Much of the bad taste exhibited by Shaftesbury's followers may be traced to their model. Various passages in the *Characteristics*, for example, deal with the use of mineral treasures, "inglorious parts of nature in the nether world"; these and similar scientific touches are partly responsible for the pseudo-science that spoils much of Thomson and Akenside and still more of Brooke. Shaftesbury's treatment of nature is usually too general for artistic effect. Introduced for evidential purposes, it rivets the attention too closely upon the mechanism of his universe. In the poetical imitations, likewise, one constantly hears the creaking of this gigantic system. The method is so general and abstract that the modern reader, who is familiar with a much more poetic treatment of the subject, feels at times that the deistic poets merely hypothecated nature as a text for a dry sermon. But this scientific habit is a fault quite natural to first efforts in this new field. Men were dealing with a universe newly revealed to human intelligence, and it is not surprising that

* *The Power of Harmony* II.246. See also Akenside's *Hymn to Science*.

at the outset the scientific facts were treated too literally and pro-
fusely while the spiritual truth was allowed to suffer by comparative brevity of treatment.

In spite of these amateurish faults in proportion, this deistic
verse, taken collectively, holds in solution the entire doctrine of
the modern romantic school. Most of these poets were clumsy
in their utterance; some of them used the couplet, which was ill-
adapted to their purpose; and all of them were too fond of "nature's wide expanse." But if nature has any larger significance
than mere sensuous delight, and if the full interpretation of
nature requires the ardor of worship in addition to keen senses
and deft phrasing, the imperfect work of the deists is not to be
despised. It represents the first stage in the evolution, a *disciplina
arcani*, through which English romanticism had to pass before the
naive and partial treatment found in our early literature could be
replaced by that combination of descriptive excellence and philosophic thought which constitutes the distinctive quality in the
modern romantic interpretation of nature.

## VI

The indebtedness of poetry to philosophy for these various
contributions has not been recognized even in the work of Thomson and Akenside. In Thomson's case there is a tendency to look
for his interpretation in merely descriptive passages. Few of these
exhibit a high degree of imagination; they are characterized rather
by conscientious realism.[63] But Thomson's contribution to the
romantic ideal, and therefore his historical importance, are to be
estimated largely, just as Wordsworth's are, by philosophical passages which express his conception of nature as a whole. Thomson's worship of nature is a religious feeling running throughout
*The Seasons.* Every scene described derives an added significance
through the informing spirit arising from the poet's general conception of the outward and visible world as a revelation of the
Deity. And to make a just estimate of this conception, we need
to keep in mind two important considerations. In the first place,
a study of Thomson must take equal account of the poets who

preceded and those who followed him. Through such a comparison it becomes evident that he was the first English poet to express at all adequately the range and the intensity of our modern reverence for nature, and that largely through him and his English and Continental * imitators this phase of modern poetry came into general favor. In the second place, greater emphasis is to be placed on the relation of Thomson's religious views to his poetry. Sometimes he is cited as the first of the romanticists. It is recognized also that he is a deist. But the two statements are never thoroughly coordinated. The truth is, Thomson was a forerunner of the romanticists in his treatment of nature because he was the first English poet to reflect at all fully the romantic tendencies inherent in deism.

In dealing with Akenside, critics have not failed to mention him also as an early romanticist; but they have refused to see that his romanticism is the direct result of his imitation of the deistic philosophers. Miss Reynolds [64] finds in *The Pleasures of the Imagination* the same "sacred order" of the universe and its spiritual effect which Wordsworth employs in *The Excursion*.[65] Again, she remarks that both *The Pleasures of the Imagination* and the *Hymn to the Naiads* [66] lay "a Wordsworthian emphasis on the effect of nature on the soul of a child." [67] On the basis of these and other analogies, she concludes with surprise that "in the middle of the century we find a statement of poetical creed which, so far as the thought is concerned, might have come from 'The Excursion' or 'The Prelude.'" But, unfortunately for a full understanding of the origin and historical development of this romantic theory which she traces, she did not observe that Akenside derived his "Wordsworthian conceptions" directly from the *Characteristics*. The whole matter of the poet's indebtedness she conveniently dismisses with the passing remark that *The Pleasures of the Imagination* "is a smooth, correct, rather frigid exposition of certain philosophical principles." To ignore Shaftesbury's re-

* See, for example, Haller's *Die Alpen* (1729) and Brockes's *Irdische Vergnügen in Gott* (1721), both of which were influenced by Thomson. Note, too, how the ideas of utility and beauty are combined.

sponsibility for this poetic creed is to stop short of the real source of a very important literary doctrine.

When we turn from Thomson and Akenside to the other members of the school, we find criticism still less inclined to recognize the full truth. In order to extol Akenside, Miss Reynolds makes an assertion which precludes a just estimate of all the other poets of this group. Akenside, she says, is "one of the first of the poets of the age to insist on the beauty of all Nature." Certainly the philosophers and the poets I have discussed make it clear that there was nothing unusual in his emphasis "on the beauty of all Nature." This had been a commonplace of learned philosophy from the time of Cudworth's *The True Intellectual System*; it underlies the dry reasoning of King; it is the mainspring of Shaftesbury's teaching; and it informs Berkeley's "language or discourse of nature." "Plastic nature," "the chain of being," "universal beauty," and their various implications had been treated also in popular literature — by writers ranging in merit from Needler to Thomson. The "sacred order" of which Miss Reynolds makes a good deal in Akenside and Wordsworth is the fundamental assumption of such theory: Shaftesbury's "universal order and coherence of things," or "sacred order," is the prevailing topic of every deistic poet discussed in the present study. Of the peculiar merits which she assigns to Akenside, the effect of nature on the plastic mind of the child is the only anticipation of nineteenth-century romanticists in which he was exceptional. In other words, if Akenside was an early romanticist, so were the other eighteenth-century poets of the deistic school.

I insist chiefly, however, on the greater fault of those who habitually misrepresent the deists as opposing and obstructing the so-called romantic attitude toward nature. Critics who do so restrict their view to advanced evolutional stages of the late eighteenth and early nineteenth century. In their anxiety to define the romanticism of the nineteenth century by contrast, they use the earlier period as a mere foil, overlooking the fact that the contrast is substantially one of diction, poetic form, descriptive skill, and other literary refinements rather than a contrast of actual interpretation. This method ignores an early and important phase of a broad historical movement that brought into popular favor an interpretation of nature involving the rationalistic and the romantic views in a complementary relation. Had there been a long interval between the first and the second step of the process, less apology would be needed for the constant insistence on the incompatibility of the rational and the imaginative interpretation. But early in the deistic movement, as I have shown, this association was clearly perceived and stated. The conclusion reached by pure reason served at once as an authoritative basis of fact for a more poetic conception of the natural universe than had ever before been at all common in any literature. That a writer was rational did not mean that he had laid by his imagination. "To state one argument is not necessarily to be deaf to all others, and that a man has written a book of travels in Montenegro, is no reason why he should never have been to Richmond." From Cudworth's "plastic nature" to Wordsworth's pantheism the development of the modern estimate of nature is consecutive.

To obtain a true historical perspective, we should compare the treatment of nature in English literature before the triumph of rationalism and afterwards. It will thus become clear that our modern sympathy for universal nature is largely an outgrowth of this philosophy. Even tolerance of mountains and other irregularities of the natural world was exceptional before the orthodox form of rationalism had begun its attack on ancient prejudices, and the apotheosis of nature as a moral and spiritual force came into our popular literature only after rationalism had passed beyond the limits sanctioned by the Church. The modern cult of nature worship is in its origin, then, unorthodox — the result of a revived pagan philosophy enriched by the discoveries of modern science.

There are in the Bible, of course, many passages pointing in the same direction and glowing with Eastern fervor; but the Church itself discouraged the pursuit of such ideas. Jealously guarding the doctrine of supernatural revelation and scenting danger in naturalism, the Fathers discountenanced any interpretation of nature approaching the fullness of modern worship. There is ample evidence to confirm Biese's remark that "to Judaism and Christianity, Nature was a fallen angel, separated as far as possible from her God." [68] It is true that early Christian literature is notable for its interest in natural scenery, that a few medieval writers showed considerable appreciation of their native Alps, and that Catholic mystics were beginning in the Middle Ages to realize the possibilities of natural revelation. But their enthusiasm was soon checked. Such appreciation clearly demonstrated that the study of nature for religious and moral purposes is likely to end in conflict with the Christian dogma. Interest of the kind, especially when associated with science, was reproved by the Councils, and in the end effectually interdicted as a heresy. [69]

The Anglican Church was no more liberal than the Roman Catholic, but through rationalism, which was invoked as a defense of her position, she was ironically betrayed into assumptions that afterwards threatened the complete overthrow of orthodox theology. When this insidious danger was completely unmasked, the English Church turned upon deism the same anathemas that had formerly silenced the Catholic mystics. Again, the reproach of heresy was used. But for various reasons — partly because the new Religion of Nature was authorized by a fuller understanding of natural law than the earlier worship of nature had been — the outcome was different. For a time the full fruition of deistic theory was delayed, but in the end the heretics were powerful enough to defy ecclesiastical authority. The final result of the fight between deism and Christianity was a compromise which liberalized English thought in various ways. With the exception of independent ethics, the most important of the additions contributed by deism is this liberal and enthusiastic appraisal of nature. Like the ethics of deism, this too has gradually outgrown the taint of heresy and been generally accepted, at least for the purposes of poetry. The theological heresy of a former age has become the poetic creed of our own.

Unavoidably I have made the change in theology and the resulting ideas in poetry appear somewhat more sudden than it really was. English deism actually began to take form as early as the fifteenth century in the writings of Reginald Pecock; but his fate was a warning to others. There were similar intimations of the new creed in the popular literature of England before the eighteenth century. Reference has already been made to some of these. Undoubtedly a thorough examination would reveal a considerable number of precursors like Vaughan, especially in the period following the Renaissance, when English thought came under the influence of Greek philosophy. But these doctrines first crystallized into a complete system in the works of the Augustan rationalists, and the historical continuity of similar ideas in popular writings dates from the imitation of this school of philosophy by deistic poets.

# ~~~III~~~

# Whig Panegyric Verse: A Phase of Sentimentalism

THOUGH of slight intrinsic value, Whig poetry of the eighteenth century constitutes a distinct chapter in the history of English literature. The earlier interest of poetry relating to affairs of state had almost invariably taken the form of personal eulogy, satire, or violent invective — types produced in extraordinary abundance during the Restoration. While such verse continued to flourish indefinitely, the complete development of the party system of government enabled poetry to acquire a much broader and more influential sphere. The great body of Whig verse written in the eighteenth century is devoted to the expression of party ideals; it is concerned with principles rather than personalities.

This change of function, deeply significant for the future relation of politics and belles lettres, arose largely from the fact that poets were irresistibly attracted by what Chevrillon calls the psychology of Whiggism. Fortunately for the Whig cause, the versifiers contrived to find in the Whig dogma the political embodiment of the most popular moral sentiments of the age. The advocacy of Whiggism thus became a phase of a sentimental movement which, beginning early in the century, eventually "spread like a mildew" over the whole surface of literature. The fusion of political and moral ideals resulted in a program especially agreeable to the bourgeoisie. As the mercantile classes ac-

quired wealth and political influence through Whig measures for
the promotion of trade, the Whig poet's audience was gradually
enlarged and the scope of his usefulness broadened. The political
ideals advocated are surprisingly modern. With the change of a
few special phrases, the principles and the sentimental arguments
used in support of them would sound curiously familiar to readers
of today. We are familiar also with the influence of a sentimental
press upon the promises, if not the actual performances, of political parties. The one unfamiliar and distinctive circumstance is
that much of the propagandist work now performed by journalists devolved at that time upon poets.

I

Professor Courthope [1] has made an excellent study of Whig
panegyric, but he leaves off at the point where the poets were
only beginning to exercise their complete function as expositors
and champions of Whig ideals. His examination is confined, virtually, to poems produced during the time of William III and of
Queen Anne, taking into account, as the nature of a general history of poetry demands, only such productions as are at least
comparatively notable for intrinsic literary value. The list includes
early poems by Montague, Addison, and Prior; notice is given
also to John Hughes and Thomas Tickell. A brief review of the
same period is included here only as a necessary introduction.

Clearness of treatment, especially of verse composed in the
initial stage, demands at the outset repetition of Mr. Courthope's
statement that the line of demarcation between Whig and Tory
was not always clear-cut. The Revolution of 1688 and the Decla-
ration of Rights (1689) were essentially Whig measures. Through
the change they produced in the government and through the
policies afterward pursued by the *roi fainéant*, William of Orange,
the Whigs attained an ascendancy which was scarcely interrupted
even by the accession of a nominal Tory ministry at the beginning of Queen Anne's reign and was never seriously imperiled
until 1710. But in this revolutionary change moderate Tories had
concurred as members of the Convention and afterward, though

reluctantly, as supporters of the foreign war precipitated by the Revolution. To have taken a different position would have been equivalent to joining the extreme, and indeed the only logical, group of Tories, the Jacobites.

The union of Whigs and moderate Tories was an instance, however, of a combination of political forces agreed, if at all, only upon a single detail of policy and incapable of cooperating after that one purpose had been effected.[2] Since the expulsion of James II was due partly to the fear that the Roman Catholic religion might be firmly re-established in England as well as to the indignation aroused by the monarch's invasion of popular liberties, with many religious safety was the chief consideration. For those in whom the religious motive was uppermost the Bill of Rights possessed significance chiefly as a guarantee of restored Protestantism, and their interest declined as soon as they regarded England reasonably safe from the Romanist plot. Even those who were actuated primarily by political convictions were not agreed necessarily except upon the fundamental maxim that an oppressed nation is justified in revolting against a tyrannical sovereign. To confirm this right, it was patently necessary to wage war against Louis XIV. But from the beginning of the war the Tories were in an awkward dilemma. While fully committed to the principal, the only ostensible, design of the war, they found themselves in the ironical position of promoting this central cause of national safety at the price of sacrificing to their Whig allies the professed interest of their own party. At every step in the successful establishment of the Dutch sovereign's policies the power of the mercantile and moneyed class was enhanced at the expense of the landed gentry. The Tories were aiding the Whigs in the destruction of Toryism.

The irony of their position was brought into clear relief at the accession of Queen Anne (1702), when Tory ministers came into power under conditions which made it necessary for them to prosecute a second foreign war, one thrust upon them by the former Whig government and designed primarily in the Whig interest. This very circumstance, however, served in the end to

fix a more definite character upon each of the two political parties and to define the political issue. It soon became evident to
the Tory statesmen in control that necessary support of the war
could be secured only from the Whigs. The new leaders themselves either became proselytes to Whiggism, as Godolphin did,
or were driven from office. Thus in the end a more definite align-
ment than had existed before was secured through division of
opinion concerning this one question of foreign policy. The
Whigs were for continuing the war, the Tories for bringing it
to a speedy conclusion.

It is easily seen why from the beginning poetical enthusiasm
was confined almost exclusively to ardent Whig poets. Obviously, too, during the early stages of literary Whiggism panegyrists were necessarily preoccupied with military affairs. As long
as British armies were engaged in a Continental war metrical
eulogy retained, almost inevitably, much of its traditional literary
character. It was written primarily to celebrate the heroism of
individuals and the valor of the British soldier or to ridicule the
enemy. The personal note is prominent. At the same time much
of the flattery was applicable to the English people as a whole.
The one national virtue certain to be signalized was the unselfish
motive that had animated the English to embark upon a foreign
war. This was said to be purely unselfish. England was not waging
a war of self-aggrandizement. She was actuated only by the noble
design of perpetuating within her own territory the most liberal
and beneficent government in the world and of imparting some
of the blessings of the Glorious Revolution to oppressed peoples
on the Continent. Poetical emphasis upon the national disinterestedness is at times delightfully egotistic. Now that St. George
had swept his own house clean in 1688, he was endeavoring to
set the houses of Europe in order. In all poems developing this
strain of flattery the encomiast intended primarily to magnify the
wisdom and humanity of the Whig patriots, those high-minded
statesmen who had expelled the tyrant James II from the English
throne and installed William III, the special agent deputed by the
Goddess of Liberty to reign over Albion in her stead. There was

at least a grain of truth in the bushel of rhetorical chaff; the Grand Monarch and Nassau, France and England, did offer points of striking contrast, and the advantages enjoyed by the English were due chiefly to the initiative of Whig leaders.

The arrival of William, champion of religious truth and political freedom, is described by his Whig subject William Walsh in the following strain:

> Firm on the rolling deck he stood,
> Unmov'd, beheld the breaking flood,
>   With blackening storms combin'd.
> "Virtue," he cry'd, "will force its way;
> The wind may for a while delay,
>   Not alter our design.
>
> "The men whom selfish hopes inflame,
> Or vanity allures to fame,
>   May be to fears betray'd:
> But here a Church for succour flies,
> Insulted Law expiring lies,
>   And loudly calls for aid.
>
> "Yes, Britons, yes, with ardent zeal,
> I come, the wounded heart to heal,
>   The wounding hand to bind:
> See tools of arbitrary sway,
> And priests, like locusts, scout away
>   Before the western wind.
>
> "Law shall again her force resume;
> Religion, clear'd from clouds of Rome,
>   With brighter rays advance.
> The British fleet shall rule the deep,
> The British youth, as rous'd from sleep,
>   Strike terrour into France." *

At the time of Walsh's writing, in 1705, this was intended as a summary of what had actually been accomplished. William III

---

* *Horace, Ode III, Book III, Imitated* (1705). Compare Walsh's ironical praise of the Tories in *The Golden Age Restored* (1703). See also George Stepney's *Epistle to Charles Montague, Esq.*, a typical Whig panegyric of William III. Steele's *The Christian Hero* (1701) and *Spectator* No. 516 (1712) are written in the same spirit.

had now been in his grave three years. What he had begun was being perfected by the "female hand" of his royal successor. The continuity of benevolent design is emphasized by two poems of Congreve's. *The Birth of the Muse*, addressed to Halifax, celebrates the virtuous achievements of William as summarized in the Treaty of Ryswick (1697) and bids

> Britannia, rise! awake, O fairest Isle,
> From iron sleep! again thy fortunes smile.
> Once more look up, the mighty man behold,
> Whose reign renews the former age of gold.

How nobly this heritage of disinterested benevolence was fostered in the next reign is set forth in Congreve's *Pindarique Ode* to the Queen (1706). Serene upon her firm throne, Anne might have looked down upon the rest of the world with contempt.

> But greatest souls, though blest with sweet repose,
> Are soonest touch'd with sense of others' woes.
>     Thus Anna's mighty mind,
>   To mercy and soft pity prone,
>   And mov'd with sorrows not her own,
> Has all her peace and downy rest resign'd
> To wake for common good, and succour human kind.
>
>   Fly, Tyranny; no more be known
>   Within Europa's blissful bound;
>   Far as th' unhabitable zone
>   Fly every hospitable ground.
> To horrid Zembla's frozen realms repair,
>     There with the baleful beldam, Night,
>       Unpeopled empire share,
>     And rob those lands of legal right.
>   For now is come the promis'd hour,
>       When Justice shall have power;
>       Justice to Earth restor'd!
>         Again Astraea reigns!
>   Anna her equal scale maintains,
> And Marlborough wields her sure-deciding sword.*

---

* Similar sentiments are expressed in Congreve's *To the Right Honourable the Earl of Godolphin*. For fulsome eulogy of the Queen, compare Samuel Cobb's *The Female Reign* (1709).

It appears from a poem by Nicholas Rowe that the new war lord, the Duke of Marlborough, was fully sustaining the unselfish character of his royal exemplar, William III:

> What vast reward, O Europe, shalt thou pay
> To him who saved thee on this glorious day!
> Bless him, ye grateful nations, where he goes,
> And heap the victor's laurel on his brows.*

If it were necessary to award first place in adulatory absurdity, it might reasonably be assigned to John Hughes, in consideration of his three poems, *The Triumph of Peace* (1697), *The Court of Neptune* (1699), and *The House of Nassau* (1702). In the midst of much metrical bombast Joseph Addison preached the Whig moral in the calmer and more dignified couplets of his *Letter from Italy* (1704). The praise conferred upon English prosperity and freedom through contrast with the miserable conditions the young traveler had beheld in Italy is the most graceful of the numerous compliments in verse addressed to Montague and his Whig colleagues. Compared with other war poems, Addison's *Campaign* (1705), though by no means a great poem, is entitled to similar praise.

## II

Only one motif of the early Whig eulogists was retained by their poetical heirs. As the War of the Spanish Succession dragged on, less emphasis came to be placed upon the altruistic motive of the English. The time came when the fiction of Marlborough's unselfishness was too threadbare even for poetical repetition. But the glorification of British liberty to the shame of France and other countries of Europe continued indefinitely to be a pleasing duty of the versifiers, and the point was elaborated in greater detail by the Georgian poets.

We could hardly expect a strict adherence to truth. At times

---

* *A Poem, On the Late Glorious Successes . . . Humbly Inscribed to the Lord Treasurer Godolphin* (1707). Compare Charles Gildon's *Libertas Triumphans* (1708). The Whig enthusiasm of Rowe's *Tamerlane* (1702) was such that until 1815 it was played annually on November 5, the anniversary of William III's landing. The Revolution is glorified also in the Prologue to Rowe's *Lady Jane Grey* (1715).

the discrepancy between the theoretic perfection described by the poet and the actual conditions is painfully great. As a modification of tyrannical doctrines of the past the Bill of Rights was undoubtedly a long stride toward modern democracy. It all but disposed of the old belief in the divine right of kings. Undoubtedly, too, English chauvinists were partly justified in their proud comparison with neighboring governments, for under the new regime they enjoyed a larger measure of self-government than existed in any of the great Continental states. But it was not true that the political millennium had been ushered in. The effects of the Revolution were, after all, superficial. No patent gain had been made except by a small governing class. Lower down in the scale there were virtually the same inequality of privilege, the same class discrimination and misery that had existed before. In some respects indeed new economic conditions aggravated the servitude of the lower classes. This limitation had to be ignored by the metrical eulogist as it had been by John Locke, the official apologist of the Revolution, in his *Two Treatises on Government* (1689–1690).

Thomson is the illustration *par excellence* of Locke's political philosophy in verse and of British egotism. There are numerous poems of his, to be sure, in which his "feeling heart" bemoans the sufferings of unfortunate Englishmen and condemns the brutality legally practiced upon them. He was, in fact, the foremost poet of his time in exposing the inhumanity of the law. Yet it was Thomson who wrote that dull and interminable poem called *Liberty* (1735–36), the most flattering of all the verse pamphlets in praise of the Whig dogma. Tracing the progress of human freedom from the earliest times, nation by nation, he comes to that glorious event of 1688. By this the fondest dreams of liberty have at last been realized. Here and now, he says in substance, Englishmen enjoy in perfection the blessing of which noble spirits of all ages have dreamed, but of which no people before has had more than a small and fugitive share in practice. From the peroration of Liberty's eloquent address to Britain, at the close of Book IV, it is clear that the cup of national blessings is full to overflowing:

> And now behold! exalted as the cope
> That swells immense o'er many-peopled earth,
> And like it free, my fabric stands complete,
> The palace of the laws. To the four heavens
> Four gates impartial thrown, unceasing crowds,
> With kings themselves the hearty peasant mixed,
> Pour urgent in. And though to different ranks
> Responsive place belongs, yet equal spreads
> The sheltering roof o'er all; while plenty flows,
> And glad contentment echoes round the whole.
> Ye floods, descend! Ye winds, confirming, blow!
> Nor outward tempest, nor corrosive time,
> Nought but the felon undermining hand
> Of dark Corruption, can its frame dissolve,
> And lay the toil of ages in the dust.

Such are the beneficent effects brought to pass by the Whig Settlement as viewed nearly a half-century later by a Whig poet.*

> The poor man's lot with milk and honey flows.

England is the

> Great nurse of fruits, of flocks, of commerce, she!
> Great nurse of men!
>
> (V.6, 81–82)

In the course of a generation, however, abstract theory had become the smallest part of poetical business. Through the general expansion of the literary program poetry was made more

---

* Parts IV and V are devoted to Britain. See also *The Castle of Indolence* II.xxiv. Compare with Thomson's tributes: Lord Lyttelton's *To the Reverend Dr. Ayscough at Oxford. Written from Paris* (1728) and *To Mr. Glover on his Poem of Leonidas* (1737); Robert Nugent's *Epistle to the Right Honourable Lord Viscount Cornbury* and *Ode to Mankind* (1739); H. Walpole's *Epistle from Florence to Thomas Ashton* (1740); Henry Fielding's *Liberty. To George Lyttelton, Esq.* (1743); Mark Akenside's *The Pleasures of the Imagination*, Bk. II (1744); Gloster Ridley's *Jovi Eleutherio, or, An Offering to Liberty* (1745); Sir James Marriott's *Verses on the Peace* (1748); Joseph Warton's *Verses Written at Montaubon* (1750); Joseph Giles's *Ode to the New Year* (1756); and Thomas Newcomb's *Vindicta Britannica* (1758). Compare also *Spectator* No. 287.

directly serviceable; it became a medium for propagating all the details of Whig practice in the conduct of national affairs. The growth of poetical responsibility becomes evident especially in the latter part of George I's reign, when verse came to be used more than ever before for practical and prosaic purposes in general. In the Whig program the chief source of inspiration for poetical propagandists was the glory of maritime commerce. At the time of Walpole's complete ascendancy, while the nation was growing opulent under the system established by William III, practically all the versifiers — influenced by the inherent poetry of the subject, and partly no doubt by patronage or the hope of it — were unremitting in their effort to express the national pride in a commerce extending throughout the world.

Most of these poems were intended as a tribute to the Whig statesmen, many of them to Walpole himself. For example, Young's *Instalment* (1726), addressed to him, contains a defense of the two favorite ministerial designs — the preservation of peace and the extension of British trade:

> If peace still smiles, by this shall commerce steer
> A finish'd course, in triumph round the sphere;
> And, gathering tribute from each distant shore,
> In Britain's lap the world's abundance pour.*

*The Universal Passion*, Satire VII (1728), contains a similar tribute to the Prime Minister, to whom it is dedicated, and sets forth the happy condition of England as the result of his guidance:

> While I survey the blessings of our isle,
> Her arts triumphant in the royal smile,
> Her public wounds bound up, her credit high,
> Her commerce spreading sails in every sky,
> The pleasing scene recalls my theme again
> And shows the madness of ambitious men,
> Who, fond of bloodshed, draw the murd'ring sword,
> And burn to give mankind a single lord.

---

* Young's loyalty is partly explained by these verses:
> My breast, O Walpole, glows with grateful fire,
> The streams of royal bounty, turn'd by thee,
> Refresh the dry domains of poesy.

The same purpose is responsible for the crude verses of Young's *Imperium Pelagi* (1730), a piece of fustian amply meriting Fielding's ridicule of it in *Tom Thumb*. One stanza is noteworthy as expressing the growing effort of the Whigs to remove the social stigma traditionally attached to the mercantile life:

> Is "merchant" an inglorious name?
> No; fit for Pindar such a theme;
> Too great for me; I pant beneath the weight.
> If loud as Ocean's were my voice,
> If words and thoughts to court my choice
> Out-number'd sands, I could not reach its height.*

His *Reflections on the Public Situation of the Kingdom* (1745) was intended to arouse the sleeping valor of the British by such appeals as the following:

> Hail to the brave! be Britain Britain still:
> Britain! high-favour'd of indulgent Heaven!
> Nature's anointed empress of the deep!
> The nurse of merchants, who can purchase crowns!
> Supreme in commerce! that exuberant source
> Of wealth, the nerve of war; of wealth, the blood,
> The circling current in a nation's veins,
> To set high bloom on the fair face of peace!

Most of the Whig poets, though less firm in their allegiance to Walpole, produced verse of this kind. The two most frequent contributors were Young and Thomson.† It is a painful commentary on the instability of Fortune that, with a sole exception, none of this enthusiastic literature of the sea has really survived,

---

* Compare *Spectator* No. 69 (1711) by Addison; *Free-Thinker*, Vol. II, No. 152, Sept. 14, 1719; Steele's *Conscious Lovers* (1722) IV.ii, V.i; Lillo's *George Barnwell* (1731) I.i, III.i, and *Fatal Curiosity* (1737) III.i; Lord Lyttelton's *Letters from a Persian* (1735), No. xlviii. Voltaire remarks with surprise in *Lettres philosophiques*, Let. x, that younger sons of noble English families do not disdain to engage in commercial pursuits. César de Saussure makes the same observation in his *Lettres*, No. viii, May 29, 1727. Montesquieu's *L'Esprit des lois* praises the national enthusiasm for trade (Bk. V, Ch. 6; Bk. XX, Chs. 7, 12), but deplores the participation of the nobility (Bk. XX, Ch. 21).

† Thomson dedicated his poem on Sir Isaac Newton to Walpole, who is described as "like Heaven, dispensing happiness to the discontented and ungrateful"; but he later withdrew the dedication and opposed the Prime

and the prolonged life of even Thomson's *Rule Britannia* is due to accident rather than independent merit. In the opinion of contemporaries (one not likely to be shared by a reader of today) mercantile enthusiasm reached the high-water mark of poetical expression in Richard Glover's *London, or, The Progress of Commerce* (1739). This long allegorical poem, a mosaic of hard words and classical allusion, narrates the birth of this Child of Neptune on an island off the Libyan coast and pursues her in the various migrations she makes until, like Thomson's Liberty of four years earlier, the Goddess of Commerce selects Albion as her permanent residence. After Glover's monumental performance only meager gleanings were left for Cornelius Arnold's *Commerce* (1751) and the second book of Dodsley's *Publick Virtue* (1754).

Though mainly responsible for nurturing commercial expansion, the Whigs had not meanwhile been left by their rivals in uncontested possession of the honor. Just as Tories insisted on seeing their own patriotic ideals reflected in Addison's Cato, whereas the Whig author of *Cato* (1713) had intended apparently to read them a severe lesson by contrast, they put in a claim also to a patriotic share in the development of Britannia's commercial prosperity. The charge was made against the Tory statesmen in authority during the last four years of Queen Anne's reign that they had thrown away the advantages acquired by numerous victories on the Continent and betrayed the commercial interest by accepting the terms of the Treaty of Utrecht (1713). Much of the obloquy attached to Prior, once an ardent Whig, but later the diplomat and finally the plenipotentiary of the other party.* The Tories, on the other hand, had all along defended their desire for peace by contending, not illogically in fact, that continuance

Minister (see *Britannia*). In addition to passages cited here in various connections, note Young's *Ocean: An Ode* (1728), *The Sea-Piece* (1733), and Thomson's *Summer*, 1005–1012, *Autumn*, 118–133, *Liberty* IV.423–450, 569–573. See Hans Marcus, "Die Entstehung von 'Rule Britannia'," etc., *Anglia Beiblatt*, XXXV (1924), 306ff.

* That Prior's business in France was not a close secret is evident from the broadside *An Excellent New Song, called Mat's Peace, or the Downfall of Trade. To the Good Old Tune of Green-Sleeves* (1711) (Br. Mus. Broadside 1876 f. 1 [59]).

of the war would only redound to the further profit of England's Dutch ally and eventually destroy British trade.

This argument is employed by Defoe in his prose tract *Reasons why this Nation Ought to Put a Speedy End to this Expensive War* (1711), a venal performance written to order for Harley and probably falsifying the author's actual sentiments. It is prominent in Arbuthnot's *Law is a Bottomless Pit* (1712). Tory poets also came to the vindication of their party. When Bolingbroke returned from Paris in 1712, he was acclaimed by William King in *Britannia's Palladium* as if the negotiations he had instituted for peace were the sole hope of a languishing commerce. Gay paid Bolingbroke a similar tribute in the Prologue to *The Shepherd's Week* (1713);* Pope welcomed the treaty in *Windsor Forest* (1713), before it was formally ratified, because sacred Peace would raise "Thames's glory to the stars"; and the same point is scored by Parnell in his poem on the Peace (1713).† But evidently Harley, Bolingbroke, and their panegyrists were reduced to the defensive. On the whole, the honor remained where it belonged historically; Whig statesmen were regarded as the creators and true sponsors of trade, and the poetry of trade came

* For other references to trade, see *Fables*, "The Man, the Cat, and the Fly," and *Epistle I. To a Lady. Occasioned by the Arrival of Her Royal Highness the Princess of Wales.*

† Compare Nicholas Tucker's *A New Poem*, etc. (1713) and M. Smith's *On the Peace: A Poem*. Dr. Johnson makes the following comment upon the surprising fact that Addison's friend Tickell composed a eulogistic poem *On the Prospect of Peace*: "How far Tickell, whom Swift afterwards mentioned as Whiggismus, had then connected himself with any party, I know not; this poem certainly did not flatter the practices, or promote the opinions, of the man by whom he was afterwards befriended. Mr. Addison, however he hated the men then in power, suffered his friendship to prevail over his public spirit, and gave in the Spectator such praises of Tickell's poem, that when . . . I laid hold on it . . . I thought it unequal to the honours which it had received. . . ." (*Life of Tickell*, Chalmers, *English Poets*, XI, 97–98). Tickell's Whig sympathies are expressed in *The Royal Progress*, praising George I, and *An Epistle from a Lady in England to a Gentleman at Avignon*, defending the Hanoverian succession. This latter, says Johnson, "stands high among party-poems; it expresses contempt without coarseness, and superiority without insolence." (*Ibid.*, p. 99.) It relates, however, only to the Whig Act of Settlement (1701), and Johnson himself was not a Jacobite. Young's *Epistle to Lansdowne* is as difficult to explain as Tickell's poem on the peace.

almost entirely from Whig singers. Whatever tenuous hold the Tories may have had upon the confidence of the moneyed class was completely shattered by the disclosure of the Jacobite treason in 1714. Thereafter the Whig claim went unchallenged, and most of the vigor left in Toryism was frittered away in Jacobite intrigue.

The national glory of maritime supremacy produced some of the most enthusiastic verse of the period; but, after all, it was not this phase of commercialism that gave the Whig cause its chief vigor in the literature of sentiment. That came rather from what the age was pleased to consider the "benevolent" aspect of the Whig program. Panegyrists saw, or professed to see, in the commercial policy the humanitarian design of ameliorating the condition of the lower classes. Since the time of Elizabeth the Poor Law had been in operation, but the results had been at best discouraging. Since the latter part of the seventeenth century there had been also a very energetic crusade to stimulate private charity. Retarded somewhat during the early years of Hanoverian rule, this movement assumed unusual activity toward the close of George I's reign, when "benevolence," "good-nature," and "charity" became the most fashionable words in the poetical vocabulary. At this juncture, to present Whiggism as a national philanthropy, supplementary to the relief of the Poor Laws and private alms and superior to either as a humanitarian expedient, was to ensure it an immediate popularity with the sentimental "benevolists."

Some idea of what was expected of a beneficent commercialism may be had from the following extracts. Young saw in it employment for the poor in the manning of ships:

> Ten thousand active hands — that hung
> In shameful sloth, with nerves unstrung,
> The nation's languid load — defy the storms,
> The sheets unfurl, and anchors weigh,
> The long-moor'd vessel wing to sea;
> Worlds, worlds salute, and peopled ocean swarms.
> *(Imperium Pelagi)*

Richard Savage's *Of Public Works* (1737) includes for praise various manifestations of public spirit, but reserves special emphasis for commerce, to which many of the undertakings he commends are merely subsidiary. Savage glorifies it chiefly for opening up an outlet for the surplus population of England, an accomplishment then recently exemplified by Oglethorpe's colonial plans:

> But now be all the generous goddess seen,
> When most diffus'd she shines, and most benign!
> Ye sons of misery, attract her view!
> Ye sallow, hollow-eyed, and meagre crew!
> Such high perfection have our arts attain'd,
> That now few sons of toil our arts demand?
> Then to the public, to itself we fear,
> Ev'n willing industry grows useless here.
> Are we too populous at length confess'd,
> From confluent strangers refug'd and redress'd?
> Has war so long withdrawn his barbarous train,
> That peace o'erstocks us with the sons of men?
> So long has plague left pure the ambient air,
> That want must prey on those disease would spare?
> Hence beauteous wretches (beauty's foul disgrace!)
> Though born the pride, the shame of human race;
> Fair wretches hence, who nightly streets annoy,
> Live but themselves and others to destroy.
>
> This Public Spirit sees, she sees and feels!
> Her breast the throb, her eye the tear reveals;
> (The patriot throb that beats, the tear that flows
> For others' welfare, and for others' woes) —
> "And what can I" (she said) "to cure their grief?
> Shall I or point out death, or point relief?
> Forth shall I lead them to some happier soil,
> To conquest lead them, and enrich with spoil?
>
> "No, no — such wars do thine, Ambition, wage!
> Go sterilize the fertile with thy rage!
> Whole nations to depopulate is thine;
> To people, culture, and protect be mine!
> Then range the world, Discovery!" Straight he goes
> O'er seas, o'er Libya's sands and Zembla's snows;

He settles where kind rays till now have smil'd
(Vain smile!) on some luxuriant houseless wild.*

The force of commerce as a mode of philanthropy was to be appreciated fully only by considering it in conjunction with allied industries. Foreign trade was merely the last detail in a comprehensive scheme extending in its remote effects to the well-being of the laboring population at large. Thomson emphasizes this close correlation of interests.

And should the big redundant flood of trade,
In which ten thousand thousand labours join
Their several currents, till the boundless tide
Rolls in a radiant deluge o'er the land;
Should this bright stream, the least inflected, point
Its course another way, o'er other lands
The various treasure would resistless pour,
Ne'er to be won again; its ancient tract
Left a vile channel, desolate, and dead,
With all around a miserable waste.

The worst effects of a defeated trade he includes in the following melancholy description of England:

Her unfrequented ports alone the sign
Of what she was; her merchants scatter'd wide;
Her hollow shops shut up; and in her streets,
Her fields, woods, markets, villages, and roads
The cheerful voice of labour heard no more.†

This large philanthropic aspect of commercialism and allied industrialism had already been argued by Defoe in essays showing that he was far ahead of his age in his comprehension of economic principle. In opposition to the indiscriminate charities that prevailed at the close of the seventeenth century, Defoe asserted

---

* Savage's eulogy of colonization was a new note. He is praised in Johnson's *Life* for having expatiated "upon a kind of beneficence not yet celebrated by any eminent poet, though it now appears more susceptible of embellishments, more adapted to exalt the ideas, and affect the passions, than many of those which have hitherto been thought worthy of the ornaments of verse." (Chalmers, XI, 277.) Savage pays other tributes to commerce in *The Wanderer*, Canto I, *An Epistle to Sir Robert Walpole*, and *The Volunteer Laureat*, No. III.

† *Britannia*, 218–227; 243–247. Compare *Autumn*, 910–928.

that promiscuous alms-giving was aggravating the very evil it sought to remedy. He urged, instead, the adoption of a national policy whereby the poor would be made permanently self-supporting. The development of manufacture and trade would, he believed, solve the whole problem of English pauperism.* The poets who lauded the Whig measures under Walpole were in a position somewhat different from that of Defoe when he began arguing the cause of trade. By their time the policy itself had become an accomplished fact. It had also produced changes in the nation which made the continued success of that policy indispensable. When once the social and economic effects of the commercial system had begun to manifest themselves in the altered condition of the English laborer, it became evident that Whiggism, while rapidly enriching the middle class and securing titles for merchant princes, had actually shouldered most of the responsibility for the poor.

For reasons so numerous that they can be barely intimated here, a change of vast historical importance was beginning to take place in the distribution and economic status of the laboring population, as a result primarily of new conditions attributable to the increasing demands for labor in the woolen and silk mills and to the gradual introduction of the capitalistic system of manufacture.[3] Conducted at first largely by Protestant refugees from the Netherlands, whose presence was at times bitterly resented by English artisans, these growing industries now absorbed more and more of the labor of the nation. The result was a gradual shift of the working classes from the rural districts to the towns and the rise of such crowded industrial centers as Birmingham, Manchester, and Leeds. Formerly the dependent classes had been distributed rather evenly throughout the country; they were now beginning to be congested in the towns. The disturbance of the old equilibrium, through what Mr. H. G. Wells has described as "the expropriation of the English peasantry and the birth of the factory

---

* *Review*, I, 83–84, 100–101; II, 10, 18; III, 9, 13–16, 92; IV, 3–16, 18–21, 23. See also *Giving Alms No Charity, and Employing the Poor a Grievance to the Nation* (1704). Addison has received much praise merely for repeating some of these arguments in *Spectator* No. 232.

system," ushered in the gravest problems of modern English society.

It is true that the change was only beginning and that the most serious difficulties were still remote, but the dislocation had begun. Although labor was usually in demand and wages were, on the whole, better than they had been formerly, the footing of the industrious poor was actually more precarious.[4] Formerly the burden of poverty had been distributed more or less evenly over the entire country; now it was localized in a few districts. Under the earlier conditions a year of famine had not produced the worst results, for the sufferings were alleviated by the country squires, the landlords, and the parish overseers, without bringing too great pressure to bear at a single point. The population at large had had little occasion for anxiety as long as most of the dependents were attached to the soil that afforded food, fuel, and clothing, and when most of the artisan's work was performed in his own cottage. With the increase of corporate enterprise, it became evident that a sudden decline in commerce, a lowering of wages, an improvement of machinery which would make it possible for one man to perform the work of a score—any of these accidents threatened a national catastrophe. Above all, any obstruction to ocean-going commerce meant the deathblow to British prosperity, and the effects would descend first upon the artisan. The Whigs, in a sense the creators of the situation, made a virtue of their necessity by defending all the measures protective of commerce and manufacture as policies absolutely essential to the preservation of the poor.

These conditions explain why sentimental poets of the Georgian period concentrated their energies mainly upon a defense of laws enacted for the protection of the woolen industry. Although some individual Whigs were among the believers in free trade, their views did not receive the sanction of the Whig party. Most of the Tories believed in a slight protection only, and it was from a few advanced thinkers of this party that the philosophy of modern free trade emanated. Before the time of Adam Smith it was a cardinal doctrine of the Whigs that native industries should

be shielded from foreign competition, especially from the manufactures of France. For the protection of the English woolen
interest there had been special statutes of Whig origin since 1678.*
Another Act was passed in 1700,† and the doctrine is embodied
in the Methuen Treaty of 1703. But the Whig protective principle was never thoroughly applied until 1721.

The preamble of the Act passed in this year declares it "most
evident that the wearing and using of printed, painted, stained,
and dyed calicoes in apparel, household stuff, furniture, and
otherwise, does manifestly tend to the great detriment of the
woollen and silk manufactures, and to the excessive increase of
the poor, and if not prevented may be the utter ruin and destruction of the said manufacturers and of many thousands whose live-
lihoods do entirely depend thereupon." ‡ This law, repeated and
explained by an Act of 1748, imposed a fine of five pounds for
wearing or using printed or dyed calico and twenty pounds for
selling it except for the purpose of exportation.§ French calicoes

* 29 and 30 Car. II, c. 1. A bill of 1689, which was finally defeated, contained this among other odd proposals, that all persons be compelled to wear
woolen garments of native manufacture from October 15 to April 15. For a
review of protective legislation by the Whigs after 1678 and the modifications made by Tory ministries, see C. B. Roylance Kent, *The Early History
of the Tories* (1908), pp. 466–468; W. J. Ashley, *Surveys Historic and Economic* (1900), pp. 268–303; W. Cunningham, *The Growth of English Industry and Commerce in Modern Times* (1912), Part I, Ch. 15. A singular
provision of the law required all corpses to be buried in woolen shrouds.
Evidently it was not strictly enforced; John Dunton remarks in his
*Mourning-Ring* (1692), p. 288, that the late Act of Parliament is *sometimes*
observed. It seems to have been applied more rigorously in the eighteenth
century. The estate of John Byrom was fined five pounds for non-
compliance (*D.N.B.*). Pope's reference to the case of Mrs. Oldfield, in
*Moral Epistles*, Ep. I (1733), is well known. The Englishman's worship of
wool is discussed at length in Henri Misson's *Mémoires et observations*
(1698), pp. 129–144. For other references, see John Ashton, *Social Life in
the Reign of Queen Anne* (1911), pp. 36–38. The rise of free trade among
Tories is discussed by Kent, pp. 469–470, and Ashley, *loc. cit.* The fact that
Walpole was somewhat less rigorous than most of his party (J. M. Robertson, *Free Trade* [1919], p. 16; *Cambridge Modern History*, Vol. VI, Ch. 2)
was a Whig grievance.
† 11 and 12 Wm. III. c. 10.
‡ 7 Geo. I. c. 7.
§ A detailed account of "The Cambric Act" is given in the *British Mag.*,
March 1749.

were so highly fashionable that violations were numerous. Paris had long been accepted as dictator of fashions in dress, and even while the two countries were at war the English beaux and belles were ready enough to sacrifice patriotism in order to be in the French mode. The Act of 1721 was really forced upon Parliament by numerous riots among unemployed and hungry weavers who not infrequently inflicted condign punishment upon women dressed in calico.* Support of the law and of the weavers by the sentimental poet was directed against the indifference of the rich upper classes to the well-being of the poor. It thus became a staple item in the program of literary sensibility and benevolence.

The one poem which adheres strictly to the text of these protectionist measures is an epistle from John Lockman to the author of the "Cambric Bill." † The immediate connection with the conditions outlined above appears from the following extracts, more

* See Mist's *Weekly Journal*, Aug. 15, 1719, May 7, 1720. The issue for March 11, 1721, reports the celebration occasioned by the passage of the bill. Accounts of riots are given in Read's *Weekly Journal*, March 19, April 9, and June 11, 1720, and in *Mercurius Politicus*, May 1720, p. 32. Read's for Nov. 7, 1719, prints "The Weavers' Complaint against the Callico Madames, as sung at the Playhouse in Lincoln's Inn Fields." The controversy engaged numerous pamphleteers. Steele contributed *The Spinster, in defence of the Woollen Manufacturers*, provoking in reply *The Female Manufacturers' Complaint*, Jan. 1719-20. Defoe, already the author of various tracts for the encouragement of the woolen industry, wrote for this special occasion *A Brief State of the Question Between the Printed and Painted Callicoes and the Woollen and the Silk Manufacture* (1719) and *The Just Complaint of the Poor Weavers Truly Represented* (1719). John Asgill replied with *A Brief Answer to a Brief State of the Question*, etc. (1719), to the second edition of which (1720) was added an Appendix upon Steele's *Spinster*. For further details, see the *Spinster* (Dublin, 1790), G. A. Aitken's *Life of Sir Richard Steele* (1889), II, 206-208, and M. Dorothy George's *London Life in the XVIIIth Century* (1925), pp. 180ff. Mandeville had little sympathy for the distressed weavers; in the *Essay on Charity and Charity Schools* (ed. 1725), p. 358, he characteristically holds them responsible for their own miseries. It was easier to secure patronage of the silk industry than of the woolen. César de Saussure wrote from England May 29, 1727, "Very few women wear woollen gowns. Even servant-maids wear silks on Sundays and holidays, when they are almost as well dressed as their mistresses" (*Letters*, tr. and ed. by Mme. Van Muyden [1902], No. viii).

† *To the long-conceal'd First Promoter of the Cambrick and Tea-Bills: An Epistle* . . . (London, 1746). The philanthropist addressed is Stephen G. Jansen. Lockman comes in for deserved ridicule in Smollett's *Advice: A Satire*.

conspicuous for their Whig enthusiasm than for any poetic
worth.

> To thee, reflexion, practice, have displayed,
> How *Manufactures* spread a foreign trade;
> How these, improv'd, give wealth with bounteous hand;
> Or slighted, crowd with beggars half a land:
> Pronounce a people, mid the nations, great;
> Or mark them, shiv'ring o'er their ruin'd state.
> When Trades are, curiously, examin'd round,
> Twixt all, or most, a strict connexion's found.*
> Let *Manufactures* (one branch) decline,
> One hundred *Trades*, thence turned adrift, wou'd pine:
> An hundred others, that on these depend,
> Must gradually, to sure destruction tend;
> For, turn'd the salutary streams of cash,
> No buyers appear, and wares become mere trash.
> *Trades* thus indulge, reciprocal, their aid;
> Shoot forth th' enliv'ning ray, or guardian shade:
> Or, one extinct, great numbers thence decay;
> And seem, as by infection, swept away.
>
> Thus all the parts of Nature's mighty frame,
> An universal, innate Power proclaim;
> Dispend this wond'rous Power, the whole wou'd fly,
> And the vast System in dread ruins lie.
>
> Impulses (O! how tender) in thee rise,
> As on a village, thou throw'st round thine eyes;
> Where Industry late cheer'd the blissful scene,
> And rosy Health danc'd, blithe, with Peace serene;
> Then sadly sunk, to poverty betray'd,
> By our worst Foe's outwitting us in Trade?
> What generous wrath, hence, fires thy patriot breast,
> To see the fop from Gallia's fabriques drest!
> View him, enwrapt, his flimzy form admire;
> And, with his comment on it, others tire.
> Sure the fantastic creature scarce can know,
> That, from such pride, a flood of evils flow;
> That whilst he stalks, with vanity elate,
> Thousands mourn, unemploy'd, their cruel fate;

---

* The author's note is that "above 130 handicrafts are employed in the
manufacture of our wool."

Encumber parishes, in sickness lie;
Frequent thro' grief, or by ill-treatment, die.
O! blast the mode, its glimmering swift suppress,
Which, on a Nation's ruin, builds success.*

The poet then comes to the selfish part played by English women of fashion:

In dangerous times, a jarring state to save,
Their richest gems Rome's spotless matrons gave:
Shall then our *British* fair, mid fierce alarms,
And heedless, tho' the poor around them sigh,
The *Gaul*, with vanity's curst gold, supply?
Ah! rather plunge such treasures in the deep,
Lest we, thro' them, should loss of freedom weep.
Ye nymphs, when in *French* ornaments ye glare,
Know, for yourselves, ye distant chains prepare;
Then hurl, like Paul, the viper swift away;
For, tho' deem'd innocent, its bite will slay.

After gloating, with moral inconsistence, over the ruin which the exclusion of French wares from England will cause in France, the author explains the happy consequences to the English laborers:

And see (inchanting contrast!) where your swains,
Who late stray'd, sorrowing, o'er the naked plains;
With deep-fall'n cheeks, sad image of their fears,
Made dreadful, by their famish'd infants tears;
Now whistling o'er their toil, whence comforts rise,
Which, conscious of their bliss, they duly prize;
Wou'd not their lot, for scenes exalted, change,
O'erjoy'd, their native fields in peace to range.

The remainder of the epistle is a violent anathema upon the heinous crime of smuggling.

Undoubtedly this political tract would sound quite as well in prose. Lockman's extreme literalness was avoided by Shenstone, in the four poems of his directly or indirectly associated with the

* Here the author adds: "France, besides plundering us of our wool, pours in upon us . . . Wines, Brandies, Cambricks, Point Laces . . . Teas. This drains us of our specie, supports the manufacture of our greatest enemy, and starves our own."

same set of laws. Declining Lord Temple's invitation to visit foreign countries, Shenstone gives as his reason:

> While others, lost to friendship, lost to love,
>     Waste their best minutes on a foreign strand,
> Be mine, with British nymph or swain to rove,
>     And court the genius of my native land.
>
> Deluded youth! that quits these verdant plains,
>     To catch the follies of an alien soil!
> To win the vice his genuine soul disdains,
>     Return exultant, and import the spoil!
>     . . . . . . . . . . . . . .
> Th' exotic folly knows its native clime;
>     An awkward stranger, if we waft it o'er;
> Why then these toils, this costly waste of time,
>     To spread soft poison on our happy shore?
>
> I covet not the pride of foreign looms;
>     In search of foreign modes I scorn to rove;
> Nor, for the worthless bird of brighter plumes,
>     Would change the meanest warbler of my grove.

This extract is from *Elegy XIV*; the same opinion is expressed in *Elegy X* and *Elegy XXI*, the latter written at a time (1746) when there was rumor of a sumptuary law.

More specific charges are contained in *Elegy XVIII*, "The song of Colin, a discerning shepherd, lamenting the state of the woollen manufactory." Possessed of every virtue but "quick-eyed Prudence," heedless Albion, says Shenstone, allows the craft of Gallia to purloin her "ponderous fleece" and foolishly supplies the sheep which now raise plaintive cries in Spain and provide fleece for a haughty foe. Thus all the English shepherd's labors go for naught.

> But Albion's youth her native fleece despise;
>     Unmoved they hear the pining shepherd's moan;
> In silky folds each nervous limb disguise,
>     Allured by every treasure but their own.

Shenstone, too, was touched most deeply by the insensibility of fashionable females.

Oft have I hurried down the rocky steep,
  Anxious to see the wintry tempest drive;
Preserve, said I, preserve your fleece, my sheep!
  Ere long will Phillis, will my love, arrive.

Ere long she came; ah! woe is me! she came,
  Robed in the Gallic loom's extraneous twine;
For gifts like these they give their spotless fame,
  Resign their bloom, their innocence resign.

Will no bright maid, by worth, by titles known,
  Give the rich growth of British hills to Fame?
And let her charms, and her example, own
    That Virtue's dress and Beauty's are the same?

Will no famed chief support this generous maid?
  Once more the patriot's arduous path resume?
And, comely from his native plains array'd,
    Speak future glory to the British loom?

The same protective principle is urged loudly in Thomson's *Britannia*, the Epilogue to his *Sophonisba*, Young's *Night Thoughts*
(II.238–255), Richard Jago's *To a Lady Working a Pair of Ruffles*,
and Joseph Reed's *A British Philippic*.

All these various aspects of poetical patriotism were finally
assembled in John Dyer's *The Fleece* (1757). This poem, divided
into four books and comprising 2,704 lines of blank verse, is
fortunately the most elaborate industrial poem, not only of the
eighteenth century, but of all English literature. The literary
method of *The Fleece* places it in a long genealogical line of
poems including John Philips's *Cyder* (1708), Somerville's *The
Chace* (1733), and Grainger's *The Sugar Cane* (1764), all influenced by Vergil's *Georgics* and composed on the assumption that
any subject can be made poetic if only it is treated in verse.* *The*

---

* *The Fleece* was praised highly by Akenside (who made some contributions to it), Wordsworth, and "Christopher North" (John Wilson); but
time has vindicated Dr. Johnson's contemptuous remark that a man cannot
"write poetically of serges and druggets" (*Life*, ed. Hill, II, 453). Of Grainger's poem he exclaimed, "What could he make of a sugar-cane? One might
as well write the 'Parsley-bed, a Poem'; or 'The Cabbage-garden, a Poem'
. . . You know there is already 'The Hop-Garden, a Poem'; and, I think,
one could say a great deal about cabbage." (*Ibid.*, p. 454.) Much of Dyer's
poem is a mere versification of ideas presented in such typical works as

*Sugar Cane,* written in direct imitation of Dyer and applying this
principle with unflinching thoroughness, should have served to
discredit the theory once for all when it descended to the vet-
erinary treatment of plantation mules and the cure of worms in
Negro slaves. Dyer's application of the doctrine stops short of
such absurdity only by a degree. *The Fleece* is a verse pamphlet
on the various departments of the woolen industry in its relation
to other forms of philanthropy, and there is not a detail of the
whole subject too petty or prosaic for the poet's attention. The
practical object is set forth in the dedicatory address:

> The care of sheep, the labours of the loom,
> And arts of trade, I sing. Ye rural nymphs,
> Ye swains, and princely merchants, aid the verse.
> And ye, high-trusted guardians of our isle,
> Whom public voice approves, or lot of birth
> To the great charge assigns: ye good, of all
> Degrees, all sects, be present to my song.
> So may distress, and wretchedness, and want
> The wide felicities of labour learn:
> So may the proud attempts of restless Gaul
> From our strong borders, like a broken wave,
> In empty foam retire.

In order to establish the importance of wool as a national asset,
Dyer reviews the history of successful peoples from

> Eldest times, when kings and hardy chiefs
> In bleating sheep-folds met

down to his own day. Beginning with Phoenicia, Syria, and
Judaea, he proves that all their greatness arose from the profits
of wool. They were succeeded by Colchis, whose prosperity
began with the arrival of Phryxus and the Thessalian ram and

Joshua Gee's *Trade and Navigation of Great Britain Considered* (1729);
*The Golden Fleece* (1736); "John London's" *Some Considerations on the
Importance of the Woollen Manufacture* (1740); William Webster's *Consequences of Trade . . . of The woollen trade in particular* (1740); *A
short Essay upon Trade in general, more particularly on the Woollen Manufactures* (1741); *A treatise on trade; or, the antiquity and honour of commerce* (1750); John Smith's *Chronicon Rusticum-Commerciale; or, Memoirs
of Wool* (2 vols.; 1747; rev. 1757).

departed when Jason and his companions of the Argonaut bore away the golden fleece. Dyer traces from this time onward the rise and decline of nations as Thomson does in *Liberty*, and in the same wearisome detail: Greece, Venice, various Asiatic empires, Spain, and the story closes with the beginning of the industry in "beauteous Albion." A considerable section is allotted to the natural advantages of English soil and climate for the production of superior grades of wool. In a patriotic outburst very different from the querulous and more intelligible attitude of Armstrong and Green, this poet praises England even for her "mists and vapours."

> Those hovering fogs, that bathe our growing vales
> In deep November (loathed by trifling Gaul,
> Effeminate) are gifts the Pleiads shed,
> Britannia's handmaids. As the beverage falls,
> Her hills rejoice, her valleys laugh and sing.
>
> (I.146–151)

Such natural advantages being given, the problem for the English government to face is how to make them most serviceable to the nation as a whole and especially to the poor. The plan encouraged by Dyer is twofold, in a general way like the proposals of Defoe: poverty is to be averted and national prosperity secured by setting the poor to work and by opening up a worldwide market for the produce of their labor.

In his direct reference to the poor Dyer is as sympathetic as any of the "benevolists" of his time. There are few arraignments of avarice more bitter than his address to selfish capitalists — "worms of pride"

> Who claim all Nature's stores, woods, waters, meads,
> All her profusion; whose vile hands would grasp
> The peasant's scantling, the weak widow's mite,
> And in the sepulchre of self entomb
> Whate'er ye can, whate'er ye cannot use.
>
> (II.476–480)

But from charity in the ordinary sense he expects little permanent benefit; that is to come rather from impressing upon the lower classes the dignity and worth of labor. True charity will teach "idle want"

> And vice the inclination to do good,
> Good to themselves, and in themselves to all,
> Through grateful toil.
>
> (II.20–22)

To the laborer's outcry against improvements in machinery he opposes an argument in need of constant repetition:

> Nor hence, ye nymphs, let anger cloud your brows;
> The more is wrought, the more is still required;
> Blithe o'er your toils, with wonted song, proceed:
> Fear not surcharge; your hands will ever find
> Ample employment. In the strife of trade,
> These curious instruments of speed obtain
> Various advantage, and the diligent
> Supply with exercise as fountains sure,
> Which ever-gliding feed the flowery lawn.
>
> (II.86–94)

He is equally practical in his severity against intemperance, which, notoriously common as it was among the needy, was seldom referred to by the sentimental "benevolists" or even the active philanthropists. It is from such practical considerations that Dyer gives his support to the workhouses provided by the Poor Law. Only in this respect is he notably different from Defoe. Defoe saw in cheap charity labor a menace to national economy; Dyer and his contemporaries were still impervious to the argument that by underselling the market workhouses took bread from the mouths of the industrious poor. His attempt to defend the "charitable rigour" of compulsory labor without offending the sensibilities of the idle is amusing. He would "compel them to happiness" and detain their "step-bruis'd feet" within the abodes prepared for them by a wise government.

> Even now the sons of trade,
> Where'er the cultivated hamlets smile,
> Erect the mansion: here soft fleeces shine;
> The card awaits you, and the comb, and wheel:
> Here shroud you from the thunder of the storm;

No rain shall wet your pillow: here abounds
Pure beverage; here your viands are prepared;
To heal each sickness the physician waits,
And priest entreats to give your Maker praise.
(II.250–258)

In developing the complementary part of his economic program, that is, supplying the raw material, manufacturing, and
marketing it, Dyer is conscientiously prolix. When he has finished
his secular "Cura Pastoralis," nothing more need be said on
methods of breeding sheep, protecting them from inclement
weather, shearing them, saving the lambs at weaning time, castrat-
ing them, treating the halt and rot. We become wearisomely
familiar with the "groves pomacious" and the spots of "rich
saponaceous loam" which determine the varying textures of wool.
The treatise on manufacture is less prosaic. It is relieved somewhat by the incidental story of the Dutch refugees who introduced the art into England and by a warm defense of them against
the occasional protests of the native artisans. In the descriptions
of machinery the style is energized at times by the clanking and
whir of the loom in a way suggestive of Walt Whitman. But
never is the reader allowed to forget the moral aspect of the subject. Woolen manufacture is a godsend to the poor because it
enables even women and children to earn a living. It is but another form of charity, a form made possible by Bishop Blaise.*

Thus, in elder time,

The reverend Blasius wore his leisure hours,
And slumbers, broken oft: till, filled at length
With inspiration, after various thought,
And trials manifold, his well-known voice
Gathered the poor, and o'er Vulcanian stoves,
With tepid lees of oil, and spiky comb,
Showed how the fleece might stretch to greater length,
And cast a glossier whiteness. Wheels went round;
Matrons and maids with songs relieved their toils;

---

* Ralph Thoresby notes in his remarks upon the customs of Leicester
that "the feast of St. Blase, a Bishop, is celebrated yearly about Candelmas
by those who deal in wool, he being said to be the first who invented the
combing thereof." *Diary*, Oct. 28, 1712, Hunter's ed., II, 166.

And every loom received the softer yarn.
What poor, what widow, Blasius, did not bless
Thy teaching hand?

(II.522–536)

If we consider long consecutive paragraphs, by far the best parts of *The Fleece* are those describing the functions of commerce. The recital is attended with parenthetic abuse of French smuggling, comments on methods of improving domestic waterways, and the advantage of opening up foreign trade by various devices, such as the construction of the Panama Canal. But the interest of the reader is gained principally by the writer's enthusiasm for the poetry of shipping. This comes out in the fourth book, one affording some apology for the tediousness of the others. Here, too, there is prolix detail; but in the comprehensiveness of the outlook there is an imaginative lure which recalls faintly the romantic voyages of the time when Elizabethan buccaneers were opening up strange lands. With "woolly treasures amply stored," British ships touch ports at the ends of the earth; the prosaic details of commerce are thus invested with the glamor of remote scenery, novel manners, and awful distance. Like other good Whigs, Dyer attempts to remove the social stigma fixed upon the business of trade. Younger sons of the nobility were engaged in it, but its gentility was still questioned in 1757. In confronting the prejudice, he bases his final argument on the moral view that commerce is the greatest civilizing and humanizing agent known to man. Its immediate influences are seen in "busy Leeds, upwafting to the clouds the incense of thanksgiving" and the "increasing walls of busy Manchester, Sheffield, and Birmingham" — all supporting thousands of industrious laborers. The remote effects of English legislation bribed to oppose commercial extension are felt even by Tartar and Chinese.

### III

In this bright picture of Britannia's merchant marine as a benevolent agency binding

The round of nations in a golden chain

unfortunately there was one dark blot. The one detail out of moral keeping was the slave traffic. The capture and sale of human beings into servitude could not be harmonized with the philanthropic spirit read into Whig policies. At the same time, the vigor of British commerce was dependent largely upon this one branch.* The conscience of the public was so blinded to the moral issue by the widespread participation in dividends that it was very difficult to bring independent judgment or sentiment to bear upon the subject.

Andrew Fletcher of Saltoun was so far from being shocked by the enslavement of Negroes that in 1698 he seriously proposed, in the interest of national economy, an extension of the system to incorrigible beggars.† Individuals might, and some did, voluntarily sell themselves as slaves in the colonies. The benevolent Berkeley owned Negroes in Rhode Island. Oglethorpe was Deputy Governor of the Royal African Company, which was under contract to deliver to the Spanish colonies 4,800 slaves annually for a period of thirty years by the terms of the Asiento Treaty (1713).[5] Besides owning slaves in South Carolina, as Oglethorpe did, George Whitefield urged the adoption of the system in Georgia.[6] The new philosophy was no more compassionate than the old religion. Thinkers who agreed with Hobbes in almost nothing else accepted without question his justification of slavery. Cumberland found a place for it in his exposition of the Laws of Nature.[7] Readers of Locke's *Two Treatises on Government* might have expected a new attitude, for the opening sentence reads, "Slavery is so vile and miserable an estate of man, and so directly opposite to the generous temper and courage of our nation, that it is hardly to be conceived that an 'Englishman,' much less a 'gentleman,' should plead for it." It is soon discovered, how-

* Much statistical information for the early period is provided by Charles D'Avenant's *Account of the rise and progress of our trade to Africa, preceding the year 1697*, in *Works* (1771) V, 83ff. See also W. E. H. Lecky, *A History of England in the Eighteenth Century* (1892), II, 242ff.

† *The Second Discourse concerning the Affairs of Scotland; written in the year 1698*. Compare Francis Hutcheson's *A System of Moral Philosophy* (1755), II, 201ff.

ever, that this is a mere flourish of the Whig philosopher's, and
that he is thinking only of liberty-loving Englishmen. Before he
concludes he finds in Nature full warrant for subjecting some "to
the absolute dominion and arbitrary power of their masters." [8]
This view seems to have continued unopposed in philosophy until
the middle of the eighteenth century.*

An apparent exception to the moral callousness of the seventeenth century is to be found in the sermons of Morgan Godwin;
but his principal concern, after all, was the Christianizing of the
Negroes and Indians.† Mrs. Behn's novel *Oroonoko* (1688) contains a powerful sentimental plea for slaves. It has been remarked
by critics, however, that Astraea's sympathy was engaged mainly
by the royal rank of her black hero and his inamorata. We may
suspect that the novelist's sole design was to tell a good story.
Neither her novel nor Southerne's dramatic version of it (1696)
had any other evident effect on folk of sensibility than to provide
them an ideal excuse for weeping copiously and happily over
miseries they had no desire to alleviate.‡ It should be remembered

* James Foster pronounced against slavery in his *Discourses on all the
principal Branches of Natural Religion and Social Virtue* (1749–1752), II,
156. A similar position is taken by Francis Hutcheson in *A System of Moral
Philosophy* (1755), I, 299–302, and by George Wallace in *A System of the
Principles of the Law of Scotland* (1760), I, 88–98. Extracts from these
writers were included in an Appendix to the American abolitionist Anthony
Benezet's *Some Historical Account of Guinea*, etc. (1762).

† *The Negro's and Indian's Advocate, sueing for their Admission into
the Church; or A persuasive to the instructing and baptizing the Negros
and Indians in our Plantations. Shewing that as the complying therewith
can be no prejudice to any man's just interest; so the wilful neglecting and
opposing of it, is no less than a manifest Apostasie from the Christian faith,*
etc. (T.C. I, 366, Nov. 1679); *Trade prefer'd before Religion and Christ
made to give place to Mammon. Reprehended in a Sermon relating to the
Plantations. First preached at Westminster Abbey*, etc. (T.C. II, 135, June
1685). Godwin is praised for his humanity by Anthony Benezet, *op. cit.*,
ed. 1771, p. 74. Baxter's counsel, in *The Christian Directory*, Part II, Ch. 14,
was widely influential in England and America; it is a plea for Christian
behavior toward slaves.

‡ Note the flippancy of the Epilogue written for Southerne's *Oroonoko*
by Congreve. The most celebrated performance of this play was given in
1749 during the visit of a young African prince and his companion who
had been redeemed from slavery by the government. The *Gentleman's Mag.*
for Feb. 1749 (XIX, 89–90) gives an elaborate account of the occasion, concluding: "They appear sometimes at the theatres, and particularly on the 1st

to the credit of Daniel Defoe's morality and audacity also that he delivered an emphatic diatribe against slavery in his prose tract *Reformation of Manners* (1702). Probably through the influence of his example, John Dunton spoke out boldly to the same purpose in *The Athenian Oracle* (1704). While conducting the *Athenian Mercury* (1691–1696) Dunton had reconciled himself to the existence of slavery by a curious, but not infrequent, form of casuistry. Without slavery, he asserted, the Negroes of Africa could never be converted to Christianity. Besides, captivity was a physical blessing in disguise; for if the Negroes were left at home "they must either be *killed* or *eaten*, or both, by their barbarous conquering enemy." [9] When, however, he was bringing out his "Notes and Queries" in collected form as *The Athenian Oracle*, he added an essay violently attacking the whole system. [10]

Another early opponent was Bernard Mandeville. If we are surprised to find *The Planter's Charity* (1704) emanating from the disciple of Hobbes and La Rochefoucauld, the satirist of Shaftesbury's and Steele's sentimentalism, and the opponent of most charities then in existence, it is probably because we have been misled into doing the character of the cynical Dutch physician an injustice.* Mandeville was not a sentimentalist, but he was

inst. were at *Covent Garden* to see the tragedy of *Oroonoko*. They were received with a loud clap of applause, which they acknowledged with a very genteel bow, and took their seats in a box. The seeing persons of their own colour on the stage, apparently in the same distress from which they had been so lately delivered, the tender interview between *Imoinda* and *Oroonoko*, who was betrayed by the treachery of a captain [as they had been], his account of his sufferings, and the repeated abuse of his placability and confidence, strongly affected them with that generous grief which pure nature always feels, and which art had not yet taught them to suppress; the young prince was so far overcome that he was obliged to retire at the end of the fourth act. His companion remained, but wept the whole time; a circumstance which affected the audience yet more than the play, and doubled the tears which were shed for *Oroonoko* and *Imoinda*."

   * Professor F. B. Kaye lists this poem, the Preface to which is signed "B.M.," among Mandeville's "Doubtful Works" but adduces good evidence for attributing it to him ("The Writings of Bernard Mandeville," *Journal of English and Germanic Philology*, XX (1921), 446–447; *The Fable of the Bees* [1924], I, xxxi). A view similar to Mandeville's had been expressed in Anthony Hill's *Afer Baptizatus: or the Negro turn'd Christian, being a Discourse showing, I. The Necessity of Instructing and Baptizing Slaves in English Plantations. II. The Folly of that Vulgar Opinion, that Slaves do*

not without sympathy, and he had Swift's contempt for pious
hypocrites. The moral thesis of his poem appears in the opening
lines:

> You that Oppress the Captive *African*,
> Abuse the BLACK, and Barbarously treat Man
> Like Beast, in spight of his great Attribute,
> Which only can distinguish him from Brute,
> Reason, the lawful Claim to Human-kind;
> As if you thought God's Image was confined
> To *European* White! Why should your Slave
> Feel your Unrighteousness beyond the Grave?
> Lay on the Burden, till you break his Back,
> And let him labour till his Sinews crack,
> Draw out the Marrow from the aking Bone,
> Feed on his Flesh, but let his Soul alone.

Evidently it was not the mere fact of slavery that provoked
Mandeville to write, although he does incidentally expose the
brutality of it; what aroused his indignation most was the cool
inhumanity of so-called Christians who refused to permit a slave
to become Christianized and by this refusal, according to their
own belief at least, condemned his soul to eternal misery.

> But says the hardened PLANTER, the Black Knave
> Knows that a *Christian* cannot be a Slave;
> He wants his Freedom; must I be undone,
> And lose that *Labour* which I live upon?
> They are my Portion by my Father's Will,
> I found 'em Slaves, and so I'll keep 'em still:
> God can be serv'd, sure, at a cheaper rate,
> Than with the loss of Right and of Estate.

Mandeville confines himself to proving that a slave does not actually become free by professing Christianity; but the total effect
of the poem is a strong protest against the whole miserable business of slavery.

These early opponents belong historically in a special category.
Any influence that might otherwise have grown out of their

*cease to be Slaves when once Baptized* (1702). That this "vulgar opinion"
persisted is evident from Sarah Fielding's *David Simple* (1744), ed. 1904, p. 147.
John Wesley notes an exception in his *Journal* for Aug. 2, 1736; but compare what is said in entries for July 3, 1736, April 23, 1737, and July 27, 1755.

attacks was neutralized by the invigoration of the slave trade
through new commercial developments culminating in the Asiento Treaty (1713).* Sympathy could not combat the powerful
argument of the purse. Compassion was limited to such suggestions as those made, for example, in *Hermit* No. 13 (1711) and
*Spectator* No. 215 (1711), that the slaves be treated humanely.
Defoe himself had apparently come to accept this compromise
when he wrote the ninth and tenth chapters of *Colonel Jacque*
(1722).† The early panegyrists of Whig commerce had nothing
to say on this one topic, but it must have been a source of moral
embarrassment. With his usual dogmatism, Young brushed the
question aside and defended the traffic in slaves by a *tu quoque*
charge against the immorality of the Negroes themselves!

> Whence Tartar Grand, or Mogul Great?
> Trade gilt their titles, power'd their State;
> While Afric's black, lascivious, slothful breed,
> To clasp their ruins, fly from toil;
> That meanest product of their soil,
> Their people sell; one half on t'other feed.
> (Imperium Pelagi, Strain V)

Some of the Whig poets, however, had the moral stamina to
oppose the system under circumstances that reflect great credit
on their sincerity. Thomson reprobates

> that cruel trade
> Which spoils unhappy Guinea of her sons.
> (Summer, 1019–1020)

Pope, not being of the Whig fraternity, could have spoken with
less occasion for embarrassment. In both *Windsor Forest* and the
*Essay on Man*, however, he seems to be moved chiefly by Spain's

---

* The provisions were explained to the public in *The Assiento; or, Con-
tract for Allowing to the Subjects of Great Britain the Liberty of Importing
Negroes into the Spanish America*, etc. (1713) and *The Assiento Contract
Considered . . . In several Letters to a Member of Parliament* (1714).

† Meanwhile Defoe had become absorbed in the commercial advantages
of the trade. Proposals for better organization are made in his *Review*, V
(Feb. 1709), 40; VII (1710), 34, 38, 40, 42, 46, etc. Various pamphlets of his
on the same subject are listed by W. P. Trent, *Cambridge Hist. of Eng. Lit.*,
Vol. IX, Bibl. for Ch. 1.

enslavement of the American Indians.[11] Richard Savage, while following in his poem *Of Public Works* (1737) the course of British vessels throughout the world, is suddenly confronted by the tortures inflicted upon African Negroes:

> Why must I Afric's sable children see
> Vended for slaves, though form'd by Nature free,
> The nameless tortures cruel minds invent,
> Those to subject, whom Nature equal meant?
> If these you dare (albeit unjust success
> Empowers you now unpunish'd to oppress)
> Revolving empire you and your's may doom.
> (Rome all subdued, yet Vandal's vanquish'd Rome)
> Yes, empire may revolve, give them the day,
> And yoke may yoke, and blood may blood repay.

The crime is treated briefly, but with evident sincerity, by Joseph Warton in the *Ode to Liberty* (1746). William Dodd's two poems (1749) upon the African prince who had been rescued from slavery by the intervention of the English government contain passages of a similar nature; but since the two epistles form an attractive romantic tale, it is natural to suspect that the author was moved quite as much by the romance and the excitement due to the presence of the liberated Negro prince in London as by the horror of the system.* The most impassioned poem occasioned at this time by the slave trade is Shenstone's *Elegy XX*, most of which was afterwards republished by Granville Sharp in the Appendix to his *Just Limitation of Slavery in the Laws of God* (1776).

Dyer consoled his conscience by pleading that this "gainful commerce" be conducted with "just humanity of heart." † His

---

* Dodd's poem, *The African prince, now in England, to Zara at her father's court*, was printed in the *Gentleman's Mag.*, July 1749, p. 323, and the companion-piece, *Zara, at the Court of Annamabboe, to the African prince, now in England*, August, p. 372. In the same year was published *The Royal African, or memoirs of the young Prince of Annamboe, his condition while a slave in Barbadoes, his reception in England*, etc.

† *The Fleece* IV.189–209. *Barbadoes, a poem*, by Mr. Weeks (1754), expressing the same sentiment, is highly applauded for its humanity in the *Monthly Review*, XI (1754), 325. Dyer is eulogized for the same reason, XVI (1757), 337.

disciple Grainger was evidently ill at ease in *The Sugar Cane*. Book IV is full of practical recommendations concerning the purchase of slaves and the best means of wringing full profit from the money invested in them. But the poet is evidently distressed by the cruelty involved. Planters are urged to "let humanity prevail." For a moment indeed he regrets that his muse lacks the power of monarchs —

> 'Twould be the fond ambition of her soul
> To quell tyrannic sway; knock off the chains
> Of heart-debasing slavery; give to man,
> Of every colour and of every clime,
> Freedom which stamps him image of his God.
> Then laws, Oppression's scourge, fair Virtue's prop,
> Offspring of Wisdom! should impartial reign,
> To knit the whole in well-accorded strife.
> Servants, not slaves; of choice, and not compell'd;
> The Blacks should cultivate the cane-land isles.
>                     (*The Sugar Cane* IV.234–243)

Churchill's *Gotham* (1764) opens with a scathing denunciation of slavery; but his sympathy, like Pope's, is expressed mainly for the native savages of America. It was only a year later that Michael Wodhul published his Rousseauistic poem entitled *The Equality of Mankind* (1765). By this time the antislavery movement was beginning to crystallize into definite form, and Sharp was ready to assume leadership in the crusade. In common with several other reforms brought to pass in the latter part of the eighteenth century, the movement against slavery owed much to the pioneer work of the poets. While the main credit has gone to a few active reformers, it is to be remembered that public sensibility had already been partly educated by a few poets who had the boldness to protest while as yet most were unready to admit that they had any scruples.*

---

\* Evidence of a growing interest may be seen in periodical literature; but it is slight, and hardly begins before the reign of George II. See *Grub-Street Journal*, Sept. 17, 1730. The *Prompter* No. 18, Jan. 10, 1735, published what purported to be "The Speech of Moses Bon Saam, a Free Negro, to the revolted Slaves in one of the most considerable Colonies of the *West Indies*," an indignant protest against the treatment of slaves. This was

IV

The most palpable evidence of the political influence acquired by the poets is the part they played in determining England's foreign policies under George II. Walpole favored peace with the Continent as a necessary condition for commercial expansion. The infringement of British rights on the high seas by Spain and France, however, led many Whigs to clamor for war. They argued that, under the circumstances, the Prime Minister's peace policy would destroy the very interest he sought to establish. This difference of opinion was the principal cause of that disaffection in the Whig ranks which developed an Opposition strong enough eventually to drive Walpole from office (1742). The poets were almost unanimously with the Opposition. Their preference was determined partly no doubt by their disapproval of Walpole's corrupt practices, partly by a sincere conviction that war was necessary, and partly by their sentimental attachment to Lord Lyttelton and the other Patriots who formed a coterie about the Prince of Wales.*

As early as 1718 hotheaded Whigs were urging an immediate attack upon Spain in the interest of British trade.[12] Thomson's *Britannia* affords sufficient evidence that by 1729 popular feeling

reprinted in the *Gentleman's Mag.* for Jan. 1735 (V, 21); a defense of the colonists was made in the number for February (p. 91). Interest was again aroused momentarily by the request of the Georgia colonists at Savannah in 1739 for an alteration of their charter which would permit the introduction of slaves. (*Ibid.*, Jan. 1741, XI, 30.) See also issues for July 1740 (X, 341); March 1741 (XI, 145); April 1741 (p. 186); Sept. 1746 (XVI, 479). Moral apathy was stirred occasionally by the exposure of extreme inhumanity, such as the report published in the *Gentleman's*, March 1759 (XXIX, 101). Seldom, however, do the remonstrants seriously question the moral right to trade in slaves. Sir Hans Sloane's *A Voyage*, etc. (2 vols.; 1707–1725), though not written against slavery, provided later opponents excellent arguments in the description of punishments inflicted upon Negroes.

* The encouragement of trade and patriotism was carried to an amusing extent by the Prince and the Princess of Wales. In order to prevent a decline in the support of the laws for protecting home industries after the war had been concluded, they issued an order that no one should appear at their court wearing any of the forbidden imports. As a further stimulation to Whig fervor, they had their children give a public performance of Addison's *Cato* from time to time. (Robert Phillimore, *Memoirs*, etc., of Lord Lyttelton [1845], II, 425.)

was lashing itself into a fury great enough to have intimidated any but a very resolute prime minister. Seldom has the British Lion roared more loudly or amusingly than he does through the 299 lines of this poem, written by a poet who once had extolled the wisdom of the Whig leader he is now denouncing for pusillanimous inactivity in the face of Spanish insults. Sitting dejectedly upon the "sea-beat shore," her bosom bare to the gale, her tresses unkempt, her azure robe torn, Britannia is so disgusted with her degenerate sons of England that at times her "copious grief" is a mere flood of question.

> What would not, Peace! the patriot bear for thee?
> What painful patience? What incessant care?
> What mixed anxiety? What sleepless toil?
> Even from the rash protected what reproach?
> For he thy value knows; thy friendship he
> To human nature: but the better thou,
> The richer of delight, sometimes the more
> Inevitable war; when ruffian force
> Awakes the fury of an injured state.
>
> . . . . . . . . . . . . .
>
> Is there the man into the lion's den
> Who dares intrude, to snatch his young away?
> And is a Briton seized? and seized beneath
> The slumbering terrors of a British fleet?
> Then ardent rise! Oh, great in vengeance rise!
> O'erturn the proud, teach rapine to restore:
> And as you ride sublimely round the world,
> Make every vessel stoop, make every state
> At once their welfare and their duty know.*

Still, although War was "greatly roused," Walpole kept him mourning his "fettered hands" for nearly a decade longer.

The tension was exceedingly high in 1735. The crisis came in

---

* *Britannia*, 147–155, 182–190. An interesting curiosity of the same year is an anonymous tract entitled *The English Cotejo; or, The Cruelties, Depredations, and Illicit Trade Charg'd upon the English in a Spanish Libel lately Published, Compared with the Murders, Robberies, Barbarities, and Clandestine Trade proved upon the Spaniards. By a Sufferer* (1729). Richard Barfield's *An Epistle to . . . Chesterfield* (1730) is a poem similar in tone to Thomson's *Britannia*.

1738. The events culminating in the War of Jenkins' Ear afforded the benevolent poets two popular arguments for fighting. The immediate provocation was the alleged brutality of the Spanish, who were said by Jenkins to have cut off his ear and sent it by him as a token of the Spaniard's contempt for England. Righteous enthusiasm was engaged by the humane idea of punishing this act of signal inhumanity and of others that soon followed in the natural course of events. In addition — and this was the chief motive — the Opposition urged that it was England's sacred duty to thwart the efforts of her rivals to repress English trade, for success on the part of the enemy meant the starvation of English laborers.

Since the war with Spain, extending later to France, was urged as a humanitarian measure, it had powerful advocates among the poets of benevolence. In the list of these it is not strange to find Tory poets as well as Whigs. In Parliament the Opposition assembled various classes who discovered a bond of common interest in their hatred of the Prime Minister; the coalition included Whigs, moderate Tories, and even Jacobites. Bolingbroke, though no longer officially connected with public affairs, was for a time after his return from exile in France the guiding genius of the Opposition. With the lapse of time and the general disintegration of the Tory party after 1714 ancient party issues had been so nearly obliterated that commercial prosperity had come to be almost the universal and unchallenged concern of the nation. Lady Mary Wortley Montagu wrote, with Whiggish exaggeration, that in 1727 there was "not one Tory left in England." [13] According to Lyttelton, "Whig" had come to mean in 1735 one who was *in* power, "Tory" one who was *out*. [14] The essential question was, not whether trade should be given all possible encouragement, but what were the wisest measures for the purpose. It is true that many of the country squires clung to the prejudices of the landed interest, but as a class they demanded slight notice except for their suspected attachment to the Pretender. Any other protest against the supremacy of commercialism was nonpolitical. It came from observers, some of them Whigs too, who shrewdly detected in it a source of national selfishness and vulgarity.* These apostles of culture deplored the growing Philistinism of the nation, but they were too few to create much impression in time of peace, and in time of threatened war they forgot their own aesthetic misgivings. Quite naturally, then, popular excitement was aggravated on the eve of war in 1738 by both the regular Whig panegyrists and their Tory allies. The free-trader Pope and the Tory Samuel Johnson were as eagerly committed as the most zealous Whig.

One of the principal instruments employed against Walpole was the broadside.[15] The more dignified poems which did most to inflame the war spirit beyond control and eventually drive him to declare war, against his own judgment, were: Mark Akenside's *A British Philippic: Occasioned by the Insults of the Spaniards and the Present Preparations for War*, the anonymous *Voice of Liberty, or A Poem, in Miltonic Verse, Occasioned by the Insults of the Spaniards*, Pope's *One Thousand Seven Hundred and Thirty-eight*, and Johnson's *London*, all of 1738.† The most influential piece of the kind, Glover's ballad of *Admiral Hosier's Ghost* (1740), was a product of the war itself. Each of these poems uses

* Even Akenside, one of the warmest advocates of Whig political principles, admits in one of his *Odes* (I.ix) (1745) that the preoccupation with trade had fostered a selfish fierceness in the national character. See, however, his *Hymn to the Naiads* (1746) and Ode i of Book II. John Brown's *Estimate* (1757) contains a severe denunciation of English commercialism. It provoked a heated reply from J. B., M.D., entitled *A Vindication of Commerce and the Arts; proving that they are the Source of the Greatness, Power, Riches, and Populousness of a State* (1758). Thomas Gray expressed great contempt for the *Estimate*, but applauded Brown's dissertation against trade (*Letters*, ed. D. C. Tovey, No. cxxxix, I, 329). Goldsmith retained the old Tory attitude. *The Bee*, No. 5, Nov. 3, 1759, observes that trade becomes a harmful influence whenever it supplies a nation with luxuries. In *The Deserted Village* he also holds commercial greed of the English responsible for the impoverishment and expatriation of the Irish peasants.

† With these may be compared the indictments against Spain and France as summarized in *A Review of all that hath pass'd between the Courts of Gt. Britain and Spain, relating to Our Trade and Navigation from the Year 1721, to the Present Convention*, etc. (1739) and Samuel Webber's *A Short Account of our Woollen Manufactures, from the Peace of Ryswick to this Time. Shewing, their former flourishing, and their present Ruinous Condition; and that they always flourished when France could not get our Wool, but declined in proportion to the Quantities of Wool Exported to them,*

one or both of the humanitarian arguments to which I have referred, and most of them, to say nothing of much mere balderdash published at the time, echo the jingoism of Thomson's *Britannia.* Concerning the actual effect of such literature on the course of events, we have the testimony of Burke. Reviewing the situation toward the close of the century, when the uselessness of the war had vindicated Walpole's judgment in opposing it, Burke declared: "There has not been in this century, any foreign peace or war, in its origin, the fruit of popular desire; except the war that was made with Spain in 1739. Sir Robert Walpole was forced into the war by the people, who were influenced to this measure by the most leading politicians, by the first orators, and the greatest poets of the time." [16] He emphasized especially the influence of Pope, Johnson, and Glover.

The indications are that by 1760 the political function of verse was beginning to wane. For particular uses it continued in popularity, notably as a medium for inciting opposition to slavery; but the evening was setting in for verse journalism of the most pedestrian kind. Except for satirical and highly sentimental purposes, the business of the political versifier gradually diminished. The growth of the romantic ideal and the consequent discouragement of didactic poetry in general was one cause. Another was the growing realization that if Whig doctrines were to be propagated in belles lettres the work could be performed more fully and convincingly by the sentimental novelist, as Henry Brooke fully demonstrated in *The Fool of Quality* (1766–1770). That the verse pamphleteers had inflicted a great hardship upon pure letters probably no reader of their lines will be disposed to question. If any apology can be made for them, it lies in the fact that the Whig panegyrists were the first group of English writers to reveal the possibilities of sentimental literature as a force for exerting the popular will in the control of national policy.

etc. (1739). Edward Philips made dramatic capital of the general excitement by bringing out his *Britons, Strike Home; or, The Sailors Rehearsal, A Farce* (1739) at the Theatre-Royal. Thomas Newcomb's *On Richelieu's Barbarities, On the French Prisoners in England,* and *On the French Cruelty to English Prisoners* are poems typical of many that appeared during the war.

# John Dunton: Pietist and Impostor

Any reliable estimate of the character and talents of John Dunton (1659–1732) can be based only upon his early work. That he eventually went mad we should at least surmise from his later works, especially the political tracts, if we had no more explicit testimony. From the year 1705 onward, indications of paranoia are increasingly pronounced. His main work as author, compiler, hack master, publisher, and factotum was performed between 1682 and 1706.

Mention of Dunton's name in histories of English literature is due almost solely to the fact that during this period he played a very active and original part in journalism. At the same time he was expending a vast deal of energy upon treatises which have long since passed into an oblivion almost undisturbed even by bibliographers. Aside from his reputation as a journalist, he was known to his contemporaries mainly as the author of numerous religious and devotional books. The momentary resurrection of these pious curiosities from long neglect is unquestionably a doubtful service to the cause of pure letters. There is nothing here without which English literature has suffered any serious deprivation. They are of some importance, however, for the additional light they shed upon the egregious dishonesty of the author and, incidentally, also upon the taste of a large English public to which he catered, with evident success, during the closing years of the seventeenth century.

I

It is a safe generalization that the further we penetrate through the elaborate deceptions Dunton built up round his character and work, the more plainly it will appear that he deserves no attention whatever as a creative writer. If a critical posterity has been unfair in its judgment, the injustice has been done chiefly in connection with his contribution to English journalism, the one phase of his activity which has attracted most attention. The historical significance of the *Athenian Gazette* (1691–1696), or the *Athenian Mercury* as he renamed his "Notes and Queries," has been admitted slowly and grudgingly. Even yet the statement is probably inadequate.* If Defoe, Steele, and Addison borrowed from their humble predecessor less openly than the editors of the *British Apollo* (1708–1711) did, beyond question they were greatly indebted to him. They owed to him the very foundation of their success in the essay.† And the obligation did not end with the hints they derived from Dunton's question-and-answer project. After a long campaign of advertising, he issued, in 1697, a volume of light, informal essays called *The Female War*, purporting to be a collection of controversial letters that had passed between the misogynist Sir Thomas and some irate champions of their sex.[1] No reader can turn from this playful dispute over paint, patches, powder, female learning, the female craze for French prose romances, and other foibles of the sex to the essays of Defoe, Steele, and Addison without realizing that *The Female War* deserves consideration. Those diverting epistles represent an important

---

* The *Athenian Gazette: or Casuistical Mercury* ran from March 17, 1690-1, to Feb. 8, 1695-6. It was revived May 14, 1697, but lasted through only ten numbers, ending June 14. For Dunton's account of this project, see *The Life and Errors*, etc. (1705), ed. J. B. Nichols (1818), I, 198–199, and *Athenianism* (1710), Project VI. The best of the questions and answers were collected and republished, with some additions, as *The Athenian Oracle* (1704). See also John Griffith Ames, *The English Literary Periodical of Morals and Manners* (1904), Ch. I and pp. 130–131, and W. P. Trent, *Cambridge Hist. of Eng. Lit.*, IX (1913), 5. The latest treatment of the subject, G. S. Marr's *Periodical Essayists of the Eighteenth Century* (1923), p. 14, is disappointingly brief.

† Dunton accused Defoe of plagiarizing his question-project (*The Life and Errors*, II, 423).

stage of transition between the brief "answers" in the *Mercury* and the completed essay-form of the *Spectator*. It is not certain, however, that even in this instance Dunton has been deprived of any rightful claim to recognition as a literary figure. Aside from the fact that few passages in the *Mercury* rise above the slipshod style practiced by other journalists of the time, we can never know whether an exceptional passage was contributed by the projector himself or by one of his Athenian collaborators. The same uncertainty attends *The Female War*; for, although Dunton was apparently responsible for the clever scheme, the advertisement of it, and the final publication of the book, it does not follow that he composed a single one of the epistles.

In a sense he was never a littérateur. He seems to have had few illusions concerning his talent as a writer, and these were rapidly dispelled. His connection with literature arose accidentally from the circumstance that he was a dealer in books. From his place behind the counter at the Sign of the Raven he formed his estimate of literature in purely commercial terms. In order to succeed in business (and at one time he was highly successful), he had to stock his shelves with what his patrons — chiefly of the lower classes — would buy. It was mainly for the purpose of supplying himself with such articles of merchandise that he assumed the additional functions of author and publisher.

Almost his sole significance is that of a shrewd entrepreneur. Whatever success or reputation he achieved is attributable mainly to two qualifications for business — a profound skill in seeing and foreseeing the trend of popular interest and a decidedly modern conception of the value and the methods of effective advertising. He discovered what his patrons liked, he provided it, and he notified them through every agency at his disposal. Dunton's title-pages are in themselves models in the art of advertisement. At the end of most books printed for him will be found a lengthy announcement of other indispensable works to be had at his shop, some of them recommended with a gusto worthy of present-day book-jackets. For the same purpose he availed himself of odd spaces in his *Athenian Mercury* and other papers, and he either established or at least controlled the *Compleat Library* (1692), a journal devoted exclusively to the review of new books.* Coming just at the time when the spirit of commercialism was beginning to manifest itself fully in the affairs of the nation, he applied it thoroughly to the business of making and selling literature.

With these modern commercial talents he combined a conveniently loose sense of *meum et tuum*. This was really a part of his genius. The slow methods of laborious honesty were precluded by his restless inventiveness. "The Mind of Man," he says, looking into his own mind, "is naturally active, and prone to Thoughts, 'tis daily forming some NEW PROJECT." [2] No sooner had he conceived one scheme for dazzling the public and attracting shillings to his till than a dozen others had suggested themselves. From beginning to end, his pathway is strewn with brilliant plans, many of which never went beyond the initial stage of the printed advertisement. His *Athenianism*, of 1710, contains a portrait of the author accompanied by "an heroic poem," proclaiming,

> Here's *Dunton's Phiz*, that new *Athenian Swain*,
> Who hatch'd Six Hundred Projects in his Brain:
> The Brood is large, but give him Time to sit
> He will Six Hundred Projects more beget.

In the mad rush to keep pace with his inventions, he sacrificed everything, honesty included, to the necessity of speedy production. Of hack writers he declares in a moment of injured righteousness, "It is very remarkable, they will either persuade you to go upon another man's *copy*, to steal his thought, or to *abridge* his *Book*, which should have got him bread for his life-time." [3]

* "A Third Project of mine, for the promotion of Learning, was a Monthly Journal of Books printed in London and beyond Sea, which was chiefly extracted out of 'The Universal *Bibliotheque*, and *Journal des Sçavans*; and it first appeared under the title of 'A Supplement to the Athenian Mercury,' but was afterwards called 'The Complete Library.' This *design* was carried on about ten months, when Monsieur *Lecrose* interfered with me, in a Monthly Journal, intituled 'The Works of the Learned'; upon which I dropped my own design, and joined with Lecrose's Bookseller in publishing 'The Works of the Learned'; but, Lecrose dying, it was discontinued, though the same design, under the same title, is yet on foot, and managed by several hands, one of which is the ingenious Mr. Ridpath . . ." (*The Life and Errors*, I, 198–199).

Yet Dunton employed such men constantly. Indeed it was due largely to him that they were first organized into a scribbling syndicate. Besides, he evidently set them an example in the works bearing his own signature.

The most tangible evidence we have had so far of his plagiarism is in connection with the Letters from New England, an account based upon a visit to Boston in 1686, but first published in *The Life and Errors* (1705).[4] Many of the best passages describing places, customs, and persons are now known to have been incorporated from works descriptive of New England and from collections of seventeenth-century prose characters.* It has been remarked also that the most elegant poems inserted in *A Voyage round the World* (1691), a farrago which is said to have influenced Laurence Sterne, were copied from Cowley and Francis Osborn.†

He himself very nearly confesses to dishonesty in the Dedication to *Athenianism* (1710). He admits that for the poems in this volume he has borrowed "many curious thoughts" from Cowley, Dryden, Congreve, Sedley, and Charles Gould; he implies that he has made free also with the religious poetry of Joseph Stennet and Isaac Watts.‡ But he makes this half-confession "without quoting the authors," that is, without attaching their names to their

---

* W. H. Whitmore pointed out a few transgressions of the kind in his edition of the eight letters (published for the Prince Society, 1867). A complete exposure was made by Chester Noyes Greenough in "John Dunton's Letters from New England," *The Colonial Society of Massachusetts*, XIV (1912), pp. 213–257. Professor Greenough summarizes the results by saying: "There are at least eighty-four cases in which Dunton incorporated borrowed material in the Letters. Of these Whitmore noted thirty-three: eighteen from Roger Williams, six from Cotton Mather, three from Josselyn, two from Increase Mather, two from J. W., one from John Eliot, and one from Joshua Moody. To these we have added fifty-one passages, — twenty from Josselyn and thirty-one from various writers of characters; namely, fourteen from Overbury, seven from Fuller, four from Earle, three from Flecknoe, and three from the author of The Ladies Calling" (p. 253).

† *The Life and Errors*, I, xiii. Dunton himself includes this among the seven books he had cause to repent of out of a total of six hundred he had published (*The Life and Errors*, I, 159). For Sterne's probable indebtedness to Dunton's mad book, see W. L. Cross, *The Life and Times of Laurence Sterne* (1909), p. 135.

‡ Professor Greenough called attention to the inclusion, besides, of four poems which had appeared in Samuel Wesley's *Maggots*, first printed for Dunton in 1685 (*op. cit.*, p. 254).

poems. The reason given by him for withholding this precise information is that he wishes to put his critics in the awkward position of never knowing whether they are criticizing him or someone else! The probable explanation is that he might thus secure credit for whatever the individual reader could not trace to its source. He then goes on to enunciate a theory somewhat after the manner of Milton's doctrine of plagiarism. "If at any time," he declares, "I have borrow'd a sparkling Thought, yet still — *The Projection, Plot,* and *Method* — of every Project (both in Prose and Verse) is entirely my own, and so for the most part are the Words; yet there's few extraordinary Thoughts in any of our modern Poets but are brought into *Duntons Athenianism*, but' they are so much alter'd, enlarg'd, or adapted to new Purposes, that the *Original Author* can't pretend any Right to 'em." He now disclaims all pretensions to the art of poetry, admitting that his muse is, at best, only a jade.* In fact, it seems to him in this moment of disillusionment that there are only five poets of any real consequence in English literature — Cowley, Dryden, Garth, Stennet, and Watts! He concludes, with charming inconsistence, by attacking pirate printers who have stolen his own wares and those of Defoe! The indications are that by 1710 Dunton's methods had become the subject of comment and that he was trying to put on the best face possible without making a frank confession. Already he had pretended to acknowledge all his sins, in *The Life and Errors*; but Dunton's confessions are models of disingenuousness. He confessed only what had already been dis-

---

* If Dunton had ever had any illusions concerning his prose style, they had vanished much earlier. "I consider the pieces I have wrote — that whatever subject I have applied to, I have generally *over-done* it, and so wrought it, that I have run it out of breath: by this means having made the thing so excessive plain, that the publick has admired it less than they might have done, had I just fleshed the hints, and left them undissected, in order for others to apply the game home themselves, and to take the pleasure of doing a little more than was already offered to their view. This, I am at last fully convinced, is the vice of an Author; for he must not *devour* his subject, if he would leave any relish in it for his Readers. This fault, of never leaving a Thought until one has worked it to death, I would by all means avoid, as I would expect that any performance of mine should be well received." This and much more pertinent self-criticism he inserted in *The Life and Errors*, I, 314f.

covered. One of many "errors" he failed to report is that near the beginning of his career he stole word for word the three separate parts of *The Informers Doom* (1683) from, respectively, Richard Bernard's *The Isle of Man* (1626); Mathew Hopkins's *The Discovery of Witches* (1647), including the illustrations; and Robert Greene's *A Quip for an Upstart Courtier* (1592).

## II

Dunton's character is nowhere more plainly revealed than in his books of piety. While editor of the *Mercury* he allotted much space to the discussion of religious topics. This was evidently his paramount interest as promoter and author. He was responsible for a greater output of solemn devotional literature than the most enterprising of his competitors among the publishers, and not a few of the treatises went under his own name. In strict accordance with the religious ideals then prevalent, he was concerned as a writer almost exclusively with the subject of death and the need of mortal man's constantly reflecting upon the dread fact of mortality. The theme was undoubtedly congenial to Dunton, for he explains that he had been haunted by the fear of dying since early childhood; some gruesome pictures of death which he had seen, probably in a typical religious treatise, had left an impression he had never been able to efface.[5] In this respect, however, he was typical of his generation. Personal predilection and public demand united to make treatises upon death the most prolific field of his literary enterprise.

In order to understand the historical significance of these lugubrious *meditationes mortis* and also to avoid an exaggeration of Dunton's pathologic tendencies, it is necessary to recall, briefly at least, the conditions existing at the time he began supplying books to the English public. We may safely assert that during the first half of the seventeenth century religious ideals had relegated all other literary interests to the background. Beginning with a large inheritance of superstitious sentiment handed down by the Elizabethans, English writers had loaded popular literature with a burden of gloomy terrorism that can now be understood fully only by examining a vast number of minor works in prose and verse which, fortunately, the historian of permanent literature is under no obligation even to mention. The entire system of religious morality was energized by the reflection that Death lies in wait for all men. The sole business of life was to be ready whenever the enemy struck. Meanwhile the ghastly moral was being emphasized by the wholesale ravages of the plague. The morbid effect of the general preoccupation can be traced in the solemnity of all departments of literature, from the work of the balladist to that of the politest poet.

At the Restoration this gloomy habit received a sudden shock. Religiosity had brought religion into disrepute. Butler became the fashion instead of Benlowes. Charles II and his friends were more interested in the art of living well than in the art and craft of dying well. Even Dryden, who had been brought up under the old regime and never wholly outgrew his puritanic training, indulged his laureate pen freely, as he afterward confessed, in the "lubricities" of the age. The masses, of course, clung to the old faith and the old superstitious bugbears, and were scandalized by the free ways of Whitehall and the press. Also devotional books of the most solemn cast continued to be produced in abundance. But the difference is that, with the exception of Milton's great poems, which really belong in spirit to the age preceding the Restoration, and various occasional pieces by Thomas Flatman, fashionable literature shows few traces of more than a perfunctory interest in religion. The old preachments were driven into the outer circle of special treatises. Puritanism was submerged. Not even the horrors of the Great Plague in 1665 were sufficient to restore the platitudes upon death to their former place as a universal *materia poetica*.

The recess was, however, comparatively brief. The Revolution of 1688 marks a change of tone in literature as well as in the policy of government. With the political triumph of Whiggism the gates were reopened for an inrush of bourgeois sentiment. The traditional pieties were gradually reinstated in spite of widespread skepticism, and the middle classes came into an influence such

as they had never exerted before. As a purveyor of religious sentiment and a restorer of the melancholy decencies, Dunton was one
of the most important figures in the transition. He had begun
six years before the Revolution, but his principal contribution
came afterward. In this department of his work he is an important link of connection between the poets of death in the pre-
Restoration period and their graveyard successors in the eighteenth
century, for, puerile as some of his disquisitions are, he made an
effort to foster a literary, as well as a religious, conscience.

Few mental peculiarities of our ancestors are more difficult for
us to grasp in their full reality than this morbid fondness of theirs
for reflecting upon death, not only in the abstract, but in its most
intimate and distressing details. We are often tempted to interpret the so-called graveyard poetry of the eighteenth century, for
example, as a literary affectation, a mere device for procuring an
artistic effect, whereas what to us is a psychological curiosity was
at that time the normal and all but universal habit of mind among
the pious. Instead of turning away from the loathsome facts of
decay and putrefaction, they dutifully envisaged the fate of body
as well as soul in order to keep themselves in a state of spiritual
preparation. Instinctive fear was deliberately fostered by religious
instruction. Attendance at funerals was a melancholy duty as well
as a pleasure. The occasion of a death was never missed for making Death terribly impressive.

From the sixteenth century onward a few sensible writers had
protested against the ceremonial of funerals as well as other elaborate rites, especially the custom of burying the dead in churches,
but their sporadic protests had made no impression.* The Frenchman Henri Misson devotes a long passage of his *Mémoires et
observations* (1698) to the strange funeral customs of the English
and their unhealthy eagerness to study dissolution at close range.†
Perhaps no record of the time throws a more amusing light upon

* See Thomas Lewis's *Seasonable Considerations on the Indecent and
Dangerous Custom of Burying in Churches and Church Fields* (1721) and
*Churches no Charnel Houses.*
† *Mémoires et observations faites par un voyageur en Angleterre . . .*
(A la Haye, 1698), pp. 129–144. The substance of this passage and other

the general morbidity than the broadside *The Noble Funeral of that Renowned Champion the Duke of Grafton* (1690). Two stanzas will serve as a commentary on the taste of Dunton's public.

> They divided his bowels, and laid at his feet,
> Whilst they imbalmed his body with spices so sweet,
> Six weeks together they kept him from the clay,
> While the Nobles appointed his funeral day,
> Twelve Lords went before him, six bore *him to th' ground*,
> While the Drums and the trumpets did solemnly sound.
>
> *In Westminster Abby* it's now call'd by name,
> The Rare Duke of Grafton was bury'd in Fame.
> They sighed and sobbed, and spent their whole day,
> While our Gracious Queen Mary came weeping away.
> When the rare Duke of *Grafton* lay deep in the clay,
> Then his soldiers went wandering every way.

Much may be learned from the funeral pomp bestowed upon Queen Mary herself in 1694 as related in the diary of Celia Fiennes [6] and from the flood of elegy evoked by her death. The ridicule of funeral customs in Steele's comedy *The Funeral, or Grief à la Mode* (1702) apparently had no effect on current fashion. That neither custom nor taste had altered by 1743 is clear from Blair's *The Grave*; one passage of this celebrated poem is nauseatingly realistic. Unless we recall this popular trait, we may underrate the broadly typical aspects of Dunton's death-books and be inclined to regard "the eccentric bookseller" as more eccentric than he actually was.

Dunton began his career as publisher very piously with *The Sufferings of Christ* (1682),* by Thomas Doolittle, one of the most "painful" preachers of the day. His third enterprise was a funeral sermon preached by another favorite of his, John Shower. At this juncture he conceived his first really ambitious design. If single funeral sermons could be sold profitably, why not venture

contemporary comment on burial customs are given by John Ashton, *Social Life in the Reign of Queen Anne* (1911), Ch. 4, which contains also some interesting illustrations.

* Licensed Nov. 1681 (T. C. I, 456, 458). Dunton's own account of his earliest publications is given in *The Life and Errors*, I, 62–63.

a collection? Besides, he had in his possession, or at least he claimed to have, numerous sermons in manuscript left by his father, John Dunton, M.A., late minister of Aston Clinton in Bucks, who had died in 1676. A strong sense of filial duty, combined probably with less generous motives, resulted in the publication of *The House of Weeping: Or, Mans last Progress to his Long Home; Fully Represented in several Funeral Discourses, With many Pertinent Ejaculations under each Head, to remind us of our Mortality and Fading State*, etc. (1682).* The lengthy title, set appropriately in a deep border of mourning, concludes with this shrewd suggestion, "Recommended as the most Proper Book yet extant to be given on *Funeral Occasions*," an idea apparently originated by Dunton's "maggoty brain."

Whether the eight sermons owe nothing, little, or everything to the pious son's ingenuity, they are no better or worse than other specimens of a kind of writing which now became more popular than it had ever been before. Dunton neglected none of the approved devices. The art of illustration had developed in England largely in connection with *memento mori* productions. The convention is honored here by the insertion of a frontispiece consisting of three separate compartments — the mourning family grouped about a coffin in the house, the procession entering the church, and the final scene at the grave. Besides the Dedication to Lady Bridget Roberts, there are four poems, signed W. S., H. C., S. S., and J. S., eulogizing the preacher and explaining the frontispiece according to the precedent established by Wither, "divine Quarles," and other emblem-writers. One of these commentaries will give a sufficient impression of the mood pervading the entire volume and also of the literary quality:

* Although dated 1682 on the title-page, *The House of Weeping* was not licensed until May 1683 (T. C. II, 12). At the same time permission was granted for *Mr. Shower's Sermon preach'd upon the Death of Mrs. Anne Barnardiston*, etc., referred to above, and five other religious works, including two funeral sermons. Apparently some at least of these were printed before they were officially authorized. *The House of Weeping* was probably suggested by *Threnoikos*. *The House of Mourning* (Arber's Tr., IV, 415, Oct. 18, 1638), a collection of funeral sermons by Daniel Featley, Richard Sibbes, etc. Forty-seven sermons (1639) were increased to fifty-three (1660).

Seest thou, frail man, the *Emblem* of thy State?
Th' exact Idea of thy hasting Fate?
The *Figure's* drawn to th' life, yea ev'ry part
Is grac'd and deckd with more than *Zeuxian* Art:
The *first* Scene showes when Man's layd out for dead,
When th' sprightly Soul from th' Body's gone & fled;
His mournful Friends no longer can endure
The lifeless Corps, therefore they do immure
And shut it close up in a *Sable Hearse*
As totally unfit for all Commerce;
O're which they showre such store of *tears* that they
Mourning, exhaust their moisture and decay.
With sorrow-wounded hearts they sob and cry
Themselves to death, they take their turns to dye.
Because one's death from th' other draws such grief,
As kills the Soul in spight of all relief:
*Next* is he brought on *shoulders* of his Friends
Along the Streets, where dismally attends
A *Croud of Mourners* to the *Church*, where they
Are twice fore-told, and warn'd they are but Clay;
*First* by the words of the *Preacher*, and the next
The Corps (tho' tacitly) repeats the *Text:*
But lo the End's more dismal than the rest,
Which brings the final *Consummatum est:*
*Earth* now is layd on *Earth*, and *dust* to *dust*,
*Earth* ope's its mouth, the *Coffin* stop it must.
This is the Lot of all, none can it flee:
*Earth's* not quite full, there's room yet left for thee.

*The House of Weeping* was so well received that the son was
encouraged to publish, two years later, eight other paternal com-
positions as *Dunton's Remains: or, The Dying Pastour's Last
Legacy to his Friends and Parishioners* (1684).\* "The Author's
Holy Life and Triumphant Death," contributed by Dunton, is of
interest mainly for what it says concerning the biographer himself. It is a fact of some importance that nearly all we know of
him and his antecedents, or think we know, is drawn from his
own reports, certainly not a thoroughly reliable source. That

---

\* Licensed Nov. 1683 (T. C. II, 38). This is another of the seven books
he repented of — apparently because of some dishonesty in connection with
it (*The Life and Errors*, I, 159).

Gildon wrote a biography of him means nothing. Gildon's methods are well known; he merely put down what he was told.

Among the eight pieces included in this volume is "A Looking-Glass for our *English* Ladies: Or, Daily Directions for their Dress and Apparel." In view especially of many passages of a similar kind in the *Athenian Mercury* and elsewhere, this essay suggests Dunton *fils* rather than Dunton *père*. The other discourses are of a convincingly clerical type — a sermon called "*Dives* Roaring in Hell Flames, whilst *Lazarus* rejoyces in *Abraham's* Bosom" (grotesquely illustrated); the story of the Penitent Prodigal (also accompanied by proper illustrations); "A Friendly Dialogue between a Moderate Conformist and one of his parishioners, concerning several Points of great Moment," one of the points being the need of accepting the dogma of predestination; the story of the bloody persecutions committed upon Protestants of the sixteenth century by the Duke of Guise; and an excruciatingly detailed account of the trial and crucifixion of Christ. Also two funeral sermons are included. The suggestion for calling one of these the author's funeral discourse upon himself probably emanated from John Donne's famous farewell sermon, "Death's Duel." The other specimen is said to be the sermon that had been preached by N. H. in memory of "that faithful and Laborious Servant of Christ, Mr. John Dunton." If there is anything in this entire collection worth noting for a gleam of literary value, it is a section entitled "Closet Employment: or Virtues and Vices . . . characterized." Although the title and the selection of topics were apparently suggested by Bishop Hall's collection of prose characters, the imitation is remote enough to be legitimate.

In the same year (1684) he brought out, undated and unlicensed, *The Pilgrim's Guide from the Cradle to his Death-bed*, one of his two monumental contributions to the cause of religion. The title indicates the ambitiousness of the design. One manual of piety had succeeded another since the time of the Reformation, each attempting to do for Protestants what had long since been accomplished by Roman Catholic treatises on practical conduct. Dunton's was merely an attempt to bring all the depressing ideals

and rules of Christianity within the compass of a single convenient volume, one that would perform the service, for example, of
Bishop Taylor's *Holy Living* and *Holy Dying*. Dunton knew
what we can now learn thoroughly only from the history of such
works, that the popularity of one creates a demand for another,
and that the English capacity for consuming melancholy advice
was unlimited. It was a question only of producing a new one big
enough and strong enough to satisfy the morbid appetite as none
of the others had done. And this is what Dunton undertook.

The title, as usual, was well chosen. For a time after the Reformation the medieval fondness for "Pilgrimages" had been checked
by the prejudice of the Reformers against a word that recalled
too painfully one of the proscribed habits of the old religion. It
came into literary popularity again, however, with Leonard
Wright's prose manual *The Pilgrimage to Paradise* (1591) and
Nicholas Breton's poem of the same title in the year following
(1592). From that time onward there was a constant succession
of Pilgrimages, leading up to Bunyan's greatest work. In this one
instance Dunton's general title indicated only a part of the entire
content of his book. The volume is made up of the following
separate divisions: (1) "The Pilgrim's Guide," (2) "The Sick
Man's Passing-Bell," (3) a set of miscellaneous pieces described in
the title as "no less than Fifty Several Treatises besides (rarely if
ever handled before)," and (4) an appendix of less than one page
called "The Sighs and Groans of a Dying Man." This last item is
another of the productions said to be inherited from Dunton
senior. Noting how useful *The House of Weeping* and *The
Dying Pastour's Last Legacy* had proved, the son was encouraged
to reoblige the world by this third composition, which was ready
for publication at the time of the author's death. With an eye to
the future, he adds that there are still other papers of his father's
to be published as soon as he can find time to decipher the short-
hand and prepare them for the press.

The mere fact that *The Pilgrim's Guide* comprises 306 pages
of closely printed matter would lead one to suspect that it was
not entirely honest. I am unable to state the full extent of plagia-

rism, but it is certain that the author borrowed without scruple. The very undignified wrangle between the Judge and a condemned sinner at the Final Assizes is an echo of a famous passage in Thomas Shepard's *The Sincere Convert.*[7] A little later we come across "Jerusalem my happy home," a hymn written as a broadside by a Roman Catholic poet early in the century.[8] The same illustrations that had been used as a frontispiece to *The House of Weeping* are again pressed into service here to illustrate the perennial topic of death, and are accompanied by fragments of two of the original commendatory poems, but now without the writers' initials. In fact, these poems seem to have been taken over as a part of Dunton's original work and permanent stock in trade.[9] The "Death-Bed Legacies," a long harangue delivered by a dying man to his wife, son, daughters, and servants, is copied from a book once attributed to Thomas Becon, *The Sicke Mans Salve*, including in full the advice given to the wife for selecting a second husband.[10] Becon's book, first published in 1561, was the most popular of the Elizabethan deathbed manuals and continued in vogue until the middle of the seventeenth century. Dunton evidently calculated that it was no longer a household treasure. One of the most readable sections in *The Pilgrim's Guide* is a long poem called "An Awaking Dialogue between the Soul and Body of a Damned Man; each laying the fault upon the other." This was plagiarized from William Crashaw's translation (1632) of *Querela sive Dialogus Animae et Corporis*, a poem attributed to St. Bernard,\* and the ornate prose introduction from James Howell's *The Vision: or A Dialog between the Soul and the Bodie* (1651). To trace all the innumerable essays, prayers, meditations, dialogues, and poems of *The Pilgrim's Guide* to their real owners would be the labor of a tedious and unprofitable lifetime. Part III alone, the fifty or more several treatises, would present a formidable task. There is ample reason for supposing

---

\* Dunton, pp. 213–224. Another translation he may have known was a broadside entitled *Saint Bernard's Vision; Or, A briefe Discourse (Dialoguewise) between the Soule and the Body of a damned man newly deceased, laying open the faults of each other; with a speech of the Divels in Hell* (*Roxburghe Ballads*, II, 490–497).

that the principal work expended by Dunton and his confederates was purely manual. It is not surprising that no reference is made to this performance in *The Life and Errors*.

The reader of *The Pilgrim's Guide* should, however, divest himself of all conventional notions of proprietorship and accept Dunton's own convenient theory. In this uncritical frame of mind he will find it an extraordinary *succès de curiosité*. While there is nothing especially distinctive in the emphasis upon death, since all human duties had long since been focused into this single point of meditation and all the "Pilgrimages" keep attention riveted upon the dire end of the journey, by stealing right and left Dunton succeeded as probably no one else had done in ringing all the possible changes upon the old subject. *Luctus ubique pavor et plurima mortis imago.* The art of the illustrator comes to the aid of prose and verse. Ministers visit the dying, passing bells are constantly tolling, dead men are "stript and laid out on the bed," wrapped in winding sheets, and laid in coffins. Directions are given for funeral processions and funeral etiquette. The writer regrets that while living in a country village, where a burial was a rarity, he had seldom had death presented to his attention. But *"London is a Library of Mortality:* Volumes of all sorts and sizes, Rich and Poor, Infants, Children, Youth, Men, Old men daily dye" (p. 160). In the course of the volume a country parson and a stranger meet on their way to London. Their decision to enliven the journey by exchanging views upon death results in a dialogue stretching over many pages. In moments of high enthusiasm the pedestrians break into poetry. One sample (p. 178) will not be amiss:

> A shirt is all remains in fine
> To victorious *Saladine;*
> At Death a piece of Linnen is
> All that great Monarch could call his:
> *Poor Prince!* who to his Son the *East* bequeaths,
> When Death had turn'd his Bays to Cypress wreaths.
> Poor prince! one Shirt must all his Trophys be,
> Deaths a far greater Conqueror than he.

The moral is pointed for us: "Let us therefore now, kind Reader, every day *make Funeral processions, or at least visit in meditation every hour our Tomb, as the place where our bodies must make so long abode. Celebrate we our selves our own Funerals, and invite to our exequies* Ambition, Pride, Choler, Luxury, Gluttony, *and all the other Passions*" (p. 195). "The entire world," says the parson, in a fit of pulpit eloquence worthy of his successor Edward Young, "is but as it were a *Coemitary* or *Church-yard*. . . . A walk into Church-yards, and Charnels, though it be sad and melancholy, by reason of the doleful objects there obvious, hath yet nevertheless something in it agreeable to content good souls, in the contemplation of those very objects, which they there find. How often have I taken pleasure to consider a great number of *Deadmens Sculls* arranged one in pile upon another with this conceit of the vanity, and arrogance, wherewith otherwhile they have been filled" (p. 196).

In such passages as this (and they are numerous) we have Dunton's nearest approach to the manner of the later graveyard poets and Hervey's prose *Meditations among the Tombs* (1746). This particular touch seems also to have been partly an addition made by Dunton himself; at least this entire dialogue bears the earmarks of his shoddy style. Strangely enough, the poets of death had not yet discovered the psychological advantage to be gained by localizing their abstractions. A few exceptions can be found, but they are remarkably few, and in no case had the possibility of a definite locale been fully utilized. This was the one discovery left for Parnell and his school. And it is here that Dunton really had something to offer these funereal successors of his. But he was not content to stop at the grave. We are treated to all the terrible signs that are to precede the Final Judgment, an account of the Trial as full as that given by Michael Wigglesworth, and also the sufferings of souls in the flames of Hell.

*Heavenly Pastimes* (1685), a combination of prose and verse, may be dismissed briefly. It is another of the numerous seventeenth-century attempts to popularize the stories of the Old Testament. Though assigned in the title to the elder John Dunton, it is more probably an enterprise of the son's, probably, too, a thoroughly dishonest enterprise.*

The last of his encyclopedic treatises on death was *A Mourning-Ring. In Memory of your Departed Friend* (1692), an awesome mass including considerable material from his previous publications. This also is "Recommended as proper to be given at funerals." The idea of introducing the use of books as funeral gifts had now been fructifying in his mind for ten years. By this time he had organized the Athenian Society. The subject had come up for discussion in this learned body, and his colleagues had heartily endorsed his opinion that a treatise on death was infinitely more appropriate at a funeral than were gifts of gloves, biscuits, wine, and the like.† For special encouragement, a blank space had been left on the title-page for inserting the name of the deceased. By this time, too, the *Compleat Library* had been established. The issue for August 1692 contains a five-page review of the book, praising it in unmeasured terms.[11] The reviewer (John Dunton

* The following description from the Term Catalogues differs somewhat from the title actually used: "A very delightful New-year's gift, entituled, Heaven's Pastimes, or Pleasant Observations on all the most remarkable passages throughout the Holy *Bible*, newly allegorized, in several pleasant Dialogues, etc. To which is added, 1. The miraculous manner of the Production of our Grandmother *Eve*, with the supposed manner of *Adam's* first Nuptial Addresses. 2. *Eve's* first Addresses to *Adam*, and industry in making Garments for her Husband. 3. *Adam* and *Eve's* Winter-Sutes, their Lodging and first Building, an account in what pretty manner they first invented fire, etc." (II, 113, Feb. 1685.) The name of the author is not given. This is another of the books Dunton afterwards regretted having published (*The Life and Errors*, I, 159).

† Quest. 1. *I have heard that several good Men have order'd* Books *to be given away after their decease,* — Query, *Whether* Books *are not more proper to be given at* Funerals, *than* Bisquits, Gloves, Rings, &c.

*Answ.* We vehemently suspect this *Query* is sent in by some *Bookseller* or other, who has either a great many Books fit for such a business, or is about to Print one that is design'd to that End. And the mischief is, we can't oblige the *Bookseller*, but we must at the same time draw upon us the Displeasure of the *Confectioners, Glovers,* and *Goldsmiths,* by intrenching on their Profits. — But to silence them, we assure 'em before-hand, the Project is ne'ere like to take, as long as Persons value their *Hands* and *Palats,* more than their *Brains;* which the generality of mankind are likely to do as long as *Bisquits* are eaten, or *Rings* are worn. — Now we have done with *them,* let's to the *Bookseller;* whose Question we Answer in the Affirmative," etc. etc. (*Athenian Mercury,* Vol. IV, No. 15, Tuesday, Nov. 17, 1691).

himself in all probability) thought it scarcely necessary to comment on the usefulness of such a treatise. "The wisest of Men said 'tis better to be in the *House of Mourning*, than the *House of Rejoycing*; and recommends the Meditations on Death and Judgment as the most effectual means, to stop even the Impetuous Current of Youth in their pursuit after the pleasures of sin. And therefore it may be presumed that a Book on this Subject needs not to be recommended to any good Christian, who makes it his work so to Live, as hourly expecting when his great Change will come." Of the author it is said that he "spent a great part of his time in Holy and Devout Contemplations upon the things of another Life, as this excellent Piece plainly shews."

Preceding the elaborate title-page, which is framed in a black border, stands a frontispiece in four transverse compartments, depicting, respectively, a corpse laid out in a winding sheet, a family group mourning around a coffin, a funeral procession, and a burial. As in several other instances, the long title enumerates various items not found in the book. In fact, of the twelve divisions announced on the title-page only six are actually printed. If the original promise had been kept, the result would have been truly appalling. We should have had, besides the present contents, "The Sick-Man's Passing-Bell" and "The Pilgrim's Guide From the Cradle to the Grave" (reprinted), "A Conference between the Mourners," "A Walk among the Tombs," and "The Author's Tears, or Meditations on his own Sickness, Death, and Funeral." Actually the ingredients are: (1) "The House of Weeping," rearranged and greatly enlarged but retaining the original title-page and illustrations; (2) "Death-Bed-Thoughts"; (3) "The Fatal Moment"; (4) "The Treatment of our Departed Friends after Their Death in Order to their Burial"; (5) "The Final Solemnity"; and (6) "An Account of the Death and last Sayings of the most Eminent Persons, from the Crucifixion of our Blessed Saviour, down to this point of time." * Charles II appears in this

---

* The make-up of this book is an interesting bibliographical curiosity in itself. Part I, "The House of Weeping," is preceded by its original frontispiece, commendatory poems, and title-page, including the date 1682. This frontispiece is very similar to that which precedes the entire volume,

galaxy of the *morituri salutamus*, but his most famous deathbed remark is not quoted.

Of the new material found in *A Mourning-Ring*, easily the best is the set of short prose pieces headed "Death-Bed-Thoughts." No reader at all familiar with the style of Dunton and his fraternity would hesitate a moment to pronounce this section an outright forgery, whether he recognized the sources or not. As a matter of fact, the "Proemium," or introductory essay, is taken bodily (with the exception of a brief sentence that escaped the eye of the copyist) from Bishop Hall's eloquent *Meditation upon Death*.[12] The contents that follow this exordium were appropriated from another work equally distinguished for its preciosity of style, *The Forerunner of Eternity, or Messenger of Death: sent to Healthy, Sick, and Dying Men*, a translation made from the Latin of Hieremias Drexelius by William Croyden in 1642.

### III

By this time Dunton must have decided that he had exhausted this particular vein or, to state the case in more practical terms, he had probably rifled all the best treatises that could be levied upon with impunity. The field was also being invaded by dan-

and the commendatory poems are used to introduce both the work as a whole and "The House of Weeping"; consequently they are repeated verbatim within the space of a few pages. The British Museum Catalogue indicates that "The House of Weeping" included in *A Mourning-Ring* (1692) is a mere reproduction from the edition of 1682; but this is not the case. The original eight sermons are here increased to eighteen, various "ejaculations" are added, and there is a complete rearrangement. On page 266 occurs "The End of the House of Weeping." But the discovery was made that three of the 1682 sermons had been omitted. A new pagination begins here (p. 1), and these missing pieces are inserted under the numbers given to them in the original edition (I, VI, VII); the result is a duplication of these numbers. The new pagination is now continued to page 296. The final portion of the volume is paginated as 161 to 256. This description is based on B. M. copy 700.a.6, which is called the second edition; but apparently it is so called with reference only to "The House of Weeping." The two other so-called second editions of *A Mourning-Ring* (852.c.15 and G-131724) show that cheaper copies were issued without the illustrations, the separate title-page for "The House of Weeping," and the three sermons inserted after page 266. *A Mourning-Ring* was licensed for publication June 1693 (T. C. II, 463). It was again entered, with twelve other books for Dunton, Nov. 1693 (II, 472).

gerous competitors. He now ventured upon a more sensational type of piety. The *Compleat Library* for December 1692 announces the forthcoming publication of "a new and singular Piece of serious Novelty, that well merits the Reflection of this loose Age." [18] The issue for the next month devotes five pages to a review of the book.[14] It is called *The Second Spira, being a fearful Example of an Atheist, who Died in Despair at Westminster, December 8th, 1692 . . . By J. S. a Minister of the Church of England, a frequent Visiter of him in his whole Sickness.* (1693).* This proved to be Dunton's best seller. He says in his *Life and Errors* that the sale amounted to 30,000 copies in six weeks.[15] It was also translated into German in 1695.

The selection of the title was a stroke of genius. Nothing else had so satisfied the morbid desire of English Calvinists to know just how a doomed "reprobate" — a soul predestined *ab aeterno* to become a vessel of divine wrath — felt at the approach of death as did a book describing in detail the dying agonies of the Italian lawyer Francis Spira, a sixteenth-century convert to the Protestant religion who finally yielded to the threats of the Roman Catholic Church, made a recantation, and thereby incurred certain destruction, as of course he was all along predestined to do. *A Relation of the Fearfull Estate of Francis Spira*, translated from the Italian by Nathaniel Bacon, was first published in 1638. Edi-

---

* As a publisher Dunton had speculated heavily in dying speeches. In June 1683 he was given permission to publish "A necessary Companion for a serious Christian . . . To which is added, The Deathbed Counsel of a late Reverend Divine to his Son, an Apprentice in *London*" (T. C. II, 24). "A Collection of the dying Speeches, Letters, and Prayers, of those Eminent Protestants who suffered in the West of *England* and elsewhere, under the cruel Sentence of the Lord *Jeffreys*" was entered May 1689 (II, 258); the same work enlarged was entered June 1689 (II, 280) and a fourth edition Nov. 1693 (II, 486). See *The Life and Errors*, I, 201–202. In Nov. 1690 (T. C. II, 330), he entered "The wonders of Free Grace, or A compleat History of all the remarkable Penitents that have been executed at *Tyburn* and elsewhere, for these last thirty years. To which is added, A Sermon preached in the hearing of a condemn'd Person immediately before his execution. By Increase Mather," and again Nov. 1693 (II, 472). At the same time he entered two books describing the trials of New England witches (II, 476). There is no record of a license for *The Second Spira*, although Dunton refers to one (*The Life and Errors*, I, 268).

tion followed edition until 1784. This is the book, it will be recalled, that almost drove John Bunyan to madness while he was
laboring under the fear that he, too, had been marked for reprobation. Bunyan's vivid account of Spira's mental torture, in *Grace
Abounding*, had done much to advertise the tragedy. The story
of Rochester's deathbed penitence as reported in Robert Parsons's
funeral sermon and Burnet's account (1680) was still good reading; * but Rochester's struggle, excellent though it was of its kind,
concluded too mildly to satisfy the greedy sensationalist. Nothing
could have been more opportune in 1692 than the discovery of a
second Spira, one near home. By this time, too, the belief in
Calvinistic reprobation had so far cooled and the growth of
skepticism become so alarming that a terrified atheist on his death-
bed was the most edifying and satisfying spectacle that could
have been presented to an orthodox public. Dunton was fishing in
excellent water. Of the content of the book it is sufficient to say
that purchasers could not have been disappointed; the horrors of
the English Spira were equal to those of his Italian prototype.†

The fact is, the sensation became too great. Readers began to
be embarrassingly inquisitive concerning the authenticity of the
story and the identity of the author. Finally Dunton came out
with an explanation, in a Key added to the actual or so-called
thirtieth edition of the tract. He had to confess that the whole
story was a fraud — not, however, of his invention. To clear his
own skirts, he put the entire responsibility upon his sister's husband, a former colleague in the Athenian Society, Richard Sault,
who had obligingly died.‡ According to Dunton, Sault had given

* Compare Thomas Flatman's poem *On the Death of the Earl of
Rochester.*

† The success of this book was probably responsible for "*Spira's* despair
revived; being a Narration of the Horror and Despair of some late Sinners
under the apprehension of Death and Judgment. By Thomas James, Minister of the Gospel" (T. C. II, 521, Nov. 1694).

‡ Sault was buried 17 May, 1702 (*D. N. B.*). Since Dunton refers to
him in his Key as "late Mathematick Professor in Cambridge," this edition
of *The Second Spira* was probably not published as early as 1700, the date
conjecturally assigned by the British Museum. See, however, *The Life and
Errors*, I, 157, where Dunton says Sault had died "about six months" before
and that he had given the culprit a chance to vindicate himself.

him the copy, declaring that he had received it from J. Sanders, the clergyman who attended the English Spira at the time of his horrible death. Thus Dunton had been made the dupe of an unscrupulous associate and his veracity unjustly impugned. He was now convinced that Sault himself, a professor of mathematics at Cambridge and an atheist, had written the report as the result of the intense fears he had suffered. To be sure, the atheist had not at the time of his writing gone through the final agonies of the deathbed, but a man terrified as he was might easily anticipate this experience by a slight exercise of the imagination. In corroboration of his theory, Dunton added to his own account a letter from the mathematician's wife, proving at least that Sault was a libertine, reports of a similar tenor "by other Persons of undoubted credit," and various other materials, evidently in the hope that the sale of the book might be made to survive the exposure of its falsehood. One addition was entitled "Double Hell, or an Essay on Despair; Occasioned by Mr. Richard Sault (the second Spira) crying out in Mr. Dunton's hearing, I am Damn'd! I am Damn'd!" This and another piece of the same kind, "A Conference between the famous Mr. John Dod and Mr. Throgmorton (then lying upon his Death-bed under Desertion)," he valued so highly that he published them again several years later in *Athenianism*. But evidently confession had killed the goose that laid the golden egg; with all these additions, the story of the second Spira failed to retain the interest of book-buyers. Whether Sault was really the author of the story and was guilty of deceiving Dunton is unknown. Certainly Dunton made a point thereafter of attacking the memory of his former colleague and relative whenever opportunity arose. The charges are repeated at length in *The Life and Errors*, where he declares he is willing to swear to the truth of them "upon all the Bibles in the Queen's dominions." [16]

*An Essay, Proving We shall Know our Friends in Heaven. Writ by a Disconsolate Widower, on the Death of his Wife, and Dedicated to her Dear Memory* (1698), besides dealing with a "subject never handled before in a distinct Treatise," has a peculiar biographical significance. The disconsolate widower was not concerned solely with the memory of his departed wife. He admits that Philaret, as he calls himself, greatly admired "the Pindarick Lady" Mrs. Singer, who was an object of tender interest likewise to Matt Prior but finally elected to become "die göttliche Rowe." Moreover, though he is silent on this topic, he had now entered into a second marriage, a very unhappy one, and was engaged in a bitter conflict with his new spouse and her mother, Mrs. Jane Nichols, "Mother Damnable." Apparently they were expected to catch a note of bitter irony in the section entitled "What I intend to do if it please God to bring me into a Married State," but the indirect rebuke had no effect. This strange memorial tract is of some importance in a study of Dunton because here, instead of quietly copying other writers, he quotes with acknowledgment from several favorite works — William Bates's *The Four Last Things*, Simon Patrick's *The Parable of the Pilgrim*, John Shower's *A Discourse of Mourning for the Dead*, Robert Bolton's *The Four Last Things*, and Joseph Stevens's *Sermons on Dives and Lazarus*. He thought well enough of the performance to reprint most of it, including the treatment of Platonic love, in *Athenianism.*

The last of Dunton's formal treatises on religion was *The New Practice of Piety. Writ in Imitation of Dr. Browne's Religio Medici: Or, The Christian Virtuoso* (1704). In his *Life and Errors* he refers to this as the production of the Society and states that it had been in preparation for ten years.* The title-page, however, refers the authorship to "a Member of the New Athenian Society," that is, John Dunton. We here have him presented in an entirely new light. No longer an old-fashioned religionist, he undertakes as a "Christian virtuoso" to effect a compromise between scriptural literalism and the new philosophy or, as he explains in the lengthy title, to discover "the Right Way to Heaven, Between all Extreams." Quite appropriately to this liberal

---

* This "fifth project" is described in *The Life and Errors*, I, 200. Evidently when writing his autobiography Dunton expected it to be printed before *The New Practice of Piety* (1704); but the order was reversed. Another inaccuracy in what he wrote as an announcement of the virtuoso philosophy is the statement that it would be dedicated to Queen Anne.

view, he inscribes the Dedication "to Mr. John Lock, Author of the Essay upon Humane Understanding," a man of large soul "Brimfull of Knowledge and Piety" who has now been on the right road for sixty years.

Again Dunton threw out excellent bait in his title. It brought together the names of two very dissimilar books of wide popularity. Bishop Lewis Bayly's *The Practice of Piety* had been in circulation nearly a century.* Everybody was familiar with it. There was a challenge to curiosity in the very proposal of a *new* Practice of Piety. *Religio Medici* was also an excellent drawing-card, but it would appeal to a somewhat different group. And if Dunton could mediate between the bishop and the physician he would accomplish a great feat. Browne's book had been under strong suspicion among the orthodox ever since Alexander Ross had drawn up his formidable indictment *Medicus Medicatus: or, The Physician's Religion Cured* (1645).† Suspicion was confirmed by one or two favorable comments upon *Religio Medici* by the notorious deist Charles Blount, and as the danger of the deistic movement increased, Browne's religion passed under still more severe scrutiny. Dunton, then, was undertaking an ambitious role. The hazard was likely to attract purchasers of very divergent views.

One passage will illustrate the influence of Browne's style upon the imitator and also points of minor difference of opinion as well as general agreement. The following is based upon a passage of *Religio Medici* so well known that it need not be repeated for the sake of comparison:

* It was licensed in 1611-12; but apparently the date of the first edition is not known. By 1613 there was a third edition, and it continued to be printed frequently until 1842. A full account is given by J. E. Bailey in "Bishop Lewis Bayly and his 'Practice of Piety'," *Manchester Quarterly*, July 1883.

† *The Religion of a Physician* (1663), a despicable poem by Edward Gayton, owes nothing to Sir Thomas Browne except the title, although he is referred to in the Introduction. The purpose of the author was to curry favor with the Anglican authorities by celebrating the festivals of the church. The prose treatise *Religio Clerici* (1681) is also the production of an ardent Anglican: it is directed principally against deists, Socinians, and atheists, and is solidly orthodox. Encouragement was given to all works of the kind by Dryden's *Religio Laici* (1682).

"I do not affect *Rhodomontadoes* in *Religion*, nor to boast the *strength* of my *Faith* [as Browne had done]: I do not covet Temptations, nor court Dangers: Yet I can exercise my *Belief* in the difficultest Point [Browne's exact phrase], when call'd to it; and walk stedfast and upright in Faith, without the *Crutch* of a visible *Miracle*. I can firmly believe in *Christ*, without going in *Pilgrimage* to his *Sepulchre*, neither need I the *Confirmation* that was vouchsaf'd to St. *Thomas*, that *Proverb* of *Unbelief*. However I do not [as Browne had done] bless myself, nor esteem my *Faith* the better, because I lived not in the *Days of Miracles*, nor ever saw *Christ* or any of his *disciples*." [17]

In their endeavor to reconcile Faith and Reason all the virtuoso philosophers were in constant danger of making out too good a case for Reason, especially in their treatment of nature as a form of the divine revelation. Bacon had advised that Religion and Science be kept severely apart. Although Browne's boast was that he had achieved this duality in perfection, allowing his faith in no way to be contaminated by pure reason, evidently this was not the impression created on his opponents, who condemned him as a deist, and indeed there was some ground for their accusation. The author of *The New Practice of Piety* was very careful in this connection. "I highly value the Sacred Scripture as the *Oracle of Divinity, and Rule of Faith*," he declares as an orthodox Christian. "Yet I esteem them not a System of Philosophy, or a Pandect of natural Science. They are able to make us Wise unto Salvation, and perfect in the Knowledge of GOD, through Faith in Christ Jesus, but they instruct us not in *Humane Curiosities*, nor acquaint us with the theory of all his Works" (p. 36). This categorical distinction would probably have satisfied Bacon himself. But when the author begins to rhapsodize over astronomy, he betrays a leaning toward the heretical Religion of Nature. In some other respects he is much more radical than Browne. Taking a leaf from the works of the Cambridge Platonists, as he had done frequently in the *Mercury*, he here boldly professes his belief in the Platonist doctrine of pre-existence. "I look upon it," he declares with warmth, "as an effect of *Gothick Barbarity* and Ignorance, which afterwards overspread all Christendom, That neither this, nor hardly any other *Point of Platonism*, were countenanced in the Christian Schools, but only the Dictates of *Aristotle* and his *Ghost Averroes*" (p. 43). In his attitude toward the "monstrosities" of creation he is hardly so catholic as Browne and the Cambridge Platonists. They decried any inclination to condemn a natural object as ugly. He admits that he has no quarrel with the old-fashioned logic of those who call a toad venomous. He adds, however (p. 64), that he himself could not hate this proverbial object of hatred since it bears the character and impress of the Divine Artificer, and, never having sinned, is better than man!

Dunton's defection from the strict orthodoxy of his other works appears most strikingly in his new treatment of death. In his philosophical role he is no longer afraid of the King of Terrors. He now holds that it is only fancy, aggravated by the pomp and circumstance of funerals (customs he had done much to encourage), that makes man afraid to die. "I have no Pannick fears of *Death* upon me," he writes, "neither am I sollicitous, how or when I shall make my *Exit* from the Stage of this *Life*; much less do I trouble my self about the manner of my *Burial*, or to which of the *Elements* I shall commit my *Carcass*." Once in this strain, the former advocate of weekly walks among the tombs as a moral prophylactic grows more and more recklessly modern until he actually declares himself in favor of the Indian custom of cremating dead bodies, this being the quickest method of resolving them back into their elements. To be on the safe side, however, he adds that he is willing, in conformity with the tradition of his church, "to undergo the tedious Conversation of *Worms* and *Serpents*, those greedy Tenants of the *Grave*, who will never be satisfied till they have eat up the *Ground-Landlord*" (p. 19). His philosophy of the resurrection had undergone a corresponding modification. He was still positive he should "rise with the same *Individual Body*" he now possessed; but it would probably not contain "one of the same *Individual Atomes*" of its present ingredients, for it would not be "Decorus to put the *Angels* on the Drudgery of *Scavengers*; as if it should at that Day be their Employment to sweep the *Graves* and *Charnel-houses*, to sift the *Elements*, and rake in all the Receptacles of the Dead, for Man's divided *Dust*" (p. 20).

Why did Dunton announce in *The Life and Errors* that this virtuoso treatise had been finished after a labor of ten years but fail to mention that the book had actually been published thirteen years earlier under a different title? He himself had boldly appropriated a long passage from it (without acknowledgment) in the essay written in memory of his wife. It had first appeared, in 1691, as *Religio Bibliopolae. By Benj. Bridgwater.*[18] The address "To the Reader" contains the information, however, that the author had lacked the necessary leisure to complete his task and that the work had been finished by another hand, "yet with all the care possible to reach the Air, and Stile of the Author, which is of that neatness and facility as must needs recommend it (were there nothing else considerable) to the taste of such an Age as this." Who was the elegant author? Arber apparently considered him a myth. As editor of the Term Catalogues he treats "Benjamin Bridgwater" as merely one of the numerous pseudonyms employed by Dunton. Hence he assigns to Dunton both *Religio Bibliopolae* and *The Secret History of the Calves Head Club* (1703), which bears the initials B. B.[19] This assumption is adopted also in the catalogue of the British Museum.

On what ground this conclusion was reached is not clear. According to the records of Trinity College, Cambridge, Benjamin Bridgwater was granted his Bachelor's degree in 1682.[20] Dunton himself gives the following account of him in the Who's Who of contemporary hacks drawn up in *The Life and Errors*: "Mr. Ben Bridgwater. He was of Trinity College in Cambridge, and M.A. His genius was very rich, and ran much upon Poetry, in which he excelled. He was, in part, Author of 'Religio Bibliopolae.' But alas! in the issue, Wine and Love were the ruin of this ingenious Gentleman." [21] Of his poetical talent we have a specimen in *A Poem Upon the Death of Her Majesty Queen Mary, of Blessed Memory. Occasioned by an Epistle to the Author from Mr. J. Tutchin* (1695). Since this elegy was not licensed, Arber had no occasion to pass judgment upon the authorship, and the British Museum does not own the poem. Is this also by Dunton? It is difficult to think so. Surely the Athenian projector was not the man to conceal himself under a pseudonym on this propitiously melancholy occasion when poets big and little were straining themselves hoarse in "Pindaricks," pastorals, and all the other known forms of elegy to express the national sorrow — and to attract favorable notice from the great. It may seem strange that Dunton did not swell the chorus; but it would be more difficult to explain that he did take part but concealed the fact. This was not Dunton's habit. There is no reason to suppose that the elegy was not composed by Mr. Ben Bridgwater. And if Bridgwater was the bona fide author of this elegy, in 1695, why should we assume that he was not the author also of a book published four years earlier under his name?

The mere fact that Dunton laid claim to it may be thrown out of consideration. That he was dishonest about the book in some measure is certain, and it is not unlikely that he was wholly so. The indications are that most of *Religio Bibliopolae* was written for Dunton by this Cambridge hack and that the final touches had to be added by the publisher or some scribbler in his employ. After "Wine and Love" had done their work on this ingenious gentleman author, Dunton saw his way, though somewhat doubtfully, to annexing the book to his own credit. He hesitated for a time between ascribing it to the Society, which no longer existed, and arrogating entire honor to himself. In the end he adopted the bolder course. Although *Religio Bibliopolae* apparently had twice been republished, in 1694 and 1702, and in any event could not have been entirely forgotten, Dunton ignored its existence and in 1704 offered *The New Practice of Piety* as an original composition.*

* It was first entered May 1704 (T. C. III, 397) as printed for S. Malthus. There were other entries Feb. 1705 (III, 444), June 1705 (III, 474), and May–June 1708 (III, 598); but these do not mean, necessarily, that the book was republished. For the known and the conjectural editions of both *Religio Bibliopolae* and *The New Practice of Piety*, see Geoffrey Keynes, *A Bibliography of Sir Thomas Browne* (1924), Appendix I.

His reason for reissuing the treatise is obvious. At this point in his career he desired to put in a word for the moderate or occasional conformists — a very perilous undertaking as Defoe had discovered by writing *The Shortest Way with the Dissenters* (1702). Defoe had come to grief with his misunderstood irony. Dunton adopted a safer course. By posing as a liberal and dedicating his book to Locke, he hoped to give his plea for religious toleration a note of complete disinterestedness. The catholicity of *The New Practice of Piety* was a mere shield for an attack on the intolerant attitude of the High Flyers toward the dissenters. With the exception of a few very slight changes in the original text, the revision of 1704 consists entirely in the addition of an introduction and a conclusion, both warmly denouncing the penal laws as an unreasonable interference with private judgment in the nonessentials of religion. The attack seems to have passed unnoticed. The Dedication prefixed to *Athenianism* announces a fourth edition, to be called *Dunton's Creed: or, the Religion of a Bookseller*; but apparently the third (1705?) was the last. On the other hand, the original *Religio Bibliopolae* was republished in 1728, 1742, and 1790 — but now without the name Benjamin Bridgwater. It was also translated into German (1737).

## IV

From the confessional intent of *The Life and Errors* (1705), composed while the author was evading the consequences of debt by a life of "solitude," we should expect a copious flow of penitential gloom. In order to confirm himself in his plans of amendment, the contrite debtor is habitually envisaging his winding sheet in the darkness of the tomb. Solemnity of mood is more prominent still in parts of *Dunton's Whipping Post*, of the next year (1706). One division of this, "The Living Elegy: Or, Dunton's Letter, Being a Word of Comfort to his Few Creditors," attains a pathetic climax in a poem reminding Wesley and other creditors that even an insolvent debtor will be rescued by death. Nowhere else has Dunton handled the old theme so effectively. But neither the fear of the law nor contrite abasement for former dereliction had changed the leopard's spots. For his "Living Elegy in Verse" he was apparently indebted to three separate sources, only one of which I have identified. Bishop King's *My Midnight Meditation* reads:

> Ill busi'd man! Why should'st thou take care
> To lengthen out thy life's short Kalendar?
> When e'ry spectacle thou lookst upon
> Presents and acts thy execution.
>     Each drooping season and each flower doth cry,
>     Fool! as I fade and wither, thou must dy.
>
> The beating of thy pulse (when thou art well)
> Is just the tolling of thy Passing Bell:
> Night is thy Hearse, whose sable Canopie
> Covers alike deceased day and thee.
>     And all those weeping dewes which nightly fall,
>     Are but the tears shed for thy funerall.[22]

This emerges from Dunton's hands uncontaminated and entire with only such exceptions as appear in the following extract:

> Then crazy Dunton, why dost take such care
> To lengthen out thy Life's short Calendar?
> Each dropping Season, and each Flower does cry,
> "John, as I fade and wither, thou must die." [23]

Dunton's star had now set. At the height of his success as a publisher and dealer, he had "abdicated" on the mistaken supposition that he had accumulated a competence. This premature retirement and his mistaken calculation that he should come into a fortune through his second marriage had reduced him to what he himself describes as the ignoble life of a scribbler. His mind was beginning to fail. Even when judged by his own low standard, his later religious works are of minor importance, most of them the pathetic efforts of a defeated man to regain his lost position. *The Hazard of a Death-Bed-Repentance* (1708) is an attack on a funeral sermon preached by Dr. Kennet in honor of the Duke of Devonshire, a titled sinner notorious for his "adulterous life." To swell the size of the pamphlet to salable proportions, the author added the dying utterances of Rochester and some other distinguished rakehells and then attempted to resolve "that nice question," one of perennial interest to him, "How far a Death-bed-Repentance is possible to be sincere?" There is much religious material also in *Athenianism* (1710), the last voluminous production "writ with his own Hand." This is described on the title-page as "an *Entire Collection of all his Writings,* both in Manuscript, and such as were formerly Printed." The announcement is correct only in saying that most of the material had appeared before.

Upon this Moment depends Eternity: or; Mr. John Dunton's *Serious Thoughts upon the Present and Future State, in a Fit of Sickness that was judg'd Mortal* (1720?) contains a suggestion of the projector in his better days. This was to have been another thesaurus. Part I is described in the title as "A New Directory for Holy Living and Dying." Part II, "The Sick-Man's Passing Bell," promises: (1) *"God be Merciful to me a Sinner:* Or, *Dunton* at Confession, in which he discovers the Secret Sins of his whole Life"; (2) *"Dunton's Legacy to his Native Country:* Or, A dying farewell"; (3) *"A Living Man following his own Corpse to the Grave:* Or, *Dunton* Represented as Dead and Buried, in *an Essay upon his own Funeral* — To which is added (for the *oddness* and *singularity* of it) A Copy of his *last Will* and *Testament* — His living *Elegy* writ with his own Hand — And the *Epitaph* designed for his Tombstone, in the *New Burying Place*"; (4) "The Real Period of Dunton's Life." Only a small part of this huge threat was executed, only enough in fact to afford the writer a slim apology for addressing an appeal to George I for patronage. This is the practical and melancholy purpose also of *Mr. John Dunton's Dying Groans from the Fleet Prison: Or The National Complaint* (1723?). In *An Essay on Death-Bed-Charity* (1728) he returns to his favorite topic. When Thomas Guy, the wealthy bookseller, bequeathed money for the founding of Guy's Hospital, tender consciences had scruples about the acceptance of the gift because of the testator's well-known failings of character. Dunton seized upon this and the similar case of Francis Bancroft to bring into question again all eleventh-hour repentance. The real purpose of this pamphlet, and also that of 1708, was to expose the sinful conduct of Mrs. Jane Nichols, who had omitted her son-in-law John Dunton from her will and left most of her estate to charity.

When the "great change" so frequently anticipated occurred in 1732, Dunton had lived long enough to see some very important developments in English literature, and he might reasonably have claimed at least a humble share of credit. Out of the rude embryo of the *Mercury* the periodical essay had come to full perfection between 1709 and 1714. As a specialist on death he had seen his judgment of public taste thoroughly vindicated in the success of more prosperous books than any of his own, but no less gloomy or dull. In this respect, as in others, he paved the way for the more fortunate. About the time he was producing *A Mourning-Ring*, his friend John Shower, the clergyman, brought out *The Mourner's Companion* (1692), and the next year appeared Thomas Doolittle's *The Mourner's Directory* (1693), both of which he must have regarded as rivals in his own special domain. A much more dangerous enemy had appeared three years earlier, William Sherlock's *A Practical Discourse concerning Death* (1689). Eventually this rose above all opposition and became the great classic on death for readers of the eighteenth century. By 1751 it had attained its twenty-seventh edition. The only serious contestant was Charles Drelincourt's book, translated from French into English by D'Assigny as *The Christian's Defence against the Fear of Death*. Though translated as far back as 1675, it seems not to have been widely known until much later. A fourth edition was issued in 1701, a seventeenth in 1751. The publishers of this work managed to secure second place for it partly by exploiting Dunton's idea of printing books to be used as funeral gifts, as will be seen by examining any edition after the ninth (1719). Drelincourt had the advantage also, it may be added, of Daniel Defoe's skill as an advertiser; most of the eighteenth-century editions were provided with Defoe's *The Apparition of Mrs. Veal*, which had been written to "recommend the perusal" of this book.*

* John Norris's *An Effectual Remedy against the Fear of Death* (1733) is in itself a work of some consequence, but the author makes a point of recommending the greater work of Drelincourt (p. 48).

There can be no question that as a dispenser of religious gloom Dunton had gauged his public well. He also lived long enough to see the morbid interest in death fully reassert itself in polite literature. With the publication of Parnell's *Night Piece on Death* (1722) the graveyard school of poetry had definitely begun. That most of Dunton's contribution was stolen is true; but as a compiler and publisher he had played a prominent part. It should be charitably remembered also that writers of pious books before his time and later had a very flexible code of morality. Thomas Jordan had stolen every line of verse in his *Death Dissected* (1650). One of the ghastliest books of piety in Dunton's time was a forgery entitled *The Visions of John Bunyan, Being his Last Remains, Giving an Account of the Glories of Heaven, and the Terrors of Hell, and of the World to Come. Recommended by him as necessary to be had in all Families* (1725).* Richard Steele did not escape the charge of having taken altogether too much of his *Ladies' Library* (1714) from Jeremy Taylor's *Holy Living* and *Holy Dying*,† and Young deliberately appropriated from Farquhar the very pathetic incident of Narcissa's burial in *Night Thoughts*.[24] Dunton merely outdid the dishonest zeal of others in the cause of religion.

---

* A reissue of *The World to Come* (1711). The example of exploiting Bunyan's name had been set in a forgery called *Meditations on the Several Ages of Man's Life: Representing the Vanity of it, from his Cradle to his Grave. Adorn'd with proper Emblems* (1701).

† See *Mr. Steele Detected: Or, the poor and oppressed Orphan's Letters . . . Complaining of the great injustice done . . . by the Ladies' Library . . . 1714.* (By R. Meredith.)

~~~ V ~~~

# The English Malady

No CHARACTERISTIC of English poetry in the mid-eighteenth century is more familiar to students of the period than the perpetual reference to melancholy. Though present in some degree in all periods of English literature, even from the time of the Anglo-Saxons, this strain had all but disappeared from polite literature after the Restoration; but now, in spite of the strenuous protests of Akenside and the other Shaftesburian optimists, it again came into fashion and indeed attained a greater vogue than it had ever had before. Whatever one's opinion of the intrinsic merit of this versified melancholy or of its genuineness as an expression of personal feeling, there can be no dispute over the quantity. Statistically, this deserves to be called the Age of Melancholy.

Some historians dismiss the entire phenomenon as nothing more than a literary fad and therefore of no significance whatever as an index of contemporary psychology. In opposition to this opinion no one will contend that the individual poet's state of mind can always be inferred from the mood expressed in his verse. Matthew Prior warns that no poet can be compelled to swear to the truth of a song. It is a well-known fact that some of the most amusing literature in the world was produced by writers in a state of mental depression, and this paradox is exemplified by the work of several of the Augustan wits of the eighteenth century, notably Prior and Swift. There is no reason to doubt that the converse is true. Presumably melancholy was sometimes affected by poets and poetasters who wished to be in fashion, once the fashion had been established. On the other hand, it would be unsafe to conclude that all of these poets were merely posturing and had entered into a conspiracy to deceive the public. Moreover, if such an assumption were possible, there would still remain the necessity of explaining why their melancholy poems were read with avidity unless they struck a sympathetic chord in the minds of their readers. Except in the case of a coterie literature, no cult can flourish if it is not rooted in popular experience. The "literature of woe" is a social as well as a literary phenomenon. When it is placed in its original setting, it will be recognized as one of several manifestations of an indigenous mood.

Either melancholy was so common as to constitute a distinctive trait of the inhabitants of the British Isles, particularly of the English, or no reliance can be placed on the testimony of foreigners or of the natives themselves. It is remarked upon in all the letters and travel-books written by Continental visitors and also the letters and diaries of Englishmen and their essays and various other publications. If the evil was exaggerated, as almost certainly it was, it was not imaginary; it posed a problem that was thought to affect the whole people and therefore engaged the efforts of all classes of public-spirited thinkers. Necessarily, the main responsibility fell upon physicians. Since the time of Henry VIII there had been a steadily increasing volume of medical literature dealing with a disease known to the English as it had been to the Greeks and the Romans as melancholy. Meanwhile, it had acquired one new name after another – "the spleen," vapors, hysteric fits, the hyp – until finally, because of its extraordinary prevalence in England, it was often referred to in the eighteenth century as the English malady.

When Dr. John Purcell brought out *A Treatise of Vapours and Hysteric Fits* (1702), the year of Queen Anne's accession, he was convinced that more of his countrymen were then afflicted with "vapours, otherwise called hysteric fits, or fits of the mother" than with any other disease whatsoever. The Dutch physician and philosopher Dr. Bernard Mandeville, author of *A Treatise of the Hypochondriack and Hysterick Passions, Vulgarly call'd the Hypo in Men and Vapours in Women* (1711), had decided to cast his lot in England because he had discovered during a visit that London was an ideal location for a specialist in nervous affections. In a treatise *Of the Spleen* (1723) Dr. William Stukeley repeated the opinion expressed by Dr. Sydenham of the Restoration, that the hysteric malady constituted fully one half of all the chronic diseases in England. Likewise Sir Richard Blackmore testified to the importance of his *Treatise of the Spleen and Vapours: Or Hypochondriacal and Hysterical Affections* (1725) by solemnly asserting that England was then notorious, not only for consumption, as it long had been, but also for "the spleen," which had gained "such universal and tyrannical dominion over both sexes" as it had established in no other country. The best known of the special studies is *The English Malady* (1733), written by Dr. George Cheyne, a Scot who came to London in 1702. "The title I have chosen for this treatise," Dr. Cheyne explains, "is a reproach universally thrown on this island by foreigners, and all our neighbours on the Continent, by whom spleen, vapours, and lowness of spirits are in derision called the English Malady."

It may be well to say in advance that these and the other specialists to be considered in this study fell short of explaining the nervous and mental disorders they were called upon to treat. They contributed so little to the advancement of scientific knowledge that most of their treatises are completely ignored in the histories of British medicine; what is more difficult to understand, there is seldom a mention even of the disease itself. As would be expected, their ideas go back in origin to the classical doctrine of the four humors in man's body, though only remnants of the old system now remained and these were rapidly disappearing. A minute study of the physiological theories they held and the controversies over them would now be of interest only to those specializing in the history of neurology and psychiatry and for the present purpose is not necessary. The intention is to make use of only such phases of medical opinion as, taken in conjunction with other sources of information, will help toward a better understanding of why the English were thought to be the most melancholy people in the world and why their melancholy poetry was considered a normal expression of the national temperament.

I

The melancholy propensity of the English had long been a source of wonder, real or feigned, to foreign visitors. The picture was drawn in very dark colors by Béat L. Muralt, a Swiss traveler, in his *Lettres sur les Anglois et les François et sur les voiages*, written in the latter part of the seventeenth century, but first published in 1726 and immediately translated as *Letters Describing the Character and Customs of the English and French Nations*. Here the gloominess of the Anglo-Saxon is emphasized by contrast with the *gaieté du coeur* of the Gallic temperament. Some of Muralt's observations were challenged in *Apologie du caractère des Anglois et des François* (1726), but the authors, Desfontaines and Brumoy, found no fault with his notes on English melancholy. Before his letters had appeared, much of the same ground had been covered in George Louis Le Sage's *Remarques sur l'état d'Angleterre* (1715), a record of the impressions the Frenchman had formed during a visit in 1713 and 1714. What most impressed these outsiders was that no satisfactory explanation had ever been offered for this national characteristic; English melancholy, though often explained, was still inexplicable. "Surely," Le Sage is said to have remarked during his visit, "the people of England are the most unhappy people on the face of the earth — with liberty, property and three meals a day." [1] When Montesquieu came over with Lord Chesterfield in the autumn of 1729, he made the usual notations on English gloominess, but was so enthusiastic in his praise of the intelligence of the people and their genius for statesmanship that his less favorable opinions were easily overlooked. He was said to have declared during his visit that there were "no men of true sense born any where but in England," [2] and later John Bull was highly pleased with himself as he appeared in *L'Esprit des lois* (1748) and elsewhere in the French philosopher's publications.[3]

None of the French writers did more to spread an ill report of the English among Continental readers than the Abbé Prévost. On different occasions Prévost spent about three years and a half in England, and was living there when he launched at Paris the *Pour et Contre* (1733–1740). It is difficult now to imagine how he could have filled the columns of this periodical during the seven years of its existence without the lugubrious habits of the British to fall back on when he was pressed for copy. He began to tap this reservoir of sensational anecdote at once and returned to it with a frequency somewhat tiresome to readers of today, though agreeable no doubt to his immediate public. The probability is that many other French readers were attracted to the *Pour et Contre*, as President Bouhier said he was, chiefly by its amusing exposé of "les extravagances angloises." [4] Simultaneously Prévost was embodying his conception of the somber temperament of the English in his novel *Clèveland* (1732–1739). The hero of this story, an Englishman of severe and upright principles but too prone to introspection and *idolâtre de sa tristesse*, is now recognized as an early draft of Lord Édouard Bomston in Rousseau's *La Nouvelle Héloïse* (1760).[5]

The most circumstantial criticism is contained in letters written by the Abbé Le Blanc during a residence in England from 1737 to 1744 and first published in 1745.[6] Most foreigners confined their observations to the upper classes; the abbé's wider knowledge enabled him to ascertain that the country boors were cast in the same funereal mold as their superiors. After commenting upon the greater comforts possessed by the English farmer as compared with the French peasant, he adds: "However, in the midst of this plenty, we easily perceive that the farmer is not so gay here, as in France; so that he may perhaps be richer, without being happier. The English of all ranks have that melancholy air, which makes part of their national character. The farmers here, shew very little mirth, even in their drunkenness; whereas in France, the farmers in several provinces drink nothing but water, and yet are as gay as possible." [7] The fault was more conspicuous in the upper classes, the natural tendency being aggravated in them by their luxury and idleness. Englishmen, he finds, are not given to laughter, and "there is a set of men in England who never laugh at all, and those are the presbyterians: they make laughing to be the eighth mortal sin. According to them, a woman who laughs commits as great a fault, as a woman would among us, in swerving from innocence and modesty." Even when the English do laugh, they seem not to be happy. "When I see an Englishman laugh, I fancy I see him hunting after joy, rather than having caught it; and this is more particularly remarkable in their women, whose temper is inclined to melancholy." [8] He admits in this letter that he has been nettled by Addison's sneer at the French as a comical nation, and that he is repaying the Spectator's insult in kind. Logic seemed to be on his side. "This cheerfulness, which is characteristic of our nation, in the eye of an Englishman passes almost for folly; but is their gloominess a greater mark of wisdom? And folly against folly, is not the most cheerful sort the best? At least if our gaiety makes them sad, they ought not to find it strange if their seriousness makes us laugh."

He could not comprehend why the English lacked a word to convey the sense of the French *ennui*. "They better express the *taedium vitae, l'ennui de la vie*, by the desperate resolution they take, when tired of life, than by any term in their language." Why had a people who had borrowed from the French so many words without any necessity for them failed to appropriate *ennui*, "which so well expresses a thing they feel every moment"? Instead, they employ those "feeble substitutes" *spleen* and *vapours*, by which they really mean "nothing else but *ennui* carried to its highest pitch, and become a dangerous and sometimes a mortal disease." [9] The abbé really answers his question by his definition: the Englishman's "spleen" (or vapors) was, potentially at least, something more than the Frenchman's *ennui*. The Duchess of Beaufort asserted that the French language was incapable of expressing fully in a single word what the English meant by *vapours*.[10] It is to be noted, too, in this connection that the word *spleen* was adopted into the French language, in 1798, and defined by the Academy as "ennui de toutes choses, maladie hypochondriaque propre aux Anglais." [11] Whether the terms were or were not quite appropriate, the English read into *spleen* and *vapours* all the *ennui de toutes choses* for which the French themselves afterward invented a new designation, *mal de siècle* — what the Germans called *Weltschmerz*.

A Frenchman's opinion of an Englishman in the eighteenth century is not worth much without confirmation, but most of the criticism made by foreign commentators might have been extracted, as some of it was, from the writings of the English themselves. If John Bull had ever been blind to his own weaknesses, the day of such ignorance had passed, and though he might still chafe under the raillery of the French, he seems to have derived a morbid pleasure from contemplating and publishing his own unhappy destiny. Steele was convinced that the "innate sullenness or stubbornness of complexion" peculiar to the national temperament was hardly to be conquered by any of his countrymen (*Tatler* No. 213). Addison speaks of melancholy as "a kind of demon that haunts the island" (*Spectator* No. 387). In one of the late numbers of the *Spectator* (558) he represents the miseries of mankind in a typical Addisonian allegory. The story runs that Jupiter issued a proclamation requiring mankind to bring all their griefs and calamities and throw them into a common heap. Under the guidance of Fancy, clothed in a flaming robe "embroidered with several figures of fiends and spectres, that discovered themselves in a thousand chimerical shapes" (signifying that all human distress is magnified by fancy), each one came obediently laden with his burden — poverty, disappointed love, old age, bodily deformities, disease, and so on. One of these packets the Spectator could not but note especially, for it "was a complication of all the diseases incident to human nature, and was in the hand of a great many fine people: This was called the Spleen."

Most of the serious essays on melancholy were composed by Addison, and his speculation on the subject led to theories of some importance to literature and literary criticism. In *Spectator*

No. 419, the last of the series of essays on the pleasures of the imagination, he observes proudly that the "gloominess and melancholy of temper" and the chimerical habits peculiar to the English have placed their poets above those of all other nations in the lively representation of fairies, demons, ghosts, and other objects that raise "a pleasing horror in the mind of the reader."

One reason for the high valuation he placed upon this accomplishment comes out in his very serious study of what method he could best use to counteract the melancholy tendency of his readers. Though at first a believer in the efficacy of humorous diversion, he later wavered. First, there was the question of moral propriety; in *Spectator* No. 47 he categorically adopts the Hobbesian view that laughter is an expression of egotistic superiority and therefore morally reprehensible. Second, he raises the question, in *Spectator* No. 163, whether as a matter of fact momentary diversion is a specific for mental depression, whether on the contrary the mind does not immediately thereafter sink to a lower depth of gloominess than before – an opinion he might have found in any one of several medical books. He was inclined to think that melancholy is more likely to be cured by indulging the mood; for while contemplating the greater miseries of others a man forgets his own and thus obtains the needed mental catharsis. St.-Évremond to the contrary, those of a gloomy temperament would probably profit more from Seneca and Plutarch than from Cervantes. To this conflict between the allopathic and the homeopathic treatment he returns over and over, and though he never arrives at a definite conclusion, the weight of argument consistently favors *Il Penseroso* over *L'Allegro*.* Besides, of this kind of writing the periodical essays offered numerous specimens, ranging in degree of melancholy from Addison's crepuscular musings among the tombs in Westminster Abbey (*Spectator* No. 26) through Steele's moving account of his father's death (*Tatler* No. 181) to Parnell's doleful allegory of grief (*Spectator* No. 501). Thus by precept and example Addison and Steele lent the weight of their authority to the literature of melancholy that

* See, e.g., *Spectator* Nos. 179, 249, 518, 519.

was already beginning to develop and was to reach a climax by the mid-century.

After the Restoration the people of England had been allowed to forget temporarily that they were more lugubrious than others, but by the beginning of the eighteenth century the traditional reputation was well on its way to complete recovery. The opinions expressed by Addison and Steele were hardly more than symptomatic. One of their contemporaries, Dr. William King, an Anglican clergyman, was so appalled by the vast number of "melancholy heads" in the British dominions that he wondered if the leaders of the Reformation should not have spared a few of the old monastic establishments so that men of severe morals and a gloomy cast of mind might have found a retreat from the world.[12] The German traveler Archenholz remarked that the extraordinary melancholy of English women made those of the Roman Catholic faith more prone to take the veil than women of any other country.[13] Horace Walpole held, on the contrary, that his countrymen were the least able of mankind to endure solitude. We are so capricious, he declares, that "we must rub off our roughnesses against one another."[14]

Critics might disagree concerning the prophylactic to be applied, but not on the need of one. In a moment of petulance Goldsmith accused the French of copying one another in a conspiracy to traduce the character of the English.[15] Whether true or not, the indictment came awkwardly from the pen of a writer who reprinted one of the Abbé Le Blanc's severest letters in the seventh number of the *Bee* (1759) and — to mention only major offenses — created the Man in Black.* If the melancholy of the national temperament was overstated, the English could blame themselves, for it is the continuous theme in all types of popular literature from the beginning to the end of the century. When Boswell enrolled as a periodical essayist in 1777, he made the following bid for popular support: "I flatter myself that *The Hypo-*

---

* *The Citizen of the World* (1762). Note especially Letter xc. Compare *The Life of Beau Nash* (1762), *passim*, and *The Vicar of Wakefield* (1766), Ch. 19.

*chondriack* may be agreeably received as a periodical essayist in England, where the malady known by the denomination of melancholy, hypochondria, spleen, or vapours has been long supposed to be universal." *

## II

In the medical vocabulary melancholy was something more than a mere mood; it was a disease, a "compound mixed malady of body and mind" that affected the imagination, often *sine causa manifesta*. Theoretically, it included only pathologic conditions short of downright madness, but the boundaries were so loosely drawn that any attempt at categorical definition would be futile. In practice it represented the little that the members of the medical profession knew about nervous and mental disorders and the much more that they did not know. Though dealing with a disease supposedly of nervous origin, they made slight if any use of the anatomical study of the brain and nerves by Dr. Willis of the Restoration. Dr. James Adair, writing late in the eighteenth century, declared, humorously, that people of fashion did not know they had nerves before the publication of Dr. Whytt's *Observations on the Nature, Cause, and Cure of those Disorders commonly called Nervous, Hypochondriac, or Hysteric* (1764).[16]

The application of numerous names to a single disease is somewhat confusing to a reader of today but is easily explained. Each of them is an allusion to some phase of the humoral pathology inherited from classical medicine, and collectively they preserve a record of the most important theories that had been proposed since the time of Galen. The variety of nomenclature had its uses: besides providing the doctor with much learned verbiage, it enabled him to make a number of necessary distinctions.

It was essential, first, in medicine as in social life to observe the proprieties by drawing a line between the upper and the lower classes. Persons of condition were supposed to be different from the common run even in their ailments. The subjects of

---

* Essay 1. Much valuable information is contained in the Introduction to Margery Bailey's edition of *The Hypochondriack* (2 vols.; 1928).

Queen Elizabeth had been content with the name used by the Greeks, melancholy, meaning black choler, the noxious humor responsible for the disease. In the reign of James I letter-writers and diarists began referring to "a new disease called the spleen," and this soon became the vogue, although the term was not adopted by medical writers until late in the seventeenth century. In reality, the new disease was new in name only, except for its social connotation; "the spleen" — alluding to the belief that the "all-mysterious spleen," as Galen calls it, was designed to regulate the supply of black choler — was nothing more than aristocratic melancholy. George Farquhar makes use of this invidious distinction in *The Beaux' Stratagem* (1707) when Archer, disguised as a valet, momentarily forgets his role and remarks that his physician has advised him to drink tea "for a remedy against the spleen." "I had thought," says Mrs. Sullen, "that distemper had been only proper to people of quality" (III.iii). Although presumably people of quality did not differ physiologically from their inferiors, there was factual ground for the belief that lords and ladies, accustomed to luxurious living and idleness, some of them afflicted with hereditary disorders, were more liable to what we call neuroses and psychoses than people in the lower ranks.

Second, in medicine as elsewhere there was need of distinguishing between the strong and the weak sex. Because of more delicate nerves, women were more subject to emotional instability than men were, especially women of the upper classes. With the exception of Dr. John Radcliffe, who made light of Princess Anne's fits of "the spleen" and for his rudeness was excused from further attendance on her royal highness,[17] the members of the profession were unanimously of Dr. Purcell's opinion that the disease was very real and that it had a peculiar "gusto for the tender sex." Dr. Mandeville and indeed most of the other high-priced specialists owed their reputation and livelihood largely to ladies of quality. Women were responsible, too, for most of the additional names used for nervous affections. Besides often being "in the spleen," they were subject to nervous paroxysms called hysteric fits, or "fits of the mother." Etymologically, hysteria (ὑστέρα,

womb) was an affliction peculiar to the female and was so regarded by Galen and also by his English disciples until the great
Dr. Sydenham decided that so-called hysteric fits were in reality
only a special manifestation of the *passio splenica.*[18] The word
*hysteria* continued in use, but now only as another name for
melancholy; for a time it was still applied exclusively to women,
but the distinction gradually faded, though even yet hysteria
carries a suggestion of effeminacy. The vapors came into fashion
at the court of William and Mary, in imitation of *les vapeurs* in
France. The appropriateness of this term is manifest: according
to Greek humoral pathology, melancholy occurs when atrabilious
vapors engendered in the hypochondrium (literally, the portion
of the body beneath the breast-bone) ascend through the hollow
nerves, cloud the clear white animal spirits, or nervous juice, and
thus cause the brain to be deceived with imaginary fears and
other illusions. At first this appellation, too, was used with reference only to women, but quite arbitrarily, and the distinction
failed to hold.

The desire for further differentiation and classification offered
every writer an ideal opportunity to display his ingenuity. Dr.
Nicholas Robinson, physician to Christ's Hospital, undertook to
correct many popular misconceptions with *A New System of
the Spleen, Vapours, and Hypochondriack Melancholy* (1729).
He classified the various degrees of mental derangement by means
of a scale of chronicity: (1) "the spleen," or vapors, is the initial
stage; (2) hypochondriac melancholy is "the spleen improv'd on
the constitution, through longer continuance of the disease"; (3)
melancholy (our melancholia) is a still more confirmed stage;
(4) madness is the tragic climax. If the review in the *Grub-Street
Journal* of February 26, 1730, is typical of critical opinion, Dr.
Robinson's graduated scale was regarded as an effort of the doctor's to explain more than he understood. An article entitled "Of
the Hyp," first published in the *Universal Spectator* of November 1732 and reprinted in the *Gentleman's Magazine* of that
month, ridicules some of the delicious absurdities resulting from
such efforts. The writer had studied physic in his younger days

and still prescribed occasionally for his neighbors in Northumberland, where doctors were scarce. "When I first dabbled in this art," he writes, "the old distemper call'd *Melancholy* was exchang'd for *Vapours*, and afterwards for the *Hypp*, and at last took up the now current appellation of the *Spleen*, which it still retains, tho' a learned doctor of the west, in a little tract he hath written, divides the *Spleen* and *Vapours*, not only into the *Hypp*, the *Hyppos*, and the *Hyppocons*; but subdivides these divisions into the *Markambles*, the *Moonpalls*, the *Strong-Fiacs*, and the *Hockogrokles*." [19]

The doctors were under the constant necessity of opposing the suspicion that they were making a great ado over a disease that did not exist. Sir Richard Blackmore steps aside from matters of cosmic magnitude in *Creation* (1712) long enough to rebuke the skeptics:

> The spleen with sullen vapours clouds the brain,
> And binds the spirits in its heavy chain,
> Howe'er the cause fantastick may appear,
> Th' effect is real and the pain sincere. [20]

More than forty years later Dr. John Shebbeare laments that this disease, "though perhaps the most affecting to the human mind, is that which draws the least compassion from our friends"; true, he adds, it seldom is the cause of death, but the greatest calamity is that the sufferer cannot die. [21] This complaint may well be symptomatic, as it probably is in Cowper's statement:

> This of all maladies that man infest,
> Claims most compassion, and receives the least. [22]

In spite of the fine sentiments in literature, there is a conspicuous vein of brutality running through the entire century. To many the vagaries of insanity were irresistibly amusing. As long as Londoners made Sunday excursions to Bedlam to divert themselves with the antics of the inmates a sympathetic understanding of the minor eccentricities of "the spleen" could hardly be expected. Besides, there was some ground for the suspicion that *la maladie à la mode* was *la maladie imaginaire*, often nothing more than a snobbish affectation, especially among ladies of quality. Queen Anne's multiple afflictions were so well known that after she came to the throne vapors were almost *de rigueur* for women of the aristocracy, and the wives and daughters of the citizens were quick to copy the example of their betters. Good health was a sign of vulgarity. So far from concealing their infirmities, both men and women advertised that they were "in the spleen" by reeking of asafetida.

Women were the chief impostors and came in for the brunt of satire. The *Humourist* (1720), after commenting on the fact that the ladies have claimed an elder brother's share of "the spleen," adds that "This harpy has a nice stomach, and loves to prey upon female flesh," sometimes killing with its company, but that ladies bear the burden because it is the mode and as necessary as a hooped petticoat, a monkey, and a pretty fellow.[23] It is often hinted that wives find their vapors an excellent device for wheedling their husbands. The female valetudinarian, surrounded by doctors and phials, boring all listeners with the recital of her imaginary ailments, was a stock figure on the comic stage. Of course no one was so naive as to take the word of a satirist literally, it being understood that he was permitted a degree of humorous exaggeration. Vaporish females themselves entered into the fun with others; indeed, as usually happens, satire of the kind flourished largely upon the patronage of those it attacked. Such ridicule does, however, point to a misunderstanding that could be cruel, even tragic. Few even of the medical faculty fully realized that the "misery habit," as William James calls it, may easily develop into a pathologic state of mind. The probability is that many of the snobbish females suspected of hypocrisy and malingering were mentally ill and in need of psychiatric treatment.

On the other hand, most neurotics suffered more from too much attention than from too little. Through ignorance of the most elementary psychology, they pursued the one course certain to aggravate their nervous ills. They made themselves melancholy by trying to avoid melancholy. The ancient tradition that every man should be his own doctor still survived. If the case was serious, the doctor would be called in, but often not before the patient had doctored himself into a parlous state of body and mind. The reason for the steady stream of treatises on nervous and mental diseases is that they were designed for family use. The number of such books is astonishing. Besides those of a general character, some were written exclusively for women, such as Dr. Ball's *The Female Physician. Or Every Woman her Own Doctress* (1770), the opening chapter of which is entitled "Nervous or Hysteric Diseases." What the dispirited introverts needed most no doubt was to get away from themselves. Instead, they spent their time checking their pulse and temperature and mulling over their favorite medical books — upon advice of counsel too.

From Burton's *The Anatomy of Melancholy* (1621), a book that had long since been discarded and forgotten, students of abnormal psychology might have learned that people predisposed to melancholy sometimes contract the disease by studying the symptoms.[24] Dr. Johnson, who learned much from Burton and also from experience, gave Boswell an excellent lecture on mental hygiene. "You are always complaining of melancholy," he says, "and I conclude from these complaints that you are fond of it." He then offers this advice: ". . . make it an invariable and obligatory law to yourself, never to mention your own mental diseases; if you are never to speak of them, you will think on them but little, and if you think little of them, they will molest you rarely." [25] This was an extraordinary view. So little thought was given to the force of mental suggestion and autohypnosis by most of the physicians of the eighteenth century that the danger involved in self-study and self-medication seems now to have been understood better by the satirists than by their medical advisers. Theoretically, it was the duty of every Briton to be on guard against the insidious approach of the melancholic distemper, watching for the first signs of its presence and ready to man the defenses. In spite of the wearisome repetition of this cliché, the anonymous author of *A Treatise on the Dismal Effects of Low-Spiritedness* (1750) feared that his readers, still not sufficiently alive to their peril, were relaxing their vigilance at the very moment when this distemper was "almost peculiar to, and epidemical, in this kingdom."

Those who heeded this counsel — and evidently many did — were inviting disaster. Their little learning was a dangerous thing. They learned just enough to keep themselves in a state of perpetual worry and frustration and therefore in danger of pathophobia. If the specialists themselves could not understand this nondescript disease, what was to be expected of the novice? Imagine, for example, the housewife's confusion of mind when she read the list of symptoms enumerated in Dr. Stukeley's *Of the Spleen* (1723): "When the head is attack'd, comas, epilepsy, apoplexy, or the numbness of a part ensues, or talkativeness, tremors, spasms, head-ach; when the heart, palpitation, swooning, anxiety; when the breast, sighing, short-breath, cough; when the diaphragm, laughing; when the belly (and more frequently, being the seat of the morbid minera) rugitis, cardalgia, colic, iliac passion, etc." (p. 70). Here she could hardly fail to discover one or more of her own symptoms. If she referred her diagnostic problem to *The Ancient Physician's Legacy* (1732), by Dr. Thomas Dover, inventor of Dover's Powders, she learned that the melancholic distemper simulates all the maladies incident to man, affecting the head, eyes, heart, lungs, gullet, intestines, kidneys, and in truth all other parts of the body.

And the confusion thickened with the passing of time. Any disease not otherwise explainable was referred to this convenient *omnium gatherum*. For instance, although melancholy was often said to be a disease without a fever, during an epidemic of intermittent fever the terms "fever on the spirits" and "the little fever or febricula" came into general use as additional synonyms for melancholy and indeed almost drove out the old familiar names.*

---

* This false identification was made by Dr. John Woodward in *The State of Physic* (1718), p. 193, and though attacked by Sir Richard Blackmore in *A Discourse upon the Plague* (1721), p. 17, and by Dr. Cockburn in *The Danger of Improving Physick* (1730), p. 27, was widely adopted by the profession. Witness, for example, Sir Richard Manningham's *The Nature, Causes, and Cure of the Febricula*, etc. (1746). The dangers of this blunder are commented upon in Dr. Charles Creighton's *History of Epidemics*, II, 67ff.

The mental effects were as varied as the somatic causes. The briefest enumeration to be found in a contemporary medical treatise is from Dr. John Arbuthnot, physician to Queen Anne. The principal signs of this "disease more terrible than death" he found to be: "Obstinate watchfulness, or short sleeps, troublesome and terrible dreams, great solicitude and anxiety of mind, with sighing, sudden fits of anger without any occasion given, love of solitude, obstinacy in defending trifling opinions, and contempt of such as are about them, suppression of usual evacuations, as menses in women and hemorrhoids in men; great heat, eyes hollow and fix'd, immoderate laughter or crying without occasion; too great loquacity, and too great taciturnity, by fits; great attention to one object, all these symptoms without a fever." [26]

Of the mental effects no physician had a better understanding than Dr. John Armstrong, who was himself a chronic hypochondriac and, like Burton, learned much merely by melancholizing. His opinions were all the more impressive because they were recorded in verse. In the fifth essay of the *Hypochondriack* Boswell quotes, among several extracts indicating that he was well read in his subject, the following passage from *The Art of Preserving Health* (1744) to show that Dr. Armstrong knew whereof he spoke:

> — the dim-ey'd fiend,
> Sour Melancholy, night and day provokes
> Her own eternal wound. The sun grows pale;
> A mournful visionary light o'erspreads
> The cheerful face of nature: earth becomes
> A dreary desart, and heaven frowns above.
> Then various shapes of curst illusion rise:
> Whate'er the wretched fears, creating fear
> Forms out of nothing; and with monsters teems
> Unknown in hell. The prostrate soul beneath
> A load of huge imagination heaves;
> And all the horrors that the guilty feel,
> With anxious flutterings wake the guiltless breast.
> (IV.92–104)

As characterized by James Thomson in *The Castle of Indolence* (1748), the poet-physician was a shy and silent man:

Oft, stung by spleen, at once away he broke,
To groves of pine, and broad o'ershadowing oak;
There, inly thrilled, he wandered all alone,
And on himself his pensive fury wroke,
Ne ever uttered word, save when first shone
The glittering star of eve — "Thank heaven! the day is done."

(I.lx)

To this same poem Armstrong himself contributed a description of "a moping mystery" —

Mother of Spleen, in robes of various dye,
Who vexed was full oft with ugly fit;
And some her frantic deemed, and some her deemed a wit.

A lady proud she was, of ancient blood,
Yet oft her fear her pride made crouchen low:
She felt, or fancied in her fluttering mood,
All the diseases which the spittles know,
And still new leeches and new drugs would try,
Her humour ever wavering to and fro:
For sometimes she would laugh, and sometimes cry,
Then sudden waxed wroth, and all she knew not why.

(I.lxxv, lxxvi)

Although the first suggestion of *melancholy* as used by physicians was a state of mental depression, something approaching our melancholia, the meaning of the term had long since overflowed the boundaries set by Hippocrates and Galen when they limited it to the mental passions sadness and fear. Potentially it covered a variety and contrariety of mood, ranging from utter despair to irrepressible gaiety. *Varium et mutabile.* For good reason it was called the Protean disease and the *je ne sais quoi.* To account for this fickleness, the neo-Galenists had developed an elaborate rationale by drawing a distinction between so-called natural and unnatural melancholy. The latter was said to arise from the adustion, or overheating, of the natural humors, the mental passion depending upon the humor or combination of humors overheated. With proper manipulation this ingenious hypothesis could be made to rationalize any type of delusional insanity. It explained the inferiority complex, megalomania, split personality, and other psychopathic phenomena that were still waiting to be named. For some reason not clear, this fiction had fallen into disuse after the Restoration and was now so generally neglected that Quincy's *Lexicon Physico-Medicum* (1719) defined *adustion* only to say that the theory was obsolete. Strangely enough, the phenomena themselves, though no longer scientifically accounted for, continued to be listed. On the whole, the word *melancholy* was apparently reverting to the original Greek meaning, the sense in which it is used today, but it should be remembered that the English were said to be the most melancholy of European people because they were not only the gloomiest, but also the most eccentric.

After the amateur had threaded his way through all this confusion to a diagnosis of his case, his tragedy was only beginning. If he doctored himself for trivial or imaginary ills, as he often did, they soon developed into substantial realities. And yet it is not certain that those who placed themselves in the hands of the family physician fared much better. A malady as polymorphous as "the spleen" offered an ideal opportunity for all the arts of quackery, and even the best of the specialists were working in the dark. Doctors of physic were, as they always had been, a favorite target for satire, and their blunders were probably exaggerated; yet it is hard to believe that the continuous stream of ridicule was entirely unmerited. Tom Brown, writing in 1700, called the medical practitioners "pensioners to death" and declared that more people "died of the doctor" than of any other disease.[27]

If Steele and Addison may be trusted, the medical men of their time, regulars as well as quacks, were with astonishingly few exceptions no better than blundering empirics preying upon the public.* Henry Fielding hounded the doctors from the beginning to the end of his career, in drama, essay, and prose fiction. The lightest of his charges is that almost every physician "hath his

* For their interest in medicine, see Fielding H. Garrison, "Medicine in the Tatler, Spectator and Guardian," *Bulletin of the Institute of Medicine*, The Johns Hopkins University, II (1934), 477–503. Typical attacks on quackery are contained in *Tatler* Nos. 240 and 241 and *Spectator* No. 195.

favourite disease to which he attributes all the victories over human nature. The gout, the rheumatism, the stone, the gravel, and the consumption, have all their several patrons in the faculty, and none more than nervous fever or the fever on the spirits." [28] Horace Walpole had as little faith in physicians as in divines, preferring to do his own quacking rather than die *secundum artem.** Lady Mary Wortley Montagu was of the same opinion. When Sir James Stewart's wife was suffering from screaming fits of hysteria, she urged him to have nothing to do with any living physician but to consult the writings of the English Hippocrates, Dr. Sydenham.[29] Some of the heaviest blows were delivered by literary men who were or had been members of the medical profession — Goldsmith, Smollett, and George Crabbe — each of whom may have been actuated by disappointed ambition.† Smollett was almost as persistent in his attacks as Fielding. He charged — how seriously, it is impossible to say — that neurotic women were systematically exploited by a syndicate composed of the doctor, the nurse, and the undertaker.[30]

This general distrust of the faculty explains why so many of the upper classes made a study of physic and also why few physicians could hold their clients. If the doctor, already on probation, did not work a speedy cure, the patient went to another and finally in desperation made the rounds of the quacks and nostrum-vendors. After Fielding had dosed himself almost a year on "the duke of Portland's medicine, as it is called" and was literally "dying of a complication of disorders," he staked his last hope on Ward's remedies and Bishop Berkeley's tar-water.[31] Concerning "the spleen" laymen were in general agreement that it was an incurable disease. If, as Mrs. Eliza Haywood complained, no two experts could agree even on the diagnosis, it was idle to expect relief from their prescriptions. After long observation and self-study she offered the readers of the *Female Spectator* (1744–

---

* For typical comments, see *Letters*, ed. Mrs. Paget Toynbee, VI, 131; VII, 37; IX, 366; XIII, 248. His opinion of French physicians (VI, 351) was equally contemptuous.

† Goldsmith's opinion is briefly summarized in *The Citizen of the World*, Letter xc (cf. lxviii); Crabbe's, in *The Library*.

1746) a *crede experto* opinion: this malady, whether real or imaginary, baffles the physicians "because the remedy is only in ourselves; and we are incapable of applying it after the disease has gathered strength." * The chronic hypochondriac had no desire to be cured; he made a luxury of his woes and would have been at a loss without them. Lady Winchilsea's *The Spleen. A Pindarick Ode* (1709), based partly at least on personal experience, so impressed Dr. Stukeley that he used it as an introduction to his treatise *Of the Spleen* (1723). Excellent as Ardelia's report on tortured nerves undoubtedly is, one of the best in its time and notably superior to Dr. Stukeley's, his choice was somewhat ironical, for here at the beginning of his book is a poem notifying readers in advance that they can expect no relief from medical science.

> In vain to chase thee ev'ry art we try,
>   In vain all remedies apply,
>   In vain the Indian leaf infuse,
>   Or the parch'd Eastern berry bruise;
> Some pass, in vain, those bounds, and nobler liquors use.
>   Now harmony, in vain, we bring,
>   Inspire the flute, and touch the string.
>   From harmony no help is had;
> Musick but soothes thee, if too sweetly sad,
> And if too light, but turns thee gayly mad.
>   Tho' the physician's greatest gains,
>   Altho' his growing wealth he sees
>   Daily increas'd by ladies' fees,
> Yet dost thou baffle all his studious pains.

Confidence had risen no higher a generation later when *The Plagues of the Spleen* was published in 1752. After describing the symptoms of the reigning malady at some length, the unknown poet concludes:

> In Heaven alone long life subsists,
> When, without potions from the Civil Lists,

* Ed. 1771, I, 279. For a slashing attack on the medical faculty, see her *Epistles for the Ladies* (1749–1750), Epistle lxi. Virtually the same charges are repeated by an anonymous physician in *The Cure of the Miliary Fever* (1751), pp. ix–xi.

Without great Cheney, Hardwicke, Bave or Lane,
Or old Hippocrates, the father of the train,
A great Sav'our, and Physician too,
Will spirits with eternal life renew.

The seriousness of public interest is best reflected in letters, diaries, and other private records not intended for publication. References to "the spleen" are to be found in almost any collection of letters, some of them as explicit as a doctor's report of his cases. Mrs. Delany points to a well-known symptom of hypochondria when she writes that her friend Mrs. Butler is really much better, "but she will not believe it." Then follows, "Oh! preserve us heaven from melancholy and its train of miseries!" A little later another of her friends was "far gone in the spleen." She herself succumbed at times to "vapours or hysteric fits" and "hysteric headache." Her dear friend the Duchess of Portland (Prior's "noble, lovely, little Peggy") "has been in such a way for two months past, such hysterics have seized her, that it has made her incapable of doing a thing." [32]

The most detailed information is supplied by the letters and household records kept by the family of the first Earl of Bristol. During the epidemic of fever in 1722 Lady Bristol wrote to her husband that she had had another fit of "fever upon the spirits" and was so weakened that she could hardly move or speak without drops or other stimulants prescribed by Dr. Freind. [33] Numerous references of the kind, together with items of expense, throw light on the conflicting theories of the doctors concerning the nervous afflictions of a noble family, the remedies they prescribed, and the failure of all of them. The evils of the family curse came to a climax in the eldest son, Lord John Hervey, remembered best perhaps as Lord Fanny, Sporus, that "mere white curd of ass's milk" and other abusive terms applied to him by Pope. For the benefit of his children he drew up, in 1731, "An Account of my Constitution and Illness," describing his colic, fainting spells, hysterical fits, and other hereditary ills which he said he could trace genealogically in his mother's family "through at least twenty yards of parchment." * A study of Lord Hervey's case would be instructive because, if for no other reason, it reveals why no definition of "the spleen" is possible and why, to quote from Dr. John Armstrong again, it was the "worst despair of physic."

### III

What disturbed the public most in connection with "Britannia's bitter bane" was that if the sufferer did not die from the effects of the disease itself he was liable to end his misery in self-destruction. Since the time of Galen mental pathologists had noted that necrophobia was a prominent symptom of melancholy but that many of its victims, unable to endure the suspense, rushed to meet what they feared most. Suicide was so prevalent in Britain, or was thought to be, that it constituted a national scandal. An article in *Mercurius Politicus* of June 1720 declares that more people kill themselves in this one country than in the rest of the entire world combined. Native and foreign critics agreed that no such wave of suicide had been known since the time of the Stoics. The chagrin expressed in Blair's *The Grave* (1743) is typical:

> Self-murder! — name it not: Our island's shame,
> That makes her the reproach of neighbouring states.

In the same year Young rebuked his countrymen in *The Complaint: Or, Night Thoughts*:

> O Britain, infamous for suicide!
> An island in thy manners! far disjoin'd
> From the whole world of rationals beside!
> In ambient waves plunge thy polluted head,
> Wash the dire stain nor shock the Continent.
> (V.442–446)

* Published with Lord Hervey's *Memoirs of the Reign of King George II*, ed. R. Sedgwick (1931), Appendix II. The editor adds a brief comment by Sir Henry Head, M.D., F.R.S., who conjectures that the colic was caused by gall-stones and that the seizures were epileptic.

Dr. Cheyne was speaking for the entire medical faculty when he expressed the hope that *The English Malady* might be of some use in halting the national mania.

An effort was made to lay this disgrace, with others, on the doorstep of the deists. A contributor to the *Universal Spectator* of August 1732, apparently in allusion to Bishop Berkeley's *Alciphron, or The Minute Philosopher* (1732), agrees with the divines and moralists in charging that the great increase in suicide is due to atheists, deists, and other "free thinkers" who, by denying a future life, have removed the only incentive to virtue.* Such heresies, however, are themselves an effect of "the spleen." But for this disease of the mind there never would have been any "free thinkers." The philosophy taught by Tindal, for example, was the immediate "inspiration of the spleen." [34] When the Prussian traveler Archenholz recorded the following observation, he was repeating a commonplace: "Deism is in a great degree the cause of suicide in England." He then adds that the English have "actually a form of prayer in which they beseech God to banish from the hearts of his servants such a frightful temptation." [35]

This sinister reputation of the deists was derived largely from the suicide of Charles Blount, who killed himself shortly after the publication of *The Oracles of Reason* (1693), a deistic treatise he had composed in collaboration with Charles Gildon and some other reprobates. Thereafter when a known deist destroyed himself, the theologians made the most of their opportunity to condemn all unorthodox thinking. The deists were no more prone to self-destruction than their opponents were, and they were not necessarily committed to a denial of the doctrine of future retribution. It is interesting to find that Charles Gildon, one of the few outspoken apologists for suicide, made a complete recantation in *The Deist's Manual* (1705). The orthodox were upon firmer ground when they argued that the will to resist the temptation had been weakened by the widespread influence of the Stoics

---

* The indictment is fully stated anonymously in *A Discourse upon Self-Murder . . . In a Letter to a Free-Thinker* (1732). See also the first letter in Young's *The Centaur Not Fabulous* (1754).

and other classical proponents of the practice. But this was not confined to "free thinkers." Even more sensational than the death of Blount was that of Thomas Creech, translator of Lucretius's *De Rerum Natura*, in 1700. In his own copy of the book he left a marginal note saying that as soon as he had completed his Commentary on this pagan poem he would take his own life,[36] and this he did by hanging himself. To the embarrassment of the moralists, however, Creech was not a deist; he was a respected clergyman of the Church of England.

Actually, the apology for suicide made less headway in England than in some of the Continental countries, partly perhaps because of the Englishman's intense fear of the thing itself. When the third edition of John Donne's *Biathanatos* came out in 1700, it was greeted by such a storm of protest that the venture was not repeated then — and has not been since. This was the fate also of *A Philosophical Discourse on Death* (1732), a defense of suicide written by one Passeran, an impoverished Italian nobleman who had taken refuge in London after he had been banished from his own country for immorality. In this instance pernicious influence was definitely established when in 1732 Richard Smith, a London bookbinder and prisoner for debt, shot his wife and hanged himself, leaving behind a note explaining that he had acted upon principles derived from the Italian philosopher. Bishop Berkeley at once pointed to this tragedy as proof that the charges he had brought against the "free thinkers" in *Alciphron* were well founded,* and for years Passeran was held up as a public enemy. Pope's protest (1738), written six years after the event, suggests that false philosophy was not the sole cause of the mania for self-destruction.

> If Blount dispatched himself, he played the man,
> And so may'st thou, illustrious Passeran!
> But shall a printer, weary of his life,

---

* *The Theory of Vision Vindicated* (1733), Sec. v. Compare the Rev. Mr. Bramston, *The Man of Taste* (1733). Smollett refers to the Smith tragedy in Bk. II, Ch. 5, of his *History of England* (1757) as "the most remarkable incident" of the year 1732.

Learn from their books, to hang himself and wife?
This, this, my friend, I cannot, must not bear;
This calls the Church to deprecate our sin,
And hurls the thunder of the laws on gin.
(*Epistle to the Satires*, Dial. I)

Otherwise, such moral comfort as prospective self-destroyers
had was provided by French philosophers. The apology for suicide drawn up by Montesquieu in the twenty-sixth of his *Lettres
persanes* (1721) – a book that reached a large English audience
in Ozell's translation (1722) – provoked so many attacks, including the anonymous English tract entitled *Queries concerning
Self-Murder Offered to a Gentleman in Distress* . . . (1741),
that the author added to the edition of 1754 a letter in refutation
of his argument. Here is to be found the germ of the better-
known debate Rousseau staged in Letters xciv and xcv of *La
Nouvelle Héloïse* (1760). How dangerous it was for a native
writer to question accepted opinion was demonstrated by the experience of David Hume. To the 1757 edition of his *Essays* he
added two heretical essays, on suicide and the immortality of the
soul; but after the book was ready for distribution, he decided
that the obnoxious material should be removed and instructed his
printer accordingly. Unfortunately for Hume, one copy escaped
correction, and the author's reputation, already dubious, was
irretrievably ruined by the hammer blows of Bishop Warburton.*

Even if philosophy lent encouragement to weaklings, the fact
remained that their weakness arose from an inherent defect of
character, some peculiarity of constitution that set the British
apart from their neighbors on the Continent. One singularity of
theirs was a source of amazement to all outsiders. Foreigners
could understand why a man should take his own life in a fit of
despondence; but Englishmen killed themselves for the most
trivial reasons, or none at all, dying by their own hands *en
cavalier* just as many of their compatriots mounted the execu-
tioner's scaffold with a jest on their lips. This nonchalance was

---

* For a full account, see *Essays Moral, Political and Literary*, ed. T. H.
Green and T. H. Grose (1889), I, 66ff. The suppressed essays were first
published in 1783 in conjunction with Rousseau's letters on suicide.

something Muralt could never comprehend. In his third letter
he repeats a well-known anecdote of a Frenchman who had lived
in London so long that he considered himself thoroughly angli-
cized; but after he had slashed his throat in attempted suicide
*à l'anglaise*, he lost his courage and pusillanimously cried out for
help — to the great amusement of his neighbors and, it proved,
too late to repair the damage. Truly, the Briton was *sui generis,*
as all foreigners soon discovered.

They begin by dwelling on the Englishman's native gloominess
and proceed to discuss his penchant for self-homicide, marveling
most at the strange motives that impel him to commit this ghastly
crime. Englishmen kill themselves, says Montesquieu, in the very
lap of fortune and happiness.[37] Baron de Poellnitz, after a visit in
1733, swells the chorus with the comment that it is a distinguishing mark of an Englishman "to be intrepid in the article of
death." [38] No doubt most of these tourists brought their opinions
with them. The suicidal habits of the barbarous islanders are exposed from all angles by Prévost in the *Pour et Contre.* They are
the theme also of Gresset's comedy *Sidnei* (1745), though oddly
enough satire is here qualified by a marked strain of sentimentalism. Everyone had some explanation to suggest. Possibly, says
Muralt, this hardihood is a strain of character inherited from the
Roman conquerors of the island. Voltaire thought that many persons made away with themselves "par humeur," out of a strange
desire to have their names appear in the newspapers.[39] All agreed
that there was some connection between this bravado and that
proverbial love of freedom and impatience of contradiction which
made it impossible for an Englishman to submit to ordinary restraint. What all this rationalization really comes to, as the *Universal Spectator* of April 26, 1735, points out, is that the giddy
English are governed by the vapors.

The carnage was said to be appalling. One of the most impressive treatments of the subject is an essay "On English Suicide:
By a Foreigner," first published in Fog's *Journal* of May 14, 1737,
and reprinted in the *Gentleman's Magazine* of that month. "I
could not, in several weeks after my arrival in the metropolis of

England," says the foreigner, the Abbé Le Blanc presumably, "master the astonishment it gave me to hear of such frequent self-murthers as happen here almost daily." He had always supposed that suicide resulted only from madness, but here people cut their throats, pistoled or stabbed themselves upon mature deliberation. The most lurid account was written by Pierre Jean Grosley in 1765. He, too, discovered that the Church of England had a form of prayer to be said for those "who labour under an excess of melancholy." Prayers notwithstanding and also fierce punitive laws, the crime was so frequent that the authorities of London had ordered all the approaches to the Thames to be boarded up. Even this precaution had failed. Workmen engaged in laying a foundation for a new bridge over the river had dug up twenty human skulls! Evidently afraid that he might be suspected of drawing the long bow, the traveler proceeds to report in detail several cases that have occurred during his short stay in the capital. Like Voltaire, he was inclined to think that many disposed of themselves for the posthumous notoriety they would achieve. If, says Grosley, any European people can be compared to the English in this respect, it is only the Italians.* In France, he adds, this is a crime almost unknown. But what could be expected in England, where self-homicide had been defended by John Donne, the celebrated Dean of St. Paul's, and practiced by the Reverend Thomas Creech? †

To what extent public hysteria was justified it is impossible to determine, for there is no reliable record of suicide in the Bills of Mortality. Whenever possible, the fact was concealed in order to shield the perpetrator and his family from disgrace and also to avoid the provisions of the laws *in terrorem* against *felo-de-se*, including the refusal of Christian burial and the confiscation of

* Lady Mary wrote from Italy in 1759 that a fashion had sprung up there "entirely new," the fashion of suicide. "You see," she concludes, "it is not in Britain alone that the spleen spreads her dominion." *Letters,* Everyman's, p. 518.

† *A Tour to London,* tr. by Thomas Nugent (1772), I, 229–234. If any other report outdid Grosley's *chronique scandaleuse,* it is a collection of stories by C. D. (A. G. Constant d'Orville) entitled *Les Nuits angloises* . . ., published at Paris in 1770.

the criminal's property. Although juries usually defeated the intent of the law, especially where property was involved, by bringing in a verdict of *non compos mentis*, it was desirable to avoid the hazard. The magazines frequently present statistics for London, but their value is doubtful, as most of the compilers admit. According to the estimate made by *Mercurius Politicus*, in the month of May 1720 six men and four women destroyed themselves. The *London Journal* of December 28, 1723, reports for the year 45 "known," 26 "found dead," and 62 "drowned."

The *annus mirabilis* was 1755, a year, as Thomas Gray says, when self-murder was "epidemical." [40] The excitement began on New Year's when Lord Mountford dispatched himself in approved style after he had gambled away his estate at White's Chocolate House. This shocking incident busied the tongues and the pens of all the gossips, filled the newspapers, and led the *Connoisseur* of January 9 to make a searching inquiry into the causes of the epidemic. Scarcely had the town recovered its breath before Sir John Bland copied his fellow-clubman's example. Needless to say, the best report of these scandals and others that followed was made by the prince of gossips, Horace Walpole. [41] While the hysteria was at its peak, an enterprising company offered insurance against self-destruction, the maximum protection, however, not to exceed £300. The good people, says Walpole, collected in front of White's expecting at any moment to see divine justice visited upon this den of iniquity. In these circumstances there was of course some exaggeration. The alarm arose less from the number of self-inflicted deaths than from the quality of the actors. If Read's *Weekly Journal* of December 22 was even near the truth in placing the estimate for the year at 47 "known" and 26 "found dead," the percentage was below rather than above the annual average; but, quite understandably, 1755 went down in the records as one of the blackest in the history of the nation, a year as memorable for English suicide as for the earthquake at Lisbon.

Exact statistical information would be of no great value if it were available; the matter of real significance is the public state of mind. Something is to be said for Voltaire's conjecture that the difference between London and Paris appeared to be even greater than it actually was because of the greater publicity given to suicide in the unrestricted English press.* What the keenest minds apparently did not grasp was the fact now obvious, that suicide is often imitative and therefore occurs in waves. People of the time read all the gruesome accounts they could find in newspapers and periodical essays under the traditional impression that the best way to avoid the crime was to become familiar with all the abhorrent details, and thus unknowingly they invited the disaster they sought to avoid.

### IV

Why were the inhabitants of the British Isles more melancholy and capricious than other people? According to medical scientists, the answer to this question was to be found in the so-called six non-naturals. Unless disease is inherited, it is brought on by one or more of these accidental causes: air, diet, lack of sufficient sleep, too little or too much exercise, defective evacuation, and the passions of the mind.† The sixth of these non-naturals, the mental passions, though recognized verbally, was so generally ignored in the diagnosis and treatment of mental disease that it may be disregarded. Underlying most medical practice is the motto *Mens sana in corpore sano*. Boswell could recall only a single treatise, Dr. Frank Nichols's *De Anima Medica* (1750), fully confirming his own judgment that although the corporeal hypothesis may explain most mental cases, "there is doubtless a madness seated much deeper, a disorder of the mind itself." In view of his admiration for Dr. Armstrong, it is surprising that he

---

* *Miscellaneous Correspondence . . . Sent to the Author of the Gentleman's Magazine*, No. I (London, 1742), pp. 70–71. Quoted by Charles Moore in *A Full Inquiry into the Subject of Suicide* (1790), p. 342. This writer estimates the average annual rate of suicide for London in the preceding twenty-eight years at only 32 (p. 351) and argues that this is exceeded in both Paris and Geneva; but he was trying to salvage the reputation of his country.

† "Why," says Sterne, "the most natural actions of a man's life should be called his Non-naturals – is another question." *Tristram Shandy*, Bk. I, Ch. 23.

did not make an exception also of *The Art of Preserving Health* (1744), for in the fourth book of this verse treatise the author clearly states his belief in autogenic mental illness and also in psychosomatic diseases. By no mere coincidence, the essay containing Boswell's profession of faith, *Hypochondriack* No. 62 (1782), opens with a florid eulogy of Burton's *Anatomy*, apparently the first of its kind in the eighteenth century.

Whether Boswell was right or not in charging the materialistic bias of the medical mind to Hippocrates, the habit had become well established beforehand and was now powerfully supported by John Locke's psychology. Occasionally a slight deviation may be found in a conventional treatise, as when Dr. Shebbeare suggests that the reading of *Joseph Andrews*, an admirable prescription "compounded by the ingenious Dr. Fielding," might be as good a cure for melancholy as a doctor's prescription; [42] but examples of the kind are rare. The principal attacks on the medical materialists were delivered by orthodox clergymen.* The physicians offered no defense of their heresy, indeed did not formally subscribe to heresy, but left the apology for their procedure to be drawn up by the real and the pretended followers of Locke.†　It is a significant commentary on the medical profession that in a period noted for hectic living – when, for instance, the passion for gambling frequently led to suicide and the whole nation was

---

* The most ambitious medical treatise opposing the physico-psychologists was written by the Rev. John Hancocke, chaplain to the Duke of Portland, with the help of some unknown collaborator, probably a physician, and entitled *Febrifugum Magnum Morbifugum Magnum* (1726). The same cause was championed by the anonymous author of *A Treatise on the Dismal Effects of Low-Spiritedness* (1750).

† The avowed purpose of Samuel Strutt's *A Philosophical Enquiry into the Physical Springs of Human Action* (1732) was to prove that man's intelligence is "nothing but matter under a peculiar manifestation" (p. 3). The ablest defenses of physical determinism were: *Man a Machine* (1748), which is a translation of La Mettrie's *L'Homme machine*; David Hartley's *Observations on Man* (1749); Joseph Priestley's *The Doctrine of Philosophical Necessity* (1777). Priestley remarks in his Preface, it is "extraordinary that the doctrine of philosophical liberty should have any adherents among persons of a liberal education, and who are at all used to reflection." John Wesley's reaction to such philosophy was "O God, how long shall this doctrine stand!" (*Works* [1865], X, 454ff.) In his *Journal* under May 12, 1759, he attacks the physicians (ed. Curnock, IV, 313).

stunned by the collapse of the South Sea bubble in 1720 – almost the only reference to the injurious effects of mental strain and anxiety is to be found in essays, sermons, poems, and other publications outside the field of medicine.*

Of the other non-naturals, two were always stressed by the etiologists, diet and climate. John Brown's very popular *Estimate of the Manners and Principles of the Times* (1757) traces the low spirits of the English to excessive eating and drinking and a general effeminacy of manners "working along with our island-climate," and in these conditions finds the cause of suicide.[43] Nine years later, as if to corroborate his estimate, he shocked the nation by taking his own life. Holbach, who took a serious interest in Britain's tragic fate, as many other Continental thinkers did, concluded that the gloominess of the British was due to climate or to "l'usage de la bière et des liqueurs fortes, des grosses viandes, des brouillards continuels, de la fumée du charbon de terre qui les enveloppe sans cesse."[44] When such statements were closely analyzed, there could be no doubt that the basic cause was a pathogenic climate, for all climatologists agreed that the diet of a nation is itself predetermined, at least in its main characteristics, by the necessities of physical environment. Therefore the inhabitants of Britain were doomed by geographic accident to be a melancholy people. Exactly how the unhealthful atmosphere worked directly upon body and indirectly upon mind eventually became the most absorbing problem of the medical men, but not until the need of such an inquiry had been forced upon them by popular opinion.

The case against the British climate was first fully presented by visiting Frenchmen, and the task was well under way long before the eighteenth century. The author of an official guidebook felt

---

* One is a humorous piece written ostensibly by Sir John Midriff, Knight, M.D., called *Observations on the Spleen and Vapours; Containing Remarkable Cases of Persons of both Sexes, and all Ranks, from the aspiring Directors to the humble Bubbler, who have been miserably afflicted with these Melancholy Disorders since the Fall of South-Sea, and other publick Stocks; with the proper Method for their Recovery, according to the new and uncommon Circumstances of each Case* (1721). Compare the broadside *A South-Sea Ballad.*

that he was bound in honor to warn his readers beforehand what to expect when they visited "the gloomy isle." James Beeverele, compiler of *Les Délices de la Grande Bretagne, et de l'Irlande* (1706) — most of it pilfered from a predecessor, Guy Miège — admits that the English live longer than other people and that their climate endows them with a unique talent for long and abstruse speculation, as had been demonstrated by their recent contributions to philosophy and science, but adds that for these benefits nature exacts a tragic price: in this ungenial atmosphere few of the inhabitants are free from the hypochondriac passion, and many of them terminate their *taedium vitae* by knife, cord, or water. The charge was made by Moreau de Brassey, author of the rival *Guide d'Angleterre* (1744), that Beeverele was a shameless plagiarist, as he undoubtedly was, but he himself was guilty of the same fault and repeated the same opinions.

Deslandes notes in his *Nouveau Voyage d'Angleterre* (1717) that London was blanketed under clouds so dense that the sun was never visible and the air so thick with coal-smoke that he could hardly draw his breath. Was it to be wondered at that a people who lived habitually in such an atmosphere, though shrewd in science and politics, should be subject to strange whims? When the Abbé Dubos, in the course of his *Réflexions critiques sur la poésie* (1719), needed proof that winds have a powerful effect on moods, he found the necessary evidence in "a neighbour country" (name not specified) where Bills of Mortality were kept: there the records showed that "out of sixty suicides in one year, fifty of them happen towards the beginning or end of winter." [45] In the five years La Mottraye spent in England on three visits made between 1698 and 1712 he discovered that the "humide et nébuleux" climate affected outsiders if they remained long. [46] His observation was confirmed by César de Saussure's unhappy experience in 1728. On the whole, Saussure was the most charitable of the French visitors. In a letter dated November 17 (the season of year usually considered the most dangerous) he characterized the air of England as "healthy, light, and agreeable on account of its temperature," free from excessive cold in winter and heat in summer.[47] This was written in the country. London was a different matter; soon after his arrival in the murky capital he was laid low by the English malady. The description he gives of his symptoms, one good enough to have been written by Dr. Cheyne, concludes with the remark that if he had been an Englishman he would have put an end to his miserable condition.[48]

The Abbé Le Blanc had no sooner set foot on these Cimmerian shores, in 1737, than he was ready with the opinion that Englishmen could not fail to be downcast, immersed as they constantly were in impenetrable fogs. As a scientist he takes it to be a self-evident truth that human beings, no less than vegetables, partake of the nature of the climate that produces them. From the same natural conditions proceed the fertility of the British soil and that melancholy disposition of the inhabitants which makes it impossible for them to submit to political or religious regimentation or to endure the ordinary misfortunes of existence. As a moralist he could not excuse their habit of killing themselves with cool courage as if this were more to be admired than the fortitude to endure calamity; nevertheless, his rebuke is tempered by understanding. He found the country depressing, the capital indescribably dreary. "Tho I have already spent upwards of eight weeks in London," he writes, "the smook and fogs have not suffered me to see the town." [49] Between melancholy in his own country and in England there was this difference, that the English fits of blue devils were more or less violent according to the direction of the wind and the season of year. Autumn and dark cloudy weather were especially to be feared. "A news-writer giving an account of several Englishmen who had killed themselves, observed pleasantly, that the thing was the more extraordinary, as the season for suicide was not yet come." [50]

It was Voltaire's extraordinary fortune to reach London on a clear day (in May 1726) in the midst of a public festival. Surely, he decided, these people could not be so glum and tongue-tied as he had been led to suppose. But the next day when he called on some of his new acquaintances, they ignored him. Apparently he had inadvertently committed some grave offense. Finally the true reason came out — the wind had shifted to the east! He went to a café. "Tout était triste et morne." At first he was inclined to laugh at this absurd notion; but alas, he confesses, "le climat opérait déjà sur moi, et je m'étonnais de ne pouvoir rire." Afterward he was given a long lecture on English meteorology by a famous court physician, who assured him: "Ce vent est la peste de notre île. Les animaux même souffrent, et ont tous l'air abattu. Les hommes qui sont assez robustes pour conserver leur sanité dans ce maudit vent perdent au moins leur bonne humeur. Chacun alors a le visage sévère, et l'esprit disposé aux résolutions désespérées." It was during an east wind, he was further informed, that Charles I was executed and James II banished. The months of November and March were the most dangerous, so depressing in fact "que presque tout le monde était réellement malade dans ces deux saisons, et qu'une mélancholie noire se répandait sur toute la nation."[51] In explanation of this phenomenon he afterward learned from Montesquieu that the humid climate occasioned a defective flow of the animal spirits,[52] a theory which he himself adopted in his *Commentaire sur L'Esprit des lois*.[53]

These French observations were confirmed by Peter Kalm in 1748;* what is more important, they were confirmed by the English themselves. A century and a half earlier the frank speech of Addison and Steele would have been construed as a breach of patriotic duty. Most Englishmen of the sixteenth century believed, with others, that the physical and mental peculiarities that distinguish different races and nations arise mainly from differences in natural environment. They did not question the classical doctrine of *milieu*, but did question what foreigners had to say of the British climate and its effects on the population. With a patriotic zeal worthy of a better cause, they insisted that both were being maligned. Gradually, however, they were convinced of their error, and once they had accepted the ugly truth, they dwelt with martyr-like zeal upon their foul climate and its depressive influence. Even yet the Elizabethan note of chauvinistic

---

* *Kalm's Account of his Visit to England*, etc., tr. by Joseph Lucas (1892), pp. 138–139.

defiance was heard occasionally, as in Robert Dodsley's *Agriculture* (1754) and John Dyer's *The Fleece* (1757), but these poets were thinking of apples, hops, and wool rather than of the people who grew them.*

That the Tatler and the Spectator connected the incorrigible melancholy of their public with climatic conditions would be evident enough from the essays already mentioned. When the demon of melancholy rides into the island, it is usually upon the wings of the east wind. In the same essay the Spectator quotes approvingly from a French novelist who, instead of opening his story as most romancers do in the flowery spring season, begins, "In the gloomy month of November, when the people of England hang and drown themselves." The crux of the Spectator's problem was to help his reader "fence against the temper of his climate or constitution." [54] Evidently recalling Congreve's defense of his comedies against the attacks of the moralists, Addison asserts in defense of his own story of a grinning-match that "the British climate, more than any other, makes entertainment of this nature in a manner necessary." [55] The censors of morals did not fail to see the comical aspect of the valetudinarian always consulting the wind to ascertain the state of his health. In *Tatler* No. 238 Swift pokes fun at a coffeehouse habitué who spends his time in discussing the weather and complaining of "the spleen." The Spectator's amusing story of a house-party attended by a group of chronic splenetics [56] may very well have given Voltaire a hint for his remarks on the east wind. It is interesting to note that toward the end of Addison's career as an essayist his prejudice against France was beginning to soften. He still thought that a taciturn Briton was worth a dozen chattering Frenchmen, but was generous enough to give unstinted praise to their climate. After complaining of the English climate, he says in reference to a recent visit to France: "I have passed one March in my life without being buffeted with the winds, and one April without being washed with the rains." [57]

* *Agriculture*, Bk. III; for *The Fleece*, see p. 129. Compare Emanuel Bowen, *A Complete System of Geography* . . . (1747), I, 2.

One of the severest critics was Lady Mary Wortley Montagu. Though a Stoic by profession, she had no philosophy to combat the demoralizing effects of British weather. Numerous conjectures have been offered to explain why she left England in 1739 to spend virtually the remainder of her life on the Continent. That she had several reasons, Pope among them and also Mr. Montagu, is evident enough, and it may be that her aversion to leaden skies was not the least of them. Complaints are numerous in the letters she wrote immediately before her departure, especially those addressed to the Countess of Pomfret, then living abroad. "We are as much blinded in England by politics and views of interest," she complains, "as we are by mist and fogs, and 'tis necessary to have a very uncommon constitution not to be tainted with the distemper of our climate." In a deeper fit of *ennui de toutes choses* she writes: "We have no news, no trade, no sun, and even our fools are all gone to play at Tunbridge, and those that remain are only miserable invalids, who talk of nothing but infirmities and remedies, as ladies who are on the point of increasing the world, who speak of only nurses and midwives." Again, "We are wrapped up in fogs and consequential stupidity, which increases so visibly, we want but little of the state of petrifaction which was said to befall an African town." [58] She was convinced that such a climate would have proved too much for the gay spirits even of Rabelais and Cervantes. As she was about to take flight from "the regions of dulness" she wrote to her friend in Paris: "I already fancy to myself the charms of the brightest conversation in the brightest climate. We have nothing here but clouds and perpetual rains, nor no news but death and sickness." [59]

Dr. Arbuthnot characterized the English perfectly when he said of John Bull that his moods depended upon the state of the air, his spirits rising and falling with the weather-glass.[60] What they feared most was "the unhealthful East that breathes the spleen." * Pope's description of the Cave of Spleen in *The Rape of the Lock* would have been lacking in realism without

* William Cowper, *The Task* (1784) IV.582.

> No cheerful breeze this sullen region knows,
> The dreaded East is all the wind that blows.
>
> (IV. 19–20)

William Somerville's poem *The Hip* begins:

> This dismal morn, when east winds blow,
> And every languid pulse beats low.

Of the sensitive poets none suffered more than Somerville's friend Shenstone, master of the Leasowes. He confides to a correspondent: "Solitary life, limited circumstances, a phlegmatic habit, and disagreeable events, have given me a melancholy turn, that is hardly dissipated by the most serene sky; but in a north-east wind is quite intolerable." When in one of his fits of gloominess, he could not but regard the deistic theory that man was intended for happiness as nothing more than another of Wollaston's "implicit lyes." [61] Thomas Gray, after standing out as long as he could, finally admitted that he trembled "at an east-wind." [62]

This article of the creed had its amusing aspects, but was nonetheless real and indeed not irrational. As soon as Laurence Sterne got up in the morning he would take a look at the weather-vane and if it pointed to the east would go back to bed. Sometimes this ill wind interfered with the goings-on at Crazy Castle when Sterne paid a visit to his crony and fellow-hypochondriac John Hall Stevenson. On one occasion Stevenson kept to his bed so long and Sterne became so bored with loneliness that he had the weather-vane fastened so that it pointed west, whereupon the good spirits of his host returned and the festivities were resumed. But later the cord broke, the wind again was in the east, the humorsome master of Crazy Castle went back to bed, and Sterne returned to Shandy Hall. [63] Some of the eccentrics realized that their fear was partly a trick of the imagination and could laugh at themselves, but, as Sterne himself illustrates, it was genuine and often amounted to a phobia.

Opinion was, of course, not entirely uniform. Besides the physico-psychologists, there were some who believed in the autonomy of mind and its direct response to environment. This

is the attitude expressed in the very popular poem *The Spleen* (1737); but the author, Matthew Green, was a humble layman, and his word had no weight in science. Of this minority group the most vocal representative in the medical profession was Dr. Armstrong. Although he was so old-fashioned as to revive the Elizabethan notion that a man's "native air," however vile it may be, is *ipso facto* best for his peculiar constitution, no one more roundly damned the air all Britons were condemned to breathe.*
Dr. Battie admits (p. 36) in *A Treatise on Madness* (1758) that he is not sure of the explanation, but warns his readers that they are gravely mistaken if they think the dread of black November days and east winds is an imaginary fear. Some went so far as to question such influences altogether. David Hume conjectured that neither climate nor any other physical agent is responsible for the mental and moral disparities of different peoples, but that these spring only from custom and education.[64] Young looked upon the doctrine of *milieu* as a denial of divine justice. After deploring the scandalous frequency of suicide, he adds:

> Blame not thy clime, nor chide the distant sun;
> The sun is innocent, thy clime absolv'd:
> Immoral climes kind Nature never made.
> *(Night Thoughts* V.250–252)

The anonymous author of *A Treatise on the Dismal Effects of Low-Spiritedness* (1750) raises the pertinent question whether the sullen climate was not being exploited as a convenient apology for evils due rather to the heavy diet for which the British were notorious. If climate was the explanation, he could not understand why the people of Holland were not as melancholy as those of England.

The need of counteracting the climatic hypothesis was felt to be particularly great in the year 1755, when the crime of self-destruction reached a high-water mark. The essay published in the *Connoisseur* of January 9 (No. 150) asserts that the British

---

* *The Art of Preserving Health* (1744), Bk. IV, 250–269. Compare *A Day: An Epistle to John Wilkes, of Aylesbury, Esq.* and *The Universal Almanac.*

climate is less gloomy than that of several north European countries — Russia, Sweden, and Greenland, for instance — where
suicide is almost unknown and that it is therefore absurd to say
in defense of the British that they are the victims of an inescap-
able destiny. Another objector, Dr. Shebbeare, held that the mind
"takes little tincture from winds or weather." [65] A similar stand
was taken in the same year by Thomas Sheridan in *British Education* (1755), a treatise written to show that the defects of character usually blamed upon the climate result from a faulty system
of education.[66] With this group may be included also Lord
Kames, who reviews the history of the climatic theory in the
introduction to *Sketches of the History of Man* (1774). The
exceptions, however, are so few that they serve mainly to emphasize by contrast the prevailing belief in the deterministic force
of climate.

## V

Beyond providing the perfect illustration, Britain contributed
little to the doctrine of *la génie des nations*. Her men of learning
offered nothing comparable to Dubos's *Réflexions critiques sur
la poésie* (1719), Montesquieu's *L'Esprit des lois* (1748), Buffon's
*Histoire naturelle* (1749ff) or Paul Henri Mallet's *Introduction à
l'histoire du Danemark* (1755). Goldsmith's work came much
later and, besides, was that of a disseminator only, for the learning
displayed in his numerous essays and *Animated Nature* (1774) is
known to have been rifled from the French.[67] Meanwhile, however, English physicians, spurred by foreign example and even
more by the urgent need of their countrymen, began to make a
more serious inquiry than had ever been made before into the
relation between climate and disease. The results, though of
minor importance to pure science, are helpful toward an understanding of the English malady. For the first time the medical
men use language that is comprehensible today. They did not
explain the mysteries of nerves and neuroticism, but they did
begin to present the problem in terms that can be restated. Any-
one curious to know what "the spleen" really was could not do

better than follow Dr. Johnson's advice to Boswell that he read Dr. Cheyne's *Essay on Health and Long Life* (1724) and *The English Malady* (1733).[68] These treatises will serve also as a basis for summarizing as briefly as possible the most important of the conclusions he and his contemporaries reached.

By the time Cheyne's work was well under way the illusion that the hypochondriac passion was *a disease*, one capable of being isolated and defined, was rapidly vanishing. Physicians of the seventeenth century had evaded the truth by resorting to mere jargon about the problem of differentiating between melancholy and various congeneric disorders of atrabilious and splenic origin. Abandoning this transparent pretense, physicians of the better sort now faced the obvious fact that melancholy, by whatever name it might be called, was a synthesis of all those maladies that enervate body and mind. It was not a disease, but a condition. Among the numerous recognized antecedents were three of the most prevalent of all English diseases: consumption, gout, and scurvy.

Notably absent from the list is what now appears to have been the most important element in the complex. Historians of medicine are apparently agreed that the disease known to the ancient Greeks and Romans as melancholy was in reality modern malaria,* and there can be little doubt that the same explanation accounts for the foothold melancholy first obtained in the British Isles. Although the word *malaria* was beginning to be used in the eighteenth century, it was only a new equivalent for melancholy and indicates no knowledge of the disease now so called.† That malaria was common is plainly evident from many clinical case histories on record. The proposed identification explains the great importance attached to the spleen in ancient and modern

---

* The arguments for the identification are summarized by W. H. S. Jones, M.D., in *Malaria and Greek Medicine* (1909). See also Fielding H. Garrison, M.D., *History of Medicine*, 4th ed. (1929), pp. 86, 94, 121; Fred B. Lund, *Greek Medicine* (1936), p. 1.

† In a letter dated 28 May, 1779, the Earl of Pembroke states that Rome and the Maremma "must be totally avoided in the Malaria season." *Letters and Diaries of Henry, Tenth Earl of Pembroke and his Circle*, ed. Lord Herbert (1939), p. 186.

treatises on melancholy and also the usual presence of such well-known malarial symptoms as jaundice, night sweats, violent disturbance of the stomach, and agues. A further correspondence is evident in the seasonal incidence of the two diseases. Equally plain also is the resemblance in the mental symptoms. There is good reason for thinking that many cases of low-spiritedness that puzzled the eighteenth-century physician would now be called malarial psychosis. The effects would have been greater than they were if the use of the Jesuit's bark (quinine) had not been introduced in the preceding century, but even so the toll must have been heavy.

A second point of agreement was that all the blood diseases contributory to "the spleen" were the consequences of the climate. One purpose Dr. Jeremiah Waineright had in publishing *A Mechanical Account of the Non-Naturals* (1707), a treatise popular enough to command six editions by 1737, was to demonstrate that the damp, saline atmosphere was responsible for that foulest of distempers, scurvy — a plague widespread among all classes of society and almost universal among sailors. Though admitting that a constant diet of salt meat aggravated the miseries of sailors, he held that the air they breathed was the *vera causa* of "the withering of the guts" and such other familiar manifestations as "red, blue or black spots on the legs, extraordinary weakness, a redness and itching, rotten gums, stinking breath, loose teeth," and so forth, and the mental depression that necessarily followed.* Dr. Cheyne himself contributed to the indictment in his first practical treatise, *Observations concerning the Nature and due Method of Treating the Gout* (1720). Already he had made up his mind that not only gout, but most of the other chronic disorders of the English people had their beginning

* "Of the Air," p. 31. For other studies, besides Dr. Cheyne's, see: Dr. Peter Shaw, *A New Practice of Physic* (1726), ed. 1728, p. 312; Bishop Berkeley, *Alciphron: or The Minute Philosopher* (1732), Dial. II, 817, and *Siris* (1744), Secs. lxxxviii, lxxxix; Dr. John Arbuthnot, *An Essay concerning the Effects of Air on Human Bodies* (1733); Dr. William Stukeley, *A Letter to Sir Hans Sloane . . . about the Cure of Gout* (1733); Sir Richard Manningham, *The Symptoms, Nature, and Cure of the Febricula*, etc. (1746), pp. vi, 16.

in one or more of three causes — diet, lack of proper exercise among the upper classes, and the gloominess and uncertainty of their climate. The most plausible explanation he and his contemporaries could offer for the climatic effects was a theory advanced in England a century earlier and probably borrowed from Sanctorius, namely, that the cold, damp, and salty atmosphere closed the pores of the skin so that normal perspiration was impossible.[69] When the "perspirable humours" are not discharged in due quantity, they stagnate and putrefy. Shenstone was speaking by the book when he said, "Spleen is often little else but obstructed perspiration." [70]

Dr. Cheyne was not a profound medical scholar; he was as little concerned with the mysteries of the nervous system as the other neurologists were. During the period of his activity some important changes were made in the physiology of mind: as early as 1702 Dr. Purcell had defied ancient tradition by denying that the spleen was the cause of the disease so named,* others attacked the theory of hollow nerves and the animal spirits, and some went so far as to repudiate the basic dogma of the four humors in man's body, contending that black bile and yellow are the same humor viewed under different conditions. Though Cheyne was not indifferent to the controversy — indeed he gave some support to the iconoclasts — he had no great interest in physiological theories *per se*. Like Dr. Sydenham, he was an empiric in a good sense of the word. Most of his knowledge he obtained from observation and experiment, beginning with a study of himself.

He was truly a tun of a man. He appears in John Gay's *Mr. Pope's Welcome from Greece* (written in 1725) as "Cheney huge of size," in Young's *Epistle to Mr. Pope* (1730) as "three ells round huge Cheyne." At the height of his good living and obesity the Aberdeen Falstaff tipped the scales at thirty-two stone and

---

* Splenectomies, most of them performed on dogs, exposed the falsity of Galen's conception of the spleen. If any life remained in the old theory, it was extinguished in 1725 by Sir Richard Blackmore's *A Critical Dissertation upon the Spleen, So far as concerns the Following Question: Whether the Spleen is necessary or useful to the Animal possessed of it?*

exhibited in his immense hulk most of the diseases in which he specialized. No better idea of that *farrago omnium morborum* called "the spleen" can be had than from the account he gives of his own case. The first "sensible shock" he experienced was an autumnal intermittent fever. This he conquered in a few weeks by "chewing the bark" and seemed to be as well as ever except that he was "jumbled and turbid." A year later he had an attack of vertigo. Thereafter he was constantly distressed by "headach, giddiness, lowness, anxiety and terror," so that he went about "like a malefactor condemn'd, or one who expected every moment to be crushed by a ponderous instrument of death, hanging over his head." He was so nervous that he could hardly endure the presence even of the members of his own household. In due course of time his legs broke out in scorbutic ulcers, "the ichor of which corroded the very skin" and baffled the skill of the entire faculty for three years. Other developments were symptomatic fever, erysipelas, swooning, sinking, gout, eructation, and a mental inquietude which reduced him to extreme melancholia — agonies too intense to be expressed and never recalled without horror.*

As most medical men of his century did, Dr. Cheyne generalized too freely, pursuing a discovery to the point of error. He was so obsessed with the tragic effects of scurvy that it became for him the root of all evil and the basis for his entire system. One of his many pronouncements on this favorite topic is that scurvy is "the fundamental distemper, the productive cause, and, as it were, the base of all the high hysterical and hypochondriacal symptoms, of all vapours, lowness of spirits, flatulence, spleen, fits, convulsions, epilepsies and apoplexies, to which the people of condition, of this various, watry and turbulent climat are subjected; and differ only according to the frame, age, and manner of living of the persons." [71] Unsatisfactory as this broad statement may appear to the modern specialist in nervous and mental disorders, it contained a large element of truth and led

---

* Included with other cases as an Appendix to *The English Malady*, pp. 325–364.

to sound practical advice. Personal experience had taught him that this national scourge could not be conquered by the conventional methods of treatment, but only by a change in diet. In his protest against the luxurious habits of the upper classes and their lack of exercise there was nothing new. Gluttony and drunkenness were already under a steady rain of fire from medical writers, essayists, and clergymen. When Dr. Purcell dismissed the spleen as the cause of the disease named for it, he, too, made a false generalization, but a very plausible one. From the days of early Greek medicine dyspepsia had been a prominent symptom of melancholy, so prominent that one type was denominated flatulent melancholy, and the list of symptoms regularly included eructation and nausea. Dr. Purcell concluded that here was the key to the whole mystery: "the spleen" was in reality nervous indigestion. This is the thesis also of his *Treatise of the Cholick* (1714). Nevertheless, all this preliminary work notwithstanding, neither the public nor the faculty was prepared for the remedy advocated by Cheyne, a proposal radical enough in fact and grossly exaggerated by his opponents.

According to them, he had the cool effrontery to recommend that beef-eating Britons abandon the fare that had made them the greatest nation in Christendom and put themselves on a diet of roots and herbs — trash they had always considered fit only for effeminate Frenchmen and Italians. Vegetarianism had been championed by Thomas Tryon in the late seventeenth century, but "old Tryon" was an ignorant artisan. It had reappeared, very cautiously, in Francis Fuller's *Medicina Gymnastica* (1705), a treatise highly honored in *Spectator* No. 115. Fuller, apparently the first Englishman to advocate physical culture as a mode of therapy, undertook to cure dyspeptic and vaporish aristocrats by a combination of systematic exercise and special diet, and he admitted that in extreme cases this might mean temporary abstention from all animal food; but this, too, is the opinion of a layman and could hardly be cited in defense of a trained physician. Cheyne had strange ideas also in regard to beverages. His recommendation of tea as a tonic for the nerves was entirely orthodox, and his prescription of asses' milk for "the spleen" standard practice.

> Before proud gates attending asses bray,
> Or arrogate with solemn pace the way;
> These grave physicians with their milky cheer
> The love-sick maid and dwindling beau repair.*

But if anything could have been more absurd than the vegetarian heresy, it was the belief that water is a beverage fit for human beings, and he adopted this heresy also. The consequence was that he was greeted with a storm of ridicule and abuse such as few physicians have had to face.

His reputation is a study in contrasts; he was at once the most famous physician of his day and the most ridiculous. He was the intimate friend of Gay, Swift, Pope, Arbuthnot, and Young. Through his practice at London and Bath he came to know more distinguished neurotics than any other physician of the time. It was to "immortal Cheyne," as Lyttelton called him, that David Hume turned for advice in 1734 after he had consulted numerous other specialists in vain concerning his scurvy, vapors, and low-spiritedness.[72] Among Cheyne's patients were Samuel Richardson, Lord Hervey, and the Countess of Huntingdon, the patroness of George Whitefield.† The last of his treatises, *The Natural Method of Cureing the Diseases of the Body* (1742), was dedicated to Lord Chesterfield. Henry Fielding, no friend of doctors or herbs, referred to him after his death as "the learned Dr. Cheyne." [73] John Wesley, one of his most faithful converts though never a patient, reproduced some of his teaching in *Primitive Physick*, published at Philadelphia in 1764. [74]

The storm of opposition first broke after the appearance of

* John Gay, *Trivia* (1716) II.13–16. Compare *Kalm's Account of his Visit to England*, p. 160.

† Many of Cheyne's letters are preserved in *The Correspondence of Samuel Richardson*, ed. Mrs. Barbauld (1804) and *Original Letters*, ed. Rebecca Warner (1817). Charles F. Mullett has edited *The Letters of Dr. George Cheyne to the Countess of Huntingdon* (1940) and *The Letters of Doctor George Cheyne to Samuel Richardson*, 1733–1743 (1943).

*An Essay on Health and Long Life* in 1724;* previously he had
given no hint of being a "vegetable man," in fact had expressed
the orthodox suspicion of such foods. The unknown author of a
ballad sung to the appropriate tune of *You Cut-Purses All* made
the very plausible charge that the doctors and apothecaries were
up in arms because they feared that nature's simple plan advocated
by Dr. Cheyne would deprive them of their livelihood. But Lady
Bristol was expressing a common attitude when she wrote from
court in 1729: "The whole world is ready to pull China [sic]
to peices for so many miserable creatures that he has brought to
death's door." [75] If Dr. Arbuthnot wrote the anonymous piece
*It cannot Rain but it Pours* (1726), as was generally supposed, he
took part in the hue and cry against "the new sect of herb-eaters."
Later, seeing that his old friend was being handled too roughly
by the critics, he brought out *An Essay concerning the Nature
of Aliments* (1731), which is said to be the first English inquiry
into the chemistry of food, in the hope that it might allay the
tempest; but his thesis that diet is a necessary branch of the
science of physic had no effect on Cheyne's opponents. "I have
been slain again and again, both in verse and prose," he says two
years later in the Preface to *The English Malady*, "but I thank
God I am still alive and well." † At this time his difficulties were
only beginning. The jest continued to the time of his death, and
long after. Occasionally a voice was lifted in his defense, but
weak and ineffective.‡ The indictment against him was fully
summarized immediately after the publication of *An Essay on
Regimen* (1740) in a tract entitled *The Tryal of Colley Cibber,
Comedian . . . and the Arraignment of George Cheyne, physi-*

* Typical of the immediate reaction are: *A Letter to George Cheyne,
M.D., Occasion'd by his Essay on Health and Long Life* (1724); Edward
Strother, M.D., *An Essay on Sickness and Health . . . in which Dr.
Cheyne's Mistaken Opinions . . . are occasionally taken Notice of . . .*
(1725); *An Epistle to Ge—ge Ch—ne, M.D. F.R.S. Upon his Essay of Health
and Long Life . . . By Pillo-Tisanus* (1725).

† A lively exchange in verse between Dr. Wynter and Dr. Cheyne is
preserved in *Original Letters*, ed. Rebecca Warner, pp. 62–63.

‡ He is eulogized by H. C. in the *Gentleman's Mag.* of April 1733 (III,
205) and by the Rev. Mr. H—e in the issue of July 1738 (VIII, 362).

*cian, at Bath for the philosophical, physical, and the logical here-sies uttered in his last book of regimen.*

Cheyne's heresies were greatly exaggerated. Reports to the contrary, he never "damn'd all meat" either as a philosopher or as a physician. Though a believer in deism, as he professes in *Philosophical Principles of Natural Religion* (1705), he had no scruples against slaughtering animals for food. And far from recommending total abstinence from animal food and alcoholic beverages for the whole population, he prescribed this Spartan regimen, as he called it, only in extreme cases and dissuaded some of his eager patients from trying it. His only real offense was that he advocated what now is called a balanced diet. Nevertheless, he was contending against a national prejudice so ingrained that his clients, never more than half-converted, were easily persuaded by their friends that they were being starved and were ready to return to conventional meat and drink and treatment. In the end Lord Hervey preferred Ward to Cheyne. Even his friends thought he had a touch of "enthusiasm." "I love him," says Pope, "as he loves Don Quixote, for the most moral and reasoning madman in the world." [76]

When Dr. Cheyne died, in 1743, he had made no signal contribution to medical science, he had failed to convert the public to his gospel of diet, and he left no worthy disciples; * yet he deserves the honor of a martyr in a noble cause. If he came miserably short of the truth when he referred all the plagues of "the spleen" to a single origin, it must be admitted that in concentrating upon scurvy he came to grips with a serious national problem and also that he was the first English physician with sufficient knowledge and courage to confront carnivorous and scorbutic Britons with the unpalatable truth about their diet. That he did have the solution of the problem was later demonstrated. One of the substantial medical accomplishments of the late eighteenth

---

* Edmond Litton, an avowed disciple of Cheyne's, weakened the cause by advocating strict vegetarianism in *Philosophical Conjectures on Aereal Influences, The Probable Origin of Diseases* (1750). The same attitude was taken by the anonymous author of *Nature the Best Physician, or, Every Man his own Doctor* (1753).

century was the virtual conquest of this loathsome disease, an achievement officially certified in 1795 when the government, very belatedly, ordered lime juice to be provided for sailors in the Royal Navy. For this discovery, honor was paid to Dr. Huxham, Dr. Lind, and others, but none to the pioneer in the movement.* When Cheyne's name was mentioned, almost invariably it was for the purpose of ridiculing his quixotism, and even such staunch admirers as Johnson and Boswell disregarded his main advice. To some extent subsequent developments also vindicated the extreme emphasis he placed upon scurvy, for as it was gradually brought under control, less and less was said of the English malady until it ceased to be the popular disease. It is more than coincidence that melancholy under various names was the reigning distemper from the middle of the sixteenth to the late eighteenth century and that during this same period the English people were eaten up with scurvy. Dr. Cheyne seems to have been born a generation too early. What he did for his contemporaries can be stated briefly and positively: he brought home to them an exaggerated impression of climatic evils without convincing them that there was any escape from their predestined fate.

## VI

This statement should not be taken to mean that the English compared themselves unfavorably with people born under brighter skies or that they asked for commiseration. On the contrary, their sense of superiority was never greater nor was *Jean Bull philosophe* ever in a more complacent mood. His egotism is amusing but also admirable. There is a note of pride even in his grumbling. If nature appeared to have discriminated against the inhabitants of the British Isles, it was only because the dis-

---

* After Huxham had seen the fleet put in at Plymouth with 1,200 scorbutic sailors, he wrote a letter to the *General Evening Post* of Sept. 30, 1747, recommending a trial of vegetables and fruit; this letter was afterward expanded into *De Scorbuto* and published at Venice in 1776. The same advice was given by Dr. John Lind in *A Treatise on the Scurvy* (1753). It was completely confirmed by the experiments of Captain Cook in his second voyage round the world (1772–1775), but not officially adopted until twenty years later.

pensation of her favors was not fully understood. By an inviolate law, good and evil are so intertwined in the web of fate that every natural benefit is accompanied by its penalty. Foreigners themselves admitted that those same environmental conditions that invested the English character with gloom and eccentricity not to be matched elsewhere were responsible, on the other hand, for a unique genius in statesmanship, natural science, and philosophy. Thus was verified once more the axiom that melancholy is the *wise disease*. The strangest of all psychological enigmas is that those bodily infirmities that enervate, even destroy, the mind often give it extreme luster.

> Great wits are sure to madness near allied,
> And thin partitions oft their bounds divide.*

Although this paradox is stated in Plato's *Phaedrus*, where the philosopher is discussing the requisites of poetry, the theory of pathologic genius was universally ascribed to Aristotle, but upon the mistaken belief that he was the author of the spurious *Problemata*, or "Aristotle's Book of Problems." [77] Since the Renaissance the English had provided the ideal exemplification of this paradox and continued to do so in the eighteenth century. Grosley made amends for all his derogatory remarks when he declared that the English illustrated "what Plutarch says after Aristotle, that none but great geniuses are subject to melancholy." †

Among the examples frequently cited were Sir Isaac Newton in science, David Hume in philosophy, and Bolingbroke and the elder Pitt in politics; but the most convincing proof was provided by members of the literary profession. The law, originally applied only to "men of parts," was now extended to include learned ladies; they were *ex hypothesi* twice vulnerable – by virtue of their sex as well as their learning – and were therefore equally liable, as Pope says, to "the hysteric or poetic fit." [78] Here, need-

---

* John Dryden, *Absalom and Achitophel* (1681), 163–164. This theory is discussed, briefly, in an article published in the *Daily Courant* of Nov. 1731 and reprinted in the *Gentleman's Mag.* of the same month (I, 190–191).

† *A Tour to London*, p. 185. For a more critical opinion, see Boswell, *Hypochondriack* No. 5 (1778).

less to say, was another motive for affectation. Without "the spleen" no man or woman was qualified to serve the muse. Underneath all the pretense and badinage, however, lay a solid substratum of erratic genius. It is ironical that a period of English literature still sometimes referred to as the age of calm rationalism and sanity numbered among its contributors more examples of abnormal psychology than can be clearly identified in any other comparable span of English history. If contemporaries were wrong in the egotistic claim that this denoted an extraordinary degree of "wit" in their generation and thus confirmed the Aristotelian law, they had good reason for seeing in the literary product further support for the thesis stated by Addison and developed more fully by the Abbé Dubos in *Réflexions critiques sur la poésie* (1719), that the essential characteristics of a people invariably find expression in the national literature.*

That the mental irregularities of some of the individual authors are perceptible in their work is generally recognized. The cases of Swift, Sterne, and Johnson are better known than any others because they have been examined more frequently and thoroughly.† Richardson's "nervous paroxysms" and "paralytic tremors" — arising, according to Dr. Cheyne, "chiefly from want of due exercise, too much head work, and great plenty" of food [79] — were matters of common knowledge and were taken by friend and foe alike to account for the "delicate sentiments" displayed in his fiction. One of the novelist's correspondents hesitated between Swift's explanation that "fine genius is the natural cause or effect of a tender constitution" and Fielding's way of stating the matter, that "the labour of the brain is necessarily productive of the malady"; but he had never met an eminent genius of sound body. [80] Dr. Delany, knowing that nothing pleased Richardson so much as praise of himself unless it was abuse of Henry Fielding, framed the perfect eulogy by combining the two themes: "I am

* This idea came into prominence in the war between the ancients and the moderns. Note Voltaire's statement in *Dictionnaire philosophique*, art. "Les anciens et les modernes."

† For an excellent account, see W. B. C. Watkins, *Perilous Balance. The Tragic Genius of Swift, Johnson and Sterne* (1939).

extremely sorry you should have such impediments, but the misfortune is, those who are fit to write delicately, must think so; those who can form a distress must be able to feel it; and as the mind and body are so united to influence one another, the delicacy is communicated, and one too often finds softness and tenderness of mind in a body equally remarkable for those qualities. Tom Jones could get drunk, and do all sorts of things, in the height of his joy for his uncle's recovery. I dare say Fielding is a robust strong man." [81] With this exegesis there can be no quarrel. Seldom has an author had so marked an influence on the course of English prose literature as Richardson, and no one, not even Sterne, has more plainly owed his reputation to a defective nervous system.

Theoretically, the extreme penalty of genius would be paid by the poets. Actually, it is difficult to establish a definable relation between the "impediments" of the individual and his poetry, but even a superficial survey will show that others as well as Swift and Johnson served a "vapoured muse." Pope's mind was as warped as his "little, tender crazy carcass." Matthew Prior, the merriest of bards and apparently the most carefree, is known to have been a sick man throughout most of his life, subject to long periodic fits of black despondence. Sir Samuel Garth, physician and wit, remembered now only for his mock-heroic poem *The Dispensary* (1699), would today be called manic-depressive; though usually agreeable in conversation, he often alarmed Pope and his other friends by complaining of the tedium of life, especially the monotony of having to tie his shoelaces daily, and on one occasion attempted to commit suicide. [82] Parnell, the intimate associate of Pope and Swift and the founder of the graveyard school of poetry, died in a state of melancholia, aggravated, it was said, by heavy drinking. His first biographer, Oliver Goldsmith, relates that the poet's fits of "the spleen" would sometimes last for weeks and that when he felt one coming on he withdrew to a remote district of his native Ireland and "there made out a gloomy kind of satisfaction in giving hideous descriptions of the solitude to which he retired." [83] Thomas Gray, whom Melancholy had

"mark'd for her own," [84] wrote up his own case in a Latin manuscript recounting his symptoms and the cures he tried upon himself, a document used to good advantage by Matthew Arnold in
explaining why the shy poet "never spoke out." Sir Charles Hanbury Williams, author of some very pleasing verses, was called
"the mad poet" because in his delusion of grandeur he wrote to
"half the crowned heads of Europe." [85] Two of the most gifted
poets, William Collins and Christopher Smart, were confined in
mental asylums. The roster of suicide contains, besides the name
of Henry Needler, those of three well-known poets — Thomas
Carey, Eustace Budgell, and Thomas Chatterton. Lady Mary
evidently contemplated the same course.[86] Cowper's tragedy was
that he failed in his attempt on his life. He confesses to his former
schoolmate Robert Lloyd that he turned to verse-writing only
in the hope that he might banish "gloomy thoughts led on by
Spleen." [87]

There developed in this atmosphere an interesting difference of
opinion concerning a question that seems to be perennial, namely,
whether the romantic or the classic type of mind is more liable
to insanity. Swift and Johnson resolutely opposed imaginative
poetry because they were convinced that whoever yields to the
allurements of the imagination in order to escape from the harsh
realities of existence is taking the plain road to mental destruction.
Johnson clearly implies in his life of Collins that this promising
young poet brought about his mental ruin through the fatal habit
of dwelling "chiefly upon works of fiction and subjects of fancy"
and of indulging "those flights of imagination which pass the
bounds of nature." * Christopher Smart took the opposite view;
in his opinion the tragedy of the *genus irritabile* arose not from

* Swift, *A Tale of a Tub* (1704), Sec. ix; Johnson, *Rasselas* (1759), Ch.
44, and *Lives of the English Poets* (1896), I, 196. For this opinion they might
have cited Plato, for he evidently had in mind the creative type of poetry
when he declared that no one can hope to succeed as a poet if he has "no
touch of the Muses' madness in his soul" and that the sane man "is nowhere
when he enters into rivalry with the madman" (*Phaedrus*, 245, tr. by B.
Jowett, *Dialogues*, I, 249). Compare Schopenhauer, *The World as Will and
Idea* (1883), III, 159, and Will Durant, *The Story of Philosophy* (1926),
p. 379.

an excess of imagination, but from a dreary literalism unrelieved by the enlivening rays of fancy.[88] Oddly enough, each of these protagonists provided evidence in refutation of his own theory. The blight seems to have settled indiscriminately upon classic and romantic alike.

The most convincing evidence of melancholy genius in this period is to be found, not in published works, either prose or poetry, but in letters and other private documents. Disregarding Lord Chesterfield's counsel of epistolary propriety, the literati communicated their miseries to their personal friends with unabashed frankness. If all the treatises of the time had been lost, a substantial portion of medical opinion concerning "the spleen" — the causes, symptoms, and cures — could be reconstructed out of the correspondence of Swift, Richardson, Shenstone, Young, and Boswell. By contrast, the poetical references now appear unreal, all the more so because of the peculiar conventions that governed Augustan poetry. In the evolution from the old to the new style no article of the neoclassic code yielded more stubbornly than the injunction that the poet avoid exposing his nakedness to public gaze. He might make free use of his amusing foibles, as Prior and Swift often do in their *vers-de-société*, but more serious self-revelation was frowned upon as a breach of decorum. Under the rule of impersonality poetry had become emotionally inarticulate except in the expression of satirical indignation.

Those of the late Augustans who felt impelled to indulge their moodiness were forced to resort to methods of indirection, which, though well enough understood at the time at home and abroad, get in the way of modern appreciation. There was, of course, no objection to a verse treatise on "the spleen" or any other subject as long as the author treated it objectively. One of the favorite devices of self-expression was allegory; more popular, because sanctioned as a religious exercise, was the *meditatio mortis* in moss-grown abbeys and country graveyards. The convenience of the religious motive as a screen for morbid emotionalism is best illustrated, however, in the work of Edward Young, the gloomiest of all poets in this period, if not in all English literature.

While he was recording his midnight meditations, lighted by a candle protruding from a human skull, it never occurred to the self-deceived poet that the "awful joy" he derived from exploring the miserable state of man was in a measure at least the effluvium of a dyspeptic mind. In the midst of all these ambages and circumlocutions, it is difficult to find a frank expression of personal unhappiness — impossible in the early part of the century except in some of the shorter poems of Lady Winchilsea. Cowper's reference to his own tragedy is less exceptional than it appears to be; his verse epistle was not intended for publication, and, besides, Cowper came late enough to escape the full force of the classical proscription. There are times when Swift and Prior are tempted to drop the mask of flippancy, but the glimpses afforded are tantalizingly brief. Shenstone, for all that has been said of his artificiality, is more autobiographically frank than most of his contemporaries. On the other hand, "Poor Collins," gifted as he was in lyric expression, almost invariably conceals himself behind allegory and other frigid conventions.[89]

What Arnold said of Gray is true of the others; they never spoke out. The consequence is that their poetry, even when professedly melancholy, seldom affects the reader of today with the lively sense of reality he derives from the melancholy Elizabethans or from the later romantics. It is interesting, however idle, to speculate on the revelations a curious world might have had if Jonathan Swift, "the unhappiest man that ever lived," or any one of a dozen other poets in this age of transition had been as uninhibited as Rousseau, Goethe, or Byron, or as Cowper finally became.

Of all the poetical artifices that were adopted the most transparent is the invocation and worship of divine Melancholy. This habit had originated much earlier out of the conception of melancholy as the source of wisdom, and most of the poetry of the kind in the eighteenth century was modeled upon Milton's *Il Penseroso*.[90] But there is a vast difference between Milton's melancholy and that of his puny imitators, the difference between gentle pensiveness and, in some instances at least, crass morbidity. Most of the poetry produced under the aegis of Milton plainly betrays the hypochondriac's enjoyment of his misery and his desire to prolong the exquisite pleasure. If anything further was needed for a confession of sheer hedonism, it was supplied by young Thomas Warton, of the new romantic group, when, discarding all pretense in *The Pleasures of Melancholy* (1747), he frankly steeped himself in midnight darkness and all the horrors he could conjure up. This poem is of some importance as at least a faint adumbration of the literary decadence traced by Mario Praz in *The Romantic Agony* (1933). That Warton was the first of his group to come out in defense of what his contemporaries were too shy to admit openly and freely is not a mere accident. Far from being a jovial impostor, as he is sometimes described, he exhibited all the earmarks of a sickly temperament. He could no more resist the morbid fascination of attending a public execution than the sadistic George Selwyn; he was the anonymous author of some gory ballads; and the same unhealthy strain manifests itself in *The Suicide* (1770), a poem written in evident allusion to the death of Chatterton. He was, in short, well qualified by temperamental peculiarities to become an early evangelist of literary algolagnia.

It was this habit of seeking and cultivating melancholy that led Walt Whitman to utter a blast against European literature in general as a "vast abnormal ward or hysterical sick-chamber." The American optimist looked upon the English as the prime offenders, though he conceded they had an unusual talent for expressing such unwholesome sentiments. He could have understood and forgiven them for discharging their woes upon the world if they had disburdened their atrabilious minds in a thunderstorm of passion and thus cleared the atmosphere as the Greeks did; instead, their poetry is "moping, sick, uncertain" and leaves behind "a secret taste for the blues, the morbid fascination, the luxury of woe."[91] As Whitman intended, this anathema applies to a large area of English literature. The distinguishing characteristic of the poetry of melancholy in the eighteenth century is the shameless depth of sensationalism to which writers eventually

descended in order to gratify a depraved appetite, foreshadowing
the gloom and ghastly terror of the Gothic romance. It is true
that similar offenses had long been committed in *memento mori*
literature; but at least the authors offered the excuse, however
lame, of a religious purpose, whereas now the only motive was
aesthetic pleasure. While citing Milton as their guide, they rev-
eled in the very mood which Milton himself condemned in
*L'Allegro* as

> loathed Melancholy,
> Of Cerberus and blackest Midnight born,
> In Stygian cave forlorn
> 'Mongst horrid shapes, and shrieks, and sights unholy.

REFERENCE NOTES AND INDEX

# Reference Notes

SHAFTESBURY AND THE ETHICAL POETS IN ENGLAND

[1] Adolph Frey, *Albrecht von Haller und seine Bedeutung für die deutsche Literatur* (Leipzig, 1879), pp. 19ff; H. Hettner, *Literaturgeschichte des 18. Jahrhunderts*, Part I (5th ed.; Braunschweig, 1894); I. C. Hatch, *Der Einfluss Shaftesburys auf Herder*, St. zur vergl. Lit.-gesch. (1901), I, 68ff; O. F. Walzel, *Shaftesbury und das deutsche Geistesleben des 18. Jahrhunderts*, G R M (1909), I, 416ff; K. Berger, *Schiller, Werke* (München, 1910), I, 106; Charles Elson, *Wieland and Shaftesbury* (Columbia Univ. Press, 1913); Herbert Grudzinski, *Shaftesburys Einfluss auf Ch. M. Wieland. Mit einer Einleitung über den Einfluss Shaftesburys auf die deutsche Literatur bis 1760* (Stuttgart, 1913).

[2] *Characteristics*, ed. J. M. Robertson (2 vols.; New York, 1900) (to which all references below), II, 89–95.

[3] *Ibid.*, II, 108.

[4] *Ibid.*, II, 22, 73, 74.

[5] *Life, Unpublished Letters, and Philosophical Regimen*, ed. Benjamin Rand (London, 1900) (referred to hereafter as *Regimen*), *passim*. He derived much also from Horace (see Letter to Pierre Costé, Oct. 1, 1706, *ibid.*, p. 355).

[6] *Characteristics*, I, 251–266. Cf. II, 135–141; also *Regimen*, pp. 403–405, 413–417.

[7] *Characteristics*, II, 41. Cf. I, 66, 287.

[8] *Ibid.*, I, 294.

[9] *Ibid.*, II, 69.

[10] *Ibid.*, I, 136.

[11] See M. F. Libby, *Influence of the Idea of Aesthetic Proportion on the Ethics of Shaftesbury* (Worcester, Mass., 1901); William G. Howard, "Good Taste and Conscience," *PMLA*, XXV (1910), 486–497.

[12] *Characteristics*, I, 243, 274.

[13] *Ibid.*, I, 73–85; II, 77–84.

[14] *Ibid.*, I, 293, 299, 304; II, 36–41, 201.

[15] *A Vindication*, etc., ed. 1740, p. 12.

[16] See F. W. Wilson, *The Importance of the Reign of Queen Anne in Church History* (1911).

[17] *An Address to Persons of Quality*, etc. (London, 1715), pp. 254–255; cf. pp. 102–104.

[18] J. M. Robertson, ed., *op. cit.*, I, xiv.

[19] *Ibid*. See also T. Fowler, *Shaftesbury and Hutcheson*, pp. 136–137.

[20] "An Account of the Augustan Age in England," the *Bee*, No. 8. Cf. J. Leland, *A View of the Principal Deistical Writers* (London, 1754), I, 71. In ridicule Berkeley rewrote some of *The Moralists* in blank verse (*Alciphron*, Dial. V, 22).

[21] *Pensées diverses, Oeuv. Comp.* (Paris, 1838), p. 626.

[22] Dedication of *The Divine Legation* (1738). Cited by T. Fowler, *op. cit.*, p. 153.

[23] *Moral and Political Dialogues*, Preface. Quoted by J. Warton, *Essay on Pope* (London, 1806), II, 198. Note also Hurd's *Dialogues on the Uses of Foreign Travel . . . Considered as a Part of an English Gentleman's Education: between Lord Shaftesbury and Mr. Locke*, etc. (London, 1764).

[24] Chalmers, *Biog. Dict.*, art. "John Brown."

[25] *Briefe zur Beförderung der Humanität*, Brief 33. See also Brief 32; *Fragmente, Zweite Sammlung*, "Von der griechischen Litteratur in Deutschland"; and *Adrastea*, I, 14: "Shaftesburi, Geist und Frohsinn."

[26] *Of Active and Retired Life, an Epistle to Henry Coventry, Esq.* (1735).

[27] The chief passages are: *Spring*, 867–962 (904–962 added in 1738); *Summer*, 1013–1025, 1630–1646; *Autumn*, 95–150, 169–176, 350–359, 1020–1029; *Winter*, 276–388, 1050–1069. Some of these are discussed briefly by Léon Morel, *James Thomson, sa vie et ses oeuvres* (Paris, 1895), p. 388. See also *To the Memory of . . . Talbot*, 117–129, 270–282, 352–362; *Liberty* III.32–70, IV.322–343, 479–573, 746–762, 1157–1176, V.235–261, 277–303, 471–483, 638–666; *Castle of Indolence* II.lxxiv, lxxv (Aldine ed.; 2 vols.; 1897).

[28] For the various texts, see O. Zippel, ed., *Seasons* (Berlin, 1908).

[29] *Winter*, 359–388.

[30] *Liberty* V.638–646.

[31] *Ibid.*, 471–483, 647–666.

[32] From Voltaire's Letter to Lyttelton, May 17, 1750. Cf. R. J. Phillimore, *Memoirs of Lord Lyttelton*, I, 323.

[33] *Adrastea*, I, 14: "Shaftesburi, Geist und Frohsinn." Cited by T. Fowler, *op. cit.*, p. 161.

[34] *Briefe zur Beförderung der Humanität*, Brief 32.

[35] *Naturhymnus von Shaftesburi* (1800).

[36] *James Thomson* (English Men of Letters), p. 96. But see W. J. Courthope, *A History of English Poetry*, V, 305–312; Morel, *op. cit.*, Ch. 6, Sec. iv.

[37] Lyttelton's Letter to Doddridge, R. J. Phillimore, *op. cit.*, I, 306–308, 407–409. See also Morel, *op. cit.*, pp. 156–157, 359–360.

[38] The following passages in the *Characteristics* reflect the author's political views: I, 73, 141–146, 153–155; II, 45–46. For further evidence see *Regimen*, Letter to Thomas Stringer, Feb. 15, 1695-6, p. 300; to Sir Rowland Gwinn, Jan. 23, 1704, pp. 318–320; to Mr. Van Twedde, Jan. 17, 1705-6, pp. 347–352; to Tiresias, Nov. 29, 1706, pp. 367–368.

[39] Prologue to *Coriolanus* (1749).

[40] *Dialogues of the Dead*, XIV.

[41] *A Poem Sacred to the Memory of Mr. James Thomson* (London, 1748). Published anonymously; for the authorship of Shiels, see Morel, *op. cit.*, p. 379n.

[42] *To Mr. Thomson* (on the publication of the second edition of *Winter*), 1726. There were four editions of *Winter* in this year.

[43] Second ed. (London, 1764).

[44] *Letters*, ed. D. C. Tovey (3 vols.; London, 1900), I, 119.

[45] *Remarks on Several Occasional Observations*, etc.

[46] Author's note on *The Power of Harmony*.

[47] *Ladies' Mag.*, IV (1753), 1.

[48] *Characteristics*, II, 287. Cf. 120–121, 176, 315–316, and I, 331–332.

[49] Letter to Mr. D., Dec. 3, 1711, *Works*, p. 216.

[50] See *Spring*, 236–241, 336–378, 387–393, 702–728; *Summer*, 220–240, 267–280, 416–422; *Autumn*, 359–457, 980–987, 1172–1207; *Winter*, 240–264, 788–793, 815–833; *Liberty* III.32–70.

[51] *Characteristics*, I, xxv. Cf. T. Fowler, *op. cit.*, p. 151; Morel, *op. cit.*, p. 399.

[52] Voltaire, *Lettres philosophiques*, Let. xxii; Warton, *Essay on Pope*, Sec. ix, and edition of Pope; Warburton, *Vindication*, etc., and edition of Pope. See Elwin's and Mark Pattison's notes on the *Essay* and Paul Vater, *Pope und Shaftesbury* (Halle, a. S., 1897).

[53] See Elwin's introductory remarks, II, 261ff.

[54] Four vols.; Philadelphia, 1841 (to which all references below).

[55] *Characteristics*, I, 90–94, 144, 185, 190–193; II, 274–275, 286.

[56] Bolingbroke, Vol. III, pp. 51, 52, 109, 116, 210, 324; Vol. IV, Frag. i, pp. 118–119, 131; Frag. ii, pp. 132–135, 137–138; Frag. vi, p. 166; Frag. viii, pp. 175–177; Frag. xx, p. 233; Frag. xli, pp. 319–322; Frag. xlvii, pp. 350–351; Frag. xlviii, pp. 355–356; Frag. xlix, pp. 356–360; Frag. l, pp. 360–363.

[57] *Idem*, Vol. IV, Frag. vi, pp. 167–168. Cf. Vol. III, pp. 396–401.

[58] *Idem*, Vol. IV, Frag. xxvi, p. 263; Frag. xxxiii, p. 290; Frag. li, pp. 369–372; Frag. lv, p. 390; Frag. lxiv, pp. 428–429.

[59] *Idem*, Vol. IV, Frag. lxv, pp. 432–433; Frag. lxvi, pp. 433–434.

[60] *Idem*, Vol. IV, Frag. xxv, p. 297.

[61] *Fragmentum, I. H. B. completum. Anti-Bolingbrokius*, etc. (London, 1769).

[62] Ch. 22, "The Happiness of a Life Led according to Nature."

[63] *Tom Jones*, Bk. XV, Ch. 1.

[64] *Peregrine Pickle*, Ch. 43; cf. Chs. 24, 57, 70. *Roderick Random*, Ch. 22.

[65] Young's *Poetical Works*, Aldine ed., I, xxxix–xl.

[66] Dr. Rand discusses Shaftesbury's own philanthropy, private and public, *Regimen*, pp. vii, viii. Note particularly the Letter to John Wheelock (Shaftesbury's steward), Nov. 6 [1703], *ibid.*, p. 315.

[67] *Regimen*, pp. xx, xxi.

[68] The Rev. Wm. M. Hatch planned a complete edition, but published only one volume of it (1871).

[69] *Regimen*, p. vii.

[70] See E. Schmidt, *Richardson, Rousseau und Goethe* (Jena, 1875), *passim*.

THE RETURN TO NATURE IN ENGLISH POETRY OF THE
EIGHTEENTH CENTURY

[1] Myra Reynolds, *The Treatment of Nature in English Poetry between Pope and Wordsworth* (Univ. of Chicago Press, 1909); R. D. Havens, "Romantic Aspects of the Age of Pope," *PMLA*, XX (Sept. 1912), 297–324.

[2] See J. C. Shairp, *On Poetic Interpretation of Nature* (1877), Chs. 9, 10; Alfred Biese, *Die Entwicklung des Naturgefühls bei den Griechern und Römern* (1882); John Veitch, *The Feeling for Nature in Scottish Poetry* (2 vols.; 1887), Vol. I, Ch. 3.

[3] Humboldt, *Kosmos* (ed. 1850), Vol. II, Part I, *passim*; Biese, *The Development of the Feeling for Nature in the Middle Ages and Modern Times* (tr.; 1905), Chs. 4, 5.

[4] *Op. cit.*, I, 6.

[5] *Modern Painters*, "Of Mountain Beauty."

[6] *Op. cit.*, p. 170.

[7] *Ibid.*, p. 176.

[8] T. S. Perry, *English Literature in the Eighteenth Century* (1883), p. 145.

[9] W. L. Phelps, *The Beginnings of the English Romantic Movement* (1893); see pp. 167–169.

[10] See Reynolds, *op. cit.*, Ch. 1; Perry, *op. cit.*, Ch. 4.

[11] Biese, *Development of the Feeling for Nature*, etc., Ch. 5.

[12] Shairp, *op. cit.*, Ch. 8, "Some of the Ways in Which Poets Deal with Nature."

[13] Veitch, *op. cit.*, Vol. I, Ch. 1, "The Feeling for Nature – Its Various Forms."

[14] Léon Morel, *James Thomson, sa vie et ses oeuvres* (Paris, 1895), p. 359.

[15] Reynolds, *op. cit.*, p. 77.

[16] Shairp, *op. cit.*, p. 115.

[17] H. A. Beers, *English Romanticism in the Eighteenth Century* (1910), p. 362. The same opinion is expressed in "A Philosopher Among the Wits" (a review of Benjamin Rand's *Berkeley and Percival*), *Nation*, C (Jan. 21, 28, 1915), 74, 104.

[18] *Critical Essays of the Eighteenth Century* (1915), p. xvii.

[19] *Essay on Pope*, I, 115, 266.

[20] *The True Intellectual System of the Universe* (3 vols.; 1845), II, 590; III, 466–528. Cf. Locke, *An Essay concerning Human Understanding*, Bk. IV, Ch. 6, Sec. 11.

[21] *An Examination of Dr. Burnet's Theory of the Earth* (Oxford, 1698), pp. 54–55. Chapter 3 is devoted to mountains.

[22] William King, *An Essay on the Origin of Evil, Translated*, etc., by Edmund Law (3d ed., 1739).

[23] For Shaftesbury's admiration of Cudworth, see *Characteristics*, ed. J. M. Robertson (2 vols.; New York, 1900) (to which all references below), II, 50, 196, and Letter to Jean Le Clerc, March 6, 1705-6, in *Life, Unpublished Letters, and Philosophical Regimen*, ed. Benjamin Rand (London, 1900) (referred to hereafter as *Regimen*), p. 352.

[24] *Pensées diverses, Oeuv. Comp.* (Paris, 1838), p. 626.

[25] *Characteristics*, II, 112.

[26] *Ibid.*, I, 279.

[27] *Ibid.*, II, 98.

[28] See Alfred Sternbeck, *Shaftesbury über Natur, Gott und Religion* (Berlin, 1904).

[29] *A History of English Thought* (2 vols.; 1902), II, 437–438.

[30] *Characteristics*, II, 119–120.

[31] See Veitch, *op. cit.*, pp. 117–118; Reynolds, *op. cit.*, pp. 18–19 and notes.

[32] *Characteristics*, II, 122.

[33] *Ibid.*, II, 287, 315–316.

[34] *Ibid.*, II, 120–121, 176.

[35] *Ibid.*, I, 331–332.

[36] *Ibid.*, II, 122.

[37] *Ibid.*, II, 9.

[38] *Ibid.*, II, 123–124. The italics are mine.

[39] *Remarks on Several Parts of Italy* (written 1705). Cited by Havens, *op. cit.*, p. 313.

[40] *The Poems of the Countess of Winchilsea*, ed. Myra Reynolds (Univ. of Chicago Press, 1903), pp. 122–123.

[41] *The Treatment of Nature*, etc., pp. 59–60.

[42] *Letters and Works*, ed. Lord Wharncliffe, I, 205.

[43] *The Letters of Thomas Gray*, ed. D. C. Tovey, I, 44.

[44] *Characteristics*, II, 125.

[45] C. A. Moore, "Berkeley's Influence on Popular Literature: A Review of a Review," *South Atlantic Quarterly*, XIV (July 1915), 3.

[46] See *Regimen*, pp. 369, 371, 384, 400–402, 420–421.

[47] See Preface to second edition.

[48] *The Treatment of Nature*, etc., p. 71.

[49] See Author's notes.

[50] For modern critics also, see Edmund Gosse, *A History of Eighteenth Century Literature* (1891), p. 311; Sir Leslie Stephen, *A History of English Thought* (1902), II, 365; W. J. Courthope, *A History of English Poetry* (1905), V, 317–318.

[51] See King's *Essay on the Origin of Evil* (as cited above), p. 216.

[52] *Op. cit.*, p. 312.

[53] *The Treatment of Nature*, etc., p. 127.

[54] Author's note, Bk. I, line 374.

[55] *Characteristics*, I, 94.

[56] *Divine Rectitude*, p. 19.

[57] *The Treatment of Nature*, etc., p. 99.

[58] *Poetry and Imagination*. Cf. Sir Leslie Stephen, *op. cit.*, II, 362.

[59] Morel, *op. cit.*, p. 360.

[60] *The Treatment of Nature*, etc., p. 78.

[61] Shairp, *op. cit.*; Ch. 3, "Poetic and Scientific Wonder"; Ch. 4, "Will Science Push Out Poetry?"

[62] Preface to *Lyrical Ballads*.

[63] See W. A. Neilson, *The Essentials of Poetry* (1912), pp. 138–142.

[64] For discussion of Akenside, see *op. cit.*, pp. 123–127.

[65] *Excursion* IV.1198–1219, 1254–1265.

[66] *The Pleasures of the Imagination* IV.38–51 (1770); *Hymn to the Naiads*, 234–249.

[67] As found in *The Prelude* I.402.

[68] Biese, *Development of the Feeling for Nature*, etc., p. 22.

[69] See Humboldt, *Kosmos* (ed. 1850), Vol. II, Part I.

## WHIG PANEGYRIC VERSE: A PHASE OF SENTIMENTALISM

[1] W. J. Courthope, *A History of English Poetry*, Vol. V, Ch. 2.

[2] See C. B. Roylance Kent, *The Early History of the Tories* (1908), Ch. 5.

[3] See W. Cunningham, *The Growth of English Industry and Commerce in Modern Times* (1912), Part I, Ch. 15, especially pp. 501ff, and L. W. Moffit, *England on the Eve of the Industrial Revolution* (1925).

[4] See W. E. H. Lecky, *A History of England in the Eighteenth Century* (1892), II, 209–211.

[5] J. R. Spears, *The American Slave Trade* (1901), p. 95.

[6] Letter of Dec. 6, 1748, *Works*, II, 208. Cited, with other references, by E. M. North, *Early Methodist Philanthropy* (1914), pp. 94–95.

[7] *De Legibus Naturae* (1672), tr. by J. Maxwell (1727), Ch. 9, Sec. xi, cites approvingly Hobbes's *De Cive*, Ch. 2, Sec. ix; Ch. 8, Secs. iii, ix.

[8] Bk. II, Ch. 1, Sec. lxxxv.

[9] Vol. VIII, No. 30 (1691).

[10] *The Athenian Oracle* (1704), I, 529–532. Reprinted at Boston, Mass., in 1705 with Samuel Sewall's *The Selling of Joseph* and also in John Hepburn's *American Defence of the Christian Golden Rule* (1714). See Mary S. Locke, *Anti-Slavery in America* (1901), pp. 18, 33.

[11] *Windsor Forest*, 408–412; *An Essay on Man* I.107–108. The first of these passages was inscribed in the frontispiece of the *Gentleman's Mag.* for 1756.

[12] *Free-Thinker*, Vol. II, No. 30, Oct. 17, 1718.

[13] Letter to the Countess of Marr, July 1727.

[14] *Persian Letters*, No. lvii.

[15] The most important have been collected by Milton Percival in *Political Ballads Illustrating the Administration of Sir Robert Walpole* (Oxford Historical and Literary Studies, 1916). For attacks on Bolingbroke also, see XXIII, XLV.

[16] *First Letter on a Regicide Peace*, in *Works* (1803), VIII, 145.

## JOHN DUNTON: PIETIST AND IMPOSTOR

[1] See *The Life and Errors*, etc. (1705), ed. J. B. Nichols (1818), I, 200.

[2] *Athenianism* (1710), Dedication, p. v.

[3] *The Life and Errors*, I, 162.

[4] I, 86–144. The manuscript, with much other material, is in the Bodleian, MS Rawl., Miscell. 71 and 72, the contents of which are catalogued by Nichols, *The Life and Errors*, II, 753f. W. H. Whitmore's edition of the eight letters was published for the Prince Society, 1867.

[5] *The Life and Errors*, I, 26.

[6] *Diary*, ed. 1888, pp. 249–251. A full description is preserved also in a folio broadside *The Form of the Proceeding to the Funeral of . . . Queen Mary II. of Blessed Memory*, etc. (1695).

[7] Dunton, pp. 76–78; Shepard, ed. 1641, pp. 87–88.

[8] Dunton, pp. 87–88; "Hierusalem my happie home. A song made by F. B. P." (Hyder E. Rollins, *Old English Ballads* [1920], No. 24.) Cf. No. 25.

[9] See *Athenianism*, p. 61.

[10] Dunton, pp. 202–208; Becon, ed. 1584, pp. 147–154.

[11] Vol. I, No. 53, pp. 265–270.

[12] *Meditations and Vowes, Divine and Morall*, etc., ed. 1621, p. 537.

[13] *Compleat Library*, II, 71.

[14] *Ibid.*, II, 75–81.

[15] *The Life and Errors*, I, 157.

[16] *Ibid.*, I, 156.

[17] *The New Practice of Piety*, p. 27. Cf. *Religio Medici*, Part I, Sec. ix, *Works*, ed. C. Sayle (1912), I, 16–17.

[18] Licensed by Dunton, June 1691 (T. C. II, 370).

[19] T. C. III, 338.

[20] *Graduati Cantabrigienses, 1659–1823*, p. 63.

[21] *The Life and Errors*, I, 77.

[22] *The English Poems of Henry King, D.D.*, ed. Lawrence Mason (1914), p. 114.

[23] Included by Nichols, *The Life and Errors*, II, 480.

[24] Night III, Aldine ed., I, 41; Farquhar's *Sir Harry Wildair* I.i. See Horace W. O'Connor, *PMLA*, XXVII (March 1919), 130–149.

## THE ENGLISH MALADY

[1] Joseph Spence, *Anecdotes* (1820), p. 251, where the remark is erroneously attributed to Alain René Le Sage.

[2] *Ibid.*, p. 182.

[3] Book IV, Chs. 12, 13. Cf. *Défense de L'Esprit des lois, Oeuv. Comp.* (1828), VI, 159; *Notes sur l'Angleterre*, VII, 236; *Pensées diverses*, VII, 467.

[4] H. Harisse, *L'Abbé Prévost* (1896), p. 221. See also George R. Havens, *The Abbé Prévost and English Literature* (1921), Ch. 2.

[5] George R. Havens, "The Sources of Rousseau's Édouard Bomston," *Modern Philology*, XVIII (1919), 125–139, and F. C. Green, *Minuet* (1935), p. 314.

[6] *Lettres d'un François*, 3 vols; an English translation followed in 1747.

[7] *Letters on the English and French Nations . . . Translated from the Original French* (1747), I, 300–301.

[8] *Ibid.*, I, 135.

[9] *Ibid.*, I, 89–90. Cf. *Letters on the English Nation: By Battista Angeloni, a Jesuit* (1755), II, 121, Letter xl (really by Dr. John Shebbeare).

[10] Reginald Blunt, *Mrs. Montagu*, etc. (1800), I, 116.

[11] Hatzfeld, 29. Cited by F. Kalkühler, *Die Natur des Spleens bei den englischen Schriftstellern*, etc. (1920), p. 3.

[12] *Political and Literary Anecdotes of His Own Times* (1818), pp. 236–237.

[13] *A Picture of England* (1789), II, 134.

[14] *Letters*, ed. Mrs. Paget Toynbee, IX, 434.

[15] *Memoirs of M. de Voltaire, Miscellaneous Works*, ed. Masson, p. 501.

[16] *Medical Cautions*, ed. 1787, p. 14.

[17] William MacMichael, *The Gold-Headed Cane* (1827), Ch. 1.

[18] *Dissertatio Epistolaris* (1682): *An Epistolary Discourse to . . . Doctor William Cole, concerning . . . Hysteric Diseases*, in *Works*, tr. by John Pechey (1734), p. 302.

[19] See also C. J. Thomson, *The Quacks of Old London* (1928), p. 110.

[20] Bk. V; Chalmers, *English Poets*, X, 364.

[21] *The Practice of Physick* (1755), II, 300.

[22] *Retirement* (1782), 301–302.

[23] *Humourist*, I, 12.

[24] Ed. A. R. Shilleto, Bohn's Library (1926), I, 38, 446.

[25] Boswell's *Life of Johnson* (1931), II, 317.

[26] *An Essay of Aliments*, 3d ed. (1736), pp. 340–341.

[27] *Amusements Serious and Comical*, Amusement XI: Physic.

[28] *Tom Jones*, Bk. II, Ch. 9. Cf. *Amelia*, Bk. III, Ch. 7.

[29] *Letters of Lady Mary Wortley Montagu*, Everyman's, p. 499.

[30] *The History of Ferdinand Count Fathom* (1759), Ch. 52.

[31] *A Voyage to Lisbon* (1755), Introduction.

[32] *Autobiography and Correspondence*, ed. Lady Lanover (1861–1862), I, 44, 450; II, 247–249, 234.

[33] *Letter-Books of John Hervey, First Earl of Bristol* (1894), II, 224.

[34] *Universal Spectator* No. 339, April 26, 1735; *Gentleman's Mag.*, of the same month.

[35] *A Picture of England*, I, 177.

[36] Voltaire, *Dictionnaire philosophique*, art. "Caton."

[37] Besides the passages referred to in note 3, see John Churton Collins, *Voltaire, Montesquieu, and Rousseau in England* (1908), p. 136n.

[38] *Memoirs*, ed. 1745, III, 286.

[39] *Oeuv. Comp.* (1877–1885), IX, 442. Cf. *Miscellaneous Correspondence . . . Sent to the Author of the Gentleman's Magazine*, No. I (London, 1742), pp. 70–71.

[40] *Letters*, ed. D. C. Tovey, I, 281.

[41] *Letters*, ed. Mrs. Paget Toynbee, III, 278–280, 284, 287–288, 344, 362.

[42] *The Practice of Physick* (1755), II, 324.

[43] Part II, Sec. iii.

[44] Quoted by Diderot, *Oeuv. Comp.* (1876), XIX, 182.

[45] Nugent's tr., II, 182.

[46] *Voyage de Sr. A. de Mottraye*, etc. (1727), I, 165.

[47] *A Foreign View of England*, etc., tr. by Mme. Van Muyden (1902), p. 313. See also René Doumic, *Études sur la littérature française*, Vol. V (1906), "La Découverte de l'Angleterre au XVIII⁰ siècle."

[48] *A Foreign View of England*, p. 196.

[49] *Lettres d'un François*, I, 195.

[50] *Ibid.*, I, 191.

[51] *Oeuv. Comp.* (1877–1885), XXII, 17–24; included with *Lettres philosophiques*, ed. G. Lanson (1909), II, 256–277.

[52] *L'Esprit des lois*, Bk. XIV, Ch. 12.

[53] *Oeuv. Comp.*, IX, 142.

[54] *Spectator* No. 387.

[55] *Spectator* No. 179. Cf. Congreve, *Amendments of Mr. Collier's False and Imperfect Citations* (1698).

[56] *Spectator* No. 424 (Steele); Nos. 429, 440 (Addison).

[57] *Guardian* No. 104. Cf. No. 102 and *Spectator* Nos. 45, 136.

[58] *Letters*, Everyman's, pp. 250–265.

[59] *Ibid.*, p. 270. Cf. p. 199.

[60] *Life and Works*, ed. G. A. Aitken (1892), p. 203.

[61] *Letters*, ed. Duncan Mallam (1939), No. cxxii.

[62] *Letters*, ed. D. C. Tovey, III, 320.

[63] Wilbur L. Cross, *The Life and Times of Laurence Sterne* (1909), p. 122.

[64] *Essays* (1741–1742), Part I, Essay 21.

[65] *Letters on the English Nation: By Battista Angeloni* (pseudonym) (1755), Letter xl.

[66] Pp. 527–529.

[67] See *New Essays by Oliver Goldsmith*, ed. Ronald S. Crane (1927), Introduction and Notes.

[68] *Life of Johnson* (1931), II, 19.

[69] William Vaughan, *The Newlanders Cure* (1630), p. 64.

[70] *Essays on Men and Manners* (1764), ed. 1804, p. 117.

[71] *The Natural Method of Cureing the Diseases of the Body* (1742), p. 192.

[72] *The Letters of David Hume*, ed. J. Y. T. Greig (1932), Letter iii.

[73] *Tom Jones*, Bk. XI, Ch. 8.

[74] See *Works* (1865), XI, 493.

[75] *Letter-Books of John Hervey, First Earl of Bristol*, III, 31–32.

[76] Letter to Lord Lyttelton, Dec. 12 [1736], *Works*, ed. Elwin and Courthope, IX, 172.

[77] The Greek text of this treatise and an English translation are included in the Loeb Classical Library, 1936. The problem referred to is XXX, 1.

[78] *The Rape of the Lock* IV.60.

[79] Cheyne's diagnosis is stated fully in *Original Letters*, ed. Rebecca Warner (1817), Letters xx–xxv.

[80] *Correspondence of Samuel Richardson*, ed. Mrs. Barbauld (1804), V, 166.

[81] *Ibid.*, III, 30.

[82] Joseph Spence, *Anecdotes*, p. 114.

[83] Quoted by G. A. Aitken, *The Poetical Works of Thomas Parnell* (1894), p. liii.

[84] *An Elegy Written in a Country Church-Yard*, "The Epitaph."

[85] E. J. Cleminson, *Elizabeth Montagu*, III, 124.

[86] See George Paston, *Lady Mary Wortley Montagu and Her Times* (1907), p. 386.

[87] *Poetical Works*, ed. John Bruce (1909), II, 305.

[88] "Fable," Chalmers, *English Poets*, XVI, 55–56. See also Lawrence Binyon, "The Case of Christopher Smart," *The English Association*, Pamphlet No. 90 (Dec. 1934), p. 11.

[89] For the forms employed, see Amy L. Reed, *The Background of Gray's Elegy: A Study in the Taste for Melancholy Poetry 1700–1751* (1924); Eleanor M. Sickels, *The Gloomy Egoist: Moods and Themes of Melancholy from Gray to Keats* (1932). Midnight, death, and horror first invaded Augustan literature through tragedy; early examples are Congreve's *The Mourning Bride* (1697) II.i and Rowe's *The Fair Penitent* (1703) V.i. The influence of the "necromantic" English poets on the literature of the Continent is discussed by P. Van Tieghem in *La Poésie de la nuit et des tombeaux en Europe au XVIII^e siècle* (1921), which was later embodied in Vol. II of *Le Préromantisme* (1930), and by F. C. Green in *Minuet* (1935), Chs. 9, 10.

[90] Raymond D. Havens, *The Influence of Milton on English Poetry* (1922), Ch. 18.

[91] *Complete Prose Works* (1898), p. 493.

# Index